Amy Ashwood Garvey
and the Future of
Black Feminist Archives

Praise for *Amy Ashwood Garvey and the Future of Black Feminist Archives*

Nydia A Swaby has woven for us the first biography of Amy Ashwood Garvey written by and for Black feminist women. Swaby's narrative seamlessly takes in the stakes and politics of Black feminist remembrance in the UK and beyond, captures the dynamism, creativity, passion and boundless, borderless energy of a brilliant peripatetic Pan-African woman, and considers the convergences of her own research and artistic practices with those of Amy Ashwood Garvey. Nydia A Swaby succeeds in illustrating how, for many of us, deepening historical knowledge shapes how we engage with the future almost as much as it equips us to navigate the present. Interweaving recent histories of Black British feminist activism in Britain with her history of the arch-feminist and Pan-Africanist Amy Ashwood Garvey in a text as theoretically stunning as the kente Amy Ashwood Garvey often wore, I cannot wait to get Nydia A Swaby's *Amy Ashwood Garvey and the Future of Black Feminist Archives* on all my reading lists – and into discussions with my students.

Dr Kesewa John, Lecturer in Black British History, Convenor MA Black British History, Goldsmiths University, London

Nydia A Swaby has been retracing Amy Ashwood Garvey's footsteps for a long time. In her love-laced narrative, she shows us all ways they have changed one another. Swaby's deft, precise and inviting prose takes us on a journey of Black feminist retrieval, revitalising the past that entombs Amy Ashwood Garvey, insisting on her continued presence in the here and now.

Dr Lola Olufemi, Black feminist writer and researcher, author of *Experiments in Imagining Otherwise* (2021) and *Feminism, Interrupted: Disrupting Power* (2020)

A twenty-first century biography for a giant of the twentieth century Pan-African world, Amy Ashwood Garvey. Swaby chronicles the life of Ashwood Garvey on both sides of the Atlantic, and her impact on the politics and culture in the cities she called home.

The book is also the lovingly written record of the Black women who continue to recover, preserve and share the histories of daughters of the diaspora and define Black feminist practice.

Kelly Foster, public historian

Radical Black Women Series

This series seeks to spotlight the contributions of radical Black women to social justice movements in Britain. It aims to redress, if even in a small way, the dire lack of resources about Black British history in general and Black women's history in particular.

The Black Cultural Archives (London, UK) are publishing partners with Lawrence Wishart for the Radical Black Women Series.

Other titles in this series:

Claudia Jones: A Life in Exile by Marika Sherwood, with a new preface by Lola Olufemi

Gerlin Bean: Mother of the Movement by A S Francis

Forthcoming:

The Making of June Givanni's Pan-African Cinema Archive by Onyeka Igwe

Amy Ashwood Garvey and the Future of Black Feminist Archives

Nydia A Swaby

Lawrence Wishart
London 2024

Lawrence and Wishart Limited
Central Books Building
Freshwater Road
Chadwell Heath
RM8 1RX

Typesetting: e-type
Cover design: Isabel Lecaros
Printing: Imprint Digital

First published 2024
© Nydia A Swaby 2024

The author has asserted her rights under the Copyright, Design and Patents Act, 1998 to be identified as the author of this work.

All rights reserved. Apart from fair dealing for the purpose of private study, research, criticism or review, no part of this publication may be reproduced, stored in a retrieval system, or transmitted, in any form or by any means, electronic, electrical, chemical, mechanical, optical, photocopying, recording or otherwise, without the prior permission of the copyright owner.

British Library Cataloguing in Publication Data.
A catalogue record for this book is available from the British Library

ISBN 9781913546397
E-ISBN 9781913546403

Contents

Preface	9
Introduction: Archival Assemblages	11
Chapter 1: Auto/biography as archival activism	35
Chapter 2: The City as a Living Archive	72
Chapter 3: Towards a Visual Archive of Diaspora	113
Chapter 4: The Future of Black Feminist Archives	164
Postscript	228
Index	231

This book is dedicated to Adali Holdbrook-Swaby.
May you find strength in the stories of the ancestors.
May your life contribute to the archives that inspire
generations to come.

PREFACE

I am the daughter of diaspora

My name is Nydia A Swaby. Nydia Ann Swaby. I am the daughter of Grace Ann Huie, the granddaughter of Mary Ann Harvey, and the great-granddaughter of Edith Ann Kent. I am the daughter of the diaspora.

I was born in Chicago, Illinois, in 1982, six years after my mother, a British subject by birth, emigrated from Jamaica, becoming a lawful permanent resident in the US. My life has been marked by a profound connection to multiple geographies – the US, the UK, and the Caribbean – a reflection of the diasporic journey that defines my heritage.

My mother Grace was born in 1958, a time when Jamaica and ten other Caribbean nations sought to forge a new political identity through the West Indies Federation, aiming to break free from British colonial rule. This pursuit of independence, interwoven with the struggle for identity and autonomy, is the foundation upon which my own sense of self and scholarly pursuits are built.

My grandmother Mary was born in Harvey River, a village in the Parish of Hanover, named after her English ancestors who migrated there in the mid 1800s. Hanover, is also the birthplace of Alexander Bustamante, Jamaica's first prime minister and a pivotal figure in the labour rebellion of 1938 that contributed to universal suffrage for Black Jamaicans. My grandmother's stories and the legacy of resistance in Hanover are etched into my understanding of the complex interplay between power, identity, and freedom throughout the African diaspora.

My great-grandmother, Edith, was born in 1896 in Westmoreland, Jamaica, and grew up on a sugar plantation in Mount Peace, four miles away from Sandy Bay, a community fonded by formerly a enslaved Africans in 1838, the year of full emancipation for Black Jamaicans. Her life, like that of many others in the diaspora, was shaped by the forces of colonisation and the struggle for freedom and dignity. These experiences are not merely historical footnotes; they are integral to my exploration of diasporic identities and the enduring legacy of colonialism in the Caribbean.

My mother is part of a generation of Jamaican women who emigrated to the US in search of opportunity, navigating the complexities of identity and belonging in a new world. Her journey, and that of countless others, is a testament to the resilience and adaptability of the diaspora – a migration and settlement that has come to define modern identities. My own path, marked by migrations across North America, Africa, the Caribbean, and Europe, has continuously redefined my sense of self and my understanding of what it means to belong.

It is from this deeply rooted diasporic identity that I approach the life and work of Amy Ashwood Garvey. Her story, much like my own, is one of movement, resistance, and the constant negotiation of identity in a world shaped by colonialism and its legacies. This book is not just an exploration of her life but a reflection of the diasporic currents that have shaped my own.

I am the daughter of the diaspora, and it is through this lens that I write.

INTRODUCTION

Archival Assemblages

IN ORDER TO KNOW

On New Year's Day 1969, Amy Ashwood Garvey wrote to her close friend and confidant Lionel M Yard with a confession. 'I would hate to write my story fully,' she said, in a typewritten letter posted from her home in Kingston, Jamaica, to her 'dear Brother' in Brooklyn, New York. 'I would have to live it over again, and it's very painful to me. I would like to get off that subject and get on to something new.' Ashwood Garvey describes feeling 'very anxious' about the biography of her life that Yard had encouraged her to write. She was hesitant to recount her relationship with Marcus Garvey, her former husband, and his second wife, her former friend Amy Jacques Garvey. 'I do not want to destroy Marcus' [sic] image, but the more I think of it, the more I realize I must somehow defend myself, for it will pass into history if I do not make special mention of his behaviour.'[1] Despite these concerns, Ashwood Garvey believed that her story should be told and she needed the money from the sale of a book, so she proposed a solution. 'Darling, can you write it? You know everything, darling. Is it too much to ask you? I only ask you to keep it dark.'

Along with the, letter Amy Ashwood Garvey enclosed a portrait of herself and a memento from her personal archive. In the postscript she explained to Yard, 'please try to take a few pictures of this, my very last picture taken in Africa, and also a copy of the magazine cover in colors. I would like to have it back. Only the cover. I can't get another.'[2] Ashwood Garvey's intentional use of photography underscores the significance she placed on visual representation. It also reflects a Black diasporic visual practice of sharing photographs to forge transnational connections and communities.[3] Through the preservation and circulation of her image, she was not only archiving her life but also actively engaging with and sustaining a sense of collective identity within the diaspora.

Amy Ashwood Garvey passed away a few months later, after an extended period of illness compounded by her financial situation. In the same letter to Yard, she explains, 'my rent, etc., is due on the 6th, and I am so forlorn. The thing is enough to drive me barmy … If I could get an advance on the book, it would help me to establish a guest house, and I could live and be able to do something constructive.' Due to her declining physical health, which naturally affected her mental health, Ashwood Garvey never managed to establish a guest house in Kingston, let alone finish her story. In Yard's biography of her life, which he later developed from the pages that she had managed to send him, he remarks that Ashwood Garvey's writing had become 'erratic, disjointed.' Several 'traumatic episodes affected her concentration', and the only thing she could commit to paper were 'brief, fragmentary episodes of a few pleasant moments that filtered through the thralldom of the emotional atmosphere that suffused her thoughts.'[4]

*

This book uses Amy Ashwood Garvey's archive to reflect on the future of Black feminist archives and archival practice. It is a biographical and methodological project that examines of the curation of archives as a way of knowing Amy Ashwood Garvey's life while attending to gaps in her archive through historical research, autoethnography, speculative narrative and arts-based research methods.

Archive(s) here refers to an assemblage of manuscripts, images, and objects that I have used to create a written and visual narrative of Amy Ashwood Garvey's life. This archive is comprised of Ashwood Garvey's writing, typed and handwritten letters, photographs, newspaper clippings and sound and moving image recordings collected from conventional archival spaces and private and digital collections.

Two biographies are also a part of this archive: *Biography of Amy Ashwood Garvey, 1897-1969: Co-founder of the Universal Negro Improvement Association* by Lionel Yard, and *Amy Ashwood Garvey: Pan-Africanist, Feminist, and Wife No. 1* by historian Tony Martin, who travelled to the places where Ashwood Garvey once lived or visited, and interviewed her political allies, family and friends. It also denotes every place she ever lived or visited, every space in which she is named and every publication in which her life and work is referenced.

I engage this archive in order to demonstrate how Black feminist knowledges can be produced in the interaction between using archives for research, curatorial and artistic purposes. Amy Ashwood Garvey's life and activism are the subject of this book, but I want readers to know her in the same way I have come to know her after more than a decade of working with her archive, and I want to show how the material it comprises might tell us everything we need to know in order to know Amy.

AMY, GUARDIE, BOAHIMAA: A SHORT BIOGRAPHY

Known affectionately as 'Guardie' by her adopted daughters, 'Aunty Amy' by the African and Caribbean students she supported and befriended, and 'Boahmiaa' by her Ghanaian allies and friends, Amy Ashwood Garvey was a well-respected Pan-Africanist, feminist, activist, orator, playwright, publisher, restaurant owner, author, art collector, sociologist and social worker. An early Black internationalist, throughout her life Ashwood Garvey moved between cities in South America, North America, West Africa, Europe and the Caribbean. She was born in Jamaica, she spent her early childhood in Panama, later migrating to the US and the UK. She had a home in London, family in Kingston, an office in Harlem and land in the Ashanti region. Each of these experiences and migrations shaped her identity and consciousness as a Black woman of the African diaspora.[5] She launched numerous projects supporting Black women's social and economic development, wrote essays and books about Black and African histories and cultures, gave lectures on women's roles in anti-colonial and Black political movements, and helped to establish several political organisations.

Amy was the first wife of the Pan-African leader Marcus Garvey. She played a pivotal role in the formation of the Universal Negro Improvement Association (UNIA), a transnational Black nationalist membership organisation that still exists today, co-founded the UNIA's newspaper, the *Negro World*, and initiated its Women's Division. Ashwood Garvey was also known for her public speaking, a skill she developed as a teenager in a debating group in Kingston. Consequently, she was often invited to participate in high-profile public events. Ashwood Garvey was a panellist at the 'Africa – New Perspectives Conference' hosted in New York by Paul Robeson under the auspices of the Council on African Affairs and was the only woman to chair a panel at the Fifth Pan-African Congress in Manchester, England, where she spoke about the economic conditions of Black women in the Caribbean.

Amy was known for her charismatic and nurturing personality, for building communities and for forging relationships. She was good friends with political activist and journalist Claudia Jones and occasionally wrote articles for Jones's London-based newspaper, the *West Indian Gazette and Afro-Asian Caribbean News*. Amy Ashwood Garvey operated a popular restaurant in London's Soho neighbourhood with her business and romantic partner, Calypso singer Sam Manning. The restaurant, named after Florence Mills, the African American cabaret singer, dancer, and comedian, was decorated with artwork that Amy had collected during her travels and offered a menu of Caribbean, African, and African American fare. It was common to see Pan-African leaders, among them Jomo Kenyatta and C L R James, involved in heated political discussions while enjoying the food and ambiance. Ashwood Garvey also ran the Afro Women's Centre and Residential Club at her home in Ladbroke Grove, which later became the Afro People's Centre, a community centre, networking and political hub for African and Caribbean migrants to Britain.

FRAGMENTS OF A LIFE: A DISPERSED ARCHIVE

Amy Ashwood Garvey's travels, business ventures and community projects often relied on the financial support of her friends and benefactors. Yet, despite her many connections, money was always tight. Amy abandoned her home in London for financial reasons, leaving behind a trove of personal papers and artefacts that were recovered by Lionel M Yard and used in his biography.[6] They were also used in the biography by Tony Martin, which is how I first came to know about Amy and her archive.

Yard notes in the conclusion of his biography that he acquired a significant portion of Amy's personal and professional archive during a research trip to London in August 1970, when he visited her former home in Ladbroke Grove. Despite previous assurances from the property service that managed the building that there was nothing worth salvaging, he felt compelled to explore the site. Inside, he discovered a chaotic scene: a vandalised kitchen, doors ripped off their hinges, and a room filled with boxes of Amy's belongings amidst old furniture covered in rugs and layers of dust. Scattered documents and a large trunk filled with theatrical clothing that had belonged to Amy's adopted son added to the disarray. Yard spent two days sorting through boxes of Amy's possessions, deciding what to discard and what to keep. He ultimately shipped five boxes of Amy's books, photographs, letters, and other personal mementos to his home in Brooklyn. Despite all precautions, one of the boxes containing a batch of letters was never received. Nevertheless, the majority of Amy's historical collection was preserved from imminent destruction, marking a pivotal moment in the development of her archive.[7]

Reading Yard's biography of Amy Ashwood Garvey was a transformative experience for me. As I turned the pages, I became deeply engrossed in the life of a woman whose legacy had been overshadowed in Black radical archives. Yard's meticulous recounting of Ashwood Garvey's journey from her early days in Panama and Jamaica to her influential role in the Pan-African movement painted a vivid picture of a complex, and dynamic woman. Yard's biography offers glimpses into Ashwood Garvey's multifaceted life – her pioneering activism, her relationships with prominent figures of her time, and her tireless efforts to unify and uplift the African diaspora. Yard's narrative, rich with anecdotes and detailed descriptions, brought Ashwood Garvey to life in a way that resonated deeply with me. I found myself imagining her not just as a historical figure, but as a living, breathing woman with passions, struggles and dreams.

One detail that particularly caught my eye was the dedication of the book to Yard's daughters, Patricia and Donna, and his grandson, Phillip Maillard. This personal touch highlighted the generational impact of Ashwood Garvey's story and sparked a curiosity in me – a desire to delve deeper into her life and the archive mentioned in the book. This newfound connection to Ashwood Garvey's legacy led me to explore further. I felt compelled to locate Yard's descendants and uncover more about the materials he had preserved. What other stories, photographs and documents lay hidden within his collection? What further insights could be gained about Ashwood Garvey's life and work? This quest to unearth more about Yard's archive became a personal mission, driven by a desire to honour and amplify the legacy of a woman whose contributions to Black feminist thought and activism were invaluable.

After much online research, I found Phillip Maillard on Facebook and promptly reached out. My email introduced myself and outlined my intentions. I explained that I was researching Amy Ashwood Garvey's life and activism and was interested in discovering whether his family still held the papers referenced in his grandfather's biography. Phillip responded graciously, expressing his belief that his mother, Patricia, still possessed boxes of books and papers left by his grandfather. He facilitated an introduction via email between Patricia and myself, paving the way for a visit to their home. Grateful for their openness and generosity, I prepared a card and a bouquet of flowers as tokens of my appreciation.

When I arrived at Patricia's home, I was welcomed warmly. Patricia showed me the boxes of books and papers, each piece a fragment of Amy Ashwood Garvey's extraordinary life. This archive was not just a collection of documents; it was a treasure trove of history and a testament to Yard's dedication to preserving Amy's legacy. As I sifted through the materials, I felt a profound connection to Amy and a deep sense of responsibility to share her story.

I reviewed what remains of this collection at Yard's family home several times between 2009 and 2011. It includes, among other things, unpublished drafts of Amy's writing on the founding days of the UNIA, letters from Ashwood Garvey to Yard, including one she sent to her 'Dear Brother' on New Year's Day, letters from Amy's close friends, and photographs from her travels in West Africa and social gatherings at her house in London. I spent hours scanning and saving digital copies of everything Yard collected and several pages of his typewritten manuscript, curating an archive of sorts on my laptop. This experience not only deepened my understanding of Amy Ashwood Garvey but also reinforced the critical importance of preserving and sharing the legacies of Black feminist leaders.

In addition to the materials held by Yard's family, Amy Ashwood Garvey has a named collection at The National Library of Jamaica, which holds manuscripts and photographs from her estate that was recovered from her property in Kingston, and a memorabilia collection at the Alma Jordan Library at the University of the West Indies in St Augustine, Trinidad, where Ashwood Garvey once lectured on 'Women as Leaders of World Thought' during her tour of the Caribbean. Rich photograph collections can also be found at the John Hope Franklin Research Center at Duke University in Durham, North Carolina, and the Schomburg Center for Research in Black Culture in Harlem, New York.

Additional archives are held in Robert A Hill Collection at the John Hope Franklin Research Center, which documents the scholars research, writing, and publications about Marcus Garvey and the founding of the UNIA, at the Moorland-Spingarn Research Library at Howard University in Washington, DC, where Amy often visited to attend UNIA meetings and socialise with friends, and the Digital Library at Indiana University in Bloomington, which holds an extensive collection on Liberia, where Ashwood Garvey spent an extended period forging a close personal and professional relationship with its president, William V S Tubman. Fragments of Amy's archive can be found throughout the UK, where Amy lived and organised for a large portion of her life. I discovered material highlighting Amy's life in London in the Local Studies Archive at the Kensington Central Library, which holds collections from the West London neighbourhood where Amy once lived, The British Newspaper Library, The National Archives, and Lambeth Archives. Additionally, I found material about Amy's involvement in the Fifth Pan-African Congress at the Manchester Central Library and the Working-Class Movement Library.

THE BIOGRAPHICAL RECOVERY OF BLACK WOMEN'S LIVES

My research on Amy Ashwood Garvey began in October 2009, when I was a master's student in Women's History at Sarah Lawrence College in Bronxville, New York. That same year, the Nubian Jak Community Trust, a commemorative plaque and sculpture initiative celebrating the historic contributions of Black people in Britain, commissioned a blue plaque to be mounted on the house in Ladbroke Grove, London that was Ashwood Garvey's primary home from 1934 to 1960.

By the summer of 2010, I was preparing for a ten-day research trip to London, where I photographed that commemorative plaque and wandered through the West London neighbourhood that Amy once called home, on the same streets walked by Yard when he came to London to do his research. I spent half a day in the Local Studies Archive at Kensington Central Library and took the tube to far-reaching places like the National Archives at Kew Gardens and the British Newspaper Library in Colindale, now part of the British Library's main building in Central London. I also explored Lambeth Archives, which used to be housed in the Minet Library and held several copies of the newspaper founded by Amy's close friend Claudia Jones, and the former location of the Black Cultural Archives (BCA) in Brixton, a dedicated archive, research library and heritage centre focused on preserving and celebrating the histories of peoples of African and Caribbean descent in Britain.

During my trip, I had the privilege of meeting renowned historians Hakim Adi, a prolific writer on Pan-Africanism, and Marika Sherwood, author of an important biography of Claudia

Jones. Together, they co-authored a biographic essay on Amy for *Pan-African History: Political Figures from Africa and the Diaspora since 1787*, a seminal book which they co-edited.[8] Additionally, I connected with Gabrielle Tierney, the filmmaker behind *Hidden Herstories*, an impactful Octavia Foundation youth-led film that highlights Amy's community activism, alongside the work of the Victorian philanthropist and social reformer Octavia Hill, trade-union activist Jayaben Desai, and Claudia Jones. As I wandered the streets of London, imagining Amy living in what was, to me, an unfamiliar place, I reflected on and made decisions that have profoundly shaped who I am today.

I submitted my master's dissertation in the spring of 2011. Since then, Amy Ashwood Garvey has been prominently featured in an ever-growing number of academic books, newspaper articles, history websites, social media posts and blogs. Amy frequently appears in digital archives and online platforms dedicated to celebrating Black women historical figures. These spaces leverage collective digital practices to piece together scattered archives, showcasing the power of digital and communal efforts in reconstructing Black women's fragmented histories and preserving their legacies.[9]

In 2021 Black Women Radicals, a US-based transnational Black feminist organisation, commemorated Amy's birthday. Thandeka Nomvele wrote an essay for the *Jamaica Gleaner*'s website highlighting Ashwood Garvey's 'exceptional contribution to Pan-Africanism,' featuring an image of Amy dressed in kente from the newspaper's archive.[10] In 2022, Ashley Everson's essay for *Black Perspectives* examined the relationship between Amy Ashwood Garvey and Claudia Jones, illustrating how their connection epitomised the revolutionary potential of transnational Black feminism. The essay included an image of Ashwood Garvey with Jones, Paul and Eslanda Robeson, from the Schomburg Center's Photographs and Prints Division.[11]

Amy has also been the subject of various artworks, a fitting tribute given her love for reciting poetry, producing musicals (such as *Brown Sugar, Hey! Hey!*, and *Black Magic*), and collecting African art. In 2016, curator Jane Bowyer commissioned Memo, a design studio run by artists Victoria Simpson and Charlotte

Hitchen, to design an illustration of Amy for *Women in Print*, an exhibition celebrating the achievements of iconic women connected to Manchester, England.[12] In 2018, Amy was the subject of *Carrying Yours and Standing Between You*, an installation by Emma Wolukau-Wanambwa for Women on Aeroplanes, an artist research project curated by the Otolith Collective at the Showroom Gallery in London. This installation presented manuscripts from Amy's archive, including fragments of my research.[13]

Historian Rhone Fraser wrote a play in 2017 entitled *The Original Mrs. Garvey*, drawing extensively on biographies by Lionel Yard and Tony Martin.[14] Fraser also penned an article, 'Where is the grave of Amy Ashwood Garvey?' for the *Jamaica Observer* in 2020.[15] Curator David Bailey featured a 1935 photograph of Ashwood Garvey, C L R James, and other members of the International Friends of Abyssinia in an installation about Black political organising in the UK at Tate Britain during the summer of 2023. Additionally, curators Aleema Grey and Mykaell Riley included a video clip of Amy in *Beyond the Bassline: 500 Years of Black British Music*, an exhibition which opened at the British Library in May 2024.[16]

The proliferation of content featuring Amy underscores the critical importance of textual, digital and physical modalities in the biographical and archival recovery of Black women's lives.[17] As these archives are created, they not only celebrate the achievements of figures like Amy Ashwood Garvey but also assert the agency of Black women activists in crafting and preserving their own narratives. Exploring Black feminist theories of the archive reveals how these collections are not just repositories of history, but also reflections of ongoing activism and resistance, where Black feminists both draw inspiration from and contribute to the ongoing curation of Black feminist archives.

BLACK FEMINIST ARCHIVES: A GENEALOGY OF PRACTICE

This book builds on existing knowledge about the life and work of Amy Ashwood Garvey by exploring the conditions of her archive.

It is a story about a Black woman, a Black internationalist, and a Black feminist whose archive, life, and activism reflect the kinds of issues I have faced undertaking Black feminist research, namely limited funds and access to resources. Without funding to support research at archives in multiple locations, my work on Amy Ashwood Garvey has often relied on the research of other Black feminist scholars. This has enabled new opportunities for collaboration and creative ways of coming to know Amy. Rather than present a traditional biographical account, I use the dispersed and fragmentary nature of Amy Ashwood Garvey's archive and how I have accessed the material to theorise Black feminist archives as sites of experimentation, speculation and collaboration.

Black feminism has been shaped by the dedicated work of Black women across disciplines such as writing, history, art, curation, archiving, and memory work. These scholars and activists have not only chronicled their own lives but also documented the communities they inhabit, enriching our understanding of Black feminist thought and activism. In my own engagement with archives, Black feminist scholarship has profoundly influenced my approach. Drawing on therapist and writer Foluke Taylor's concept of 'instinctual wayfinding', I navigate archival materials through an embodied, emotional, and affective lens.[18] This approach allows me to deeply connect with the narratives and experiences of Black women preserved in these archives, challenging traditional historical inquiry and interpretation.

The preservation of Black feminist archives has evolved remarkably over time, beginning with grassroots efforts in the early twentieth century. Black women activists not only chronicled their own lives, they also documented the communities they inhabited, enriching our understanding of Black feminist thought and activism. Figures like Amy Ashwood Garvey, who wrote essays about women in Africa and the diaspora, were instrumental in creating spaces where Black women's voices could be heard, and their achievements recorded. Initial endeavours were informal and community-based, relying on personal networks and local organisations. As global movements for civil rights and decolonisation gained momentum in the mid twentieth century, the importance of preserving Black women's history became more widely recognised. This period saw the establishment of formal archives and collections within historically Black colleges and universities (HBCUs) in the US, community centres and cultural institutions worldwide. These organisations began actively collecting documents, photographs and oral histories highlighting Black women's pivotal roles in social justice and liberation movements.[19]

The late twentieth and early twenty-first centuries witnessed further professionalisation and expansion of Black feminist archives. Academic institutions, public libraries, and museums increasingly acknowledged these collections' value, leading to dedicated archival projects and digital repositories. Technological advancements enabled the digitisation of materials, making them accessible to a global audience.[20] Amy Ashwood Garvey's early efforts to launch an international women's magazine laid the foundation for these developments, demonstrating the importance of preserving Black women's voices and histories.

In recent years, there has been a deliberate effort to decolonise archival practices, ensuring that Black feminist archives are preserved and interpreted by community members. This shift involved collaborations between Black scholars, activists and archivists to develop more inclusive and representative archival methodologies.[21] Projects like the Heart of the Race Collection at the Black Cultural Archives (BCA) exemplify these efforts, documenting the oral history of the Black women's movement in Britain. Working with a collective of archivists of African descent, The Heart of the Race project conducted thirty-six oral history interviews with women involved in the UK Black women's movement of the 1970s and 1980s, focusing on themes explored in *The Heart of The Race* by Beverley Bryan, Stella Dadzie and Suzanne Scafe, which examined Black women's lives in Britain using oral testimony.[22] BCA also holds the papers of Stella Dadzie and Jan McKenley, key figures in London's Black feminist and Black Power movements.

Located at One Windrush Square in Brixton, South London – so named after the passenger ship that famously brought the largest group of migrants from the Caribbean to the UK – BCA emerged as a response to the myriad challenges and injustices faced by Black communities. From the tragic New Cross Massacre in

1981, to the racist policing of Black communities and the systemic underachievement of Black children in schools throughout the UK, the need for a dedicated space celebrating Black heritage and culture became evident. Len Garrison and other visionaries recognised this, thus birthing the BCA as a repository where the African and Caribbean diaspora in Britain could see their stories, legacies and cultures reflected and honoured.[23]

The BCA collections, especially those highlighting the contributions of Black women, stand as powerful testimonies to the lineage of Black feminist archival practices in Britain. From its humble beginnings as a Black bookshop and supplementary school to an office space in Kennington, to becoming a cornerstone cultural institution in Brixton, a neighbourhood known for Black culture and activism in London, BCA has ardently worked to reclaim and celebrate the narratives of Black women. This dedication is exemplified in exhibitions like the 2014 inaugural show, 'Re-imag[ining]: Black Women in Britain,' which paid homage to the freedom fighters, activists, musicians, and writers who have shaped our collective history. Through these collections, the BCA doesn't just preserve history; it actively participates in the vital and transformative project of Black feminist archiving in the UK.[24]

Another significant initiative is the Remembering Olive Collective (ROC), named in honour of the community leader in the Black feminist, Black Power, and squatters' rights movements of the 1970s, who tragically lost her life to cancer at a very young age. Through research and documentation of Olive Morris and her era, ROC deepened their understanding of each other and the significance of preserving women's histories. Their meetings featured speakers who shared memories of Olive Morris and their own personal histories. During this period, ROC established the Olive Morris Collection, now housed at Lambeth Archives. This collection includes a curated selection of Olive Morris's personal documents and photographs, generously donated by Olive's friend and fellow activist Liz Obi, alongside thirty oral history interviews. These initiatives underscore the importance of community-centered archival practices in capturing and preserving marginalised histories.[25]

These practices are embodied in the work of Black creative practitioners who engage with Black feminist archives in their work. Oumou Longley's work on Olive Morris exemplifies the convergence of Black feminist theory and creative archival practices. Using a Black feminist framework to curate the Olive Morris Collection at Lambeth Archives as a therapeutic space, their installation, *Olive Morris: Voices from the Archive*, utilised an historic sound system to blend memories, radio static, original music and immersive sound design, bringing Olive Morris to life through the vibrant community that remembers her. By generating a layered, dynamic conversation and installing this work in a public space, Longley underscores that Black history, and Black feminist archives, are living, changing and shared. Longley's creative engagement with archives not only inspires a deeper understanding of Olive Morris but also profoundly influences my own Black feminist archival and creative practices.[26]

The evolution of Black feminist archives mirrors a broader recognition of the necessity to document and celebrate the contributions of Black women. From grassroots initiatives to institutional collections and creative interpretations, preserving these archives has become essential to understanding and honouring Black feminist thought and activism. In 'Sister to Sister: Developing a Black Feminist Archival Consciousness,' Yula Burin and Ego Ahaiwe Sowinski reflect on their experiences as Black British feminists in grassroots organising. The closure of the Lambeth Women's Project (LWP), a vital space for Black women to mobilise for social and political change, highlighted the fragility of feminist libraries and archives. This loss underscored the vulnerability of these repositories of activist herstories, which risk disappearing without dedicated preservation efforts.

To address these challenges, Yula and Ego advocate for the establishment of a Black British feminist herstory and archive association. This organisation would document and safeguard the diversity of Black feminist organising and activism in the UK, elevating the lives and experiences of Black women, often marginalised in mainstream narratives. For them, archiving serves not only as historical preservation but also as therapy and empowerment for Black women. It provides a space for healing from traumatic experiences, such as the LWP's closure, ensuring that the contributions of Black women to the feminist movement are not erased.[27]

Archives also play an active role in shaping the future of Black feminist narratives by engaging in community outreach and collaboration. By working with Black feminist organisations and activists, archives can help document ongoing struggles and achievements, ensuring that contemporary voices are preserved for future generations. The existence of Black feminist archives inspires and empowers current and future generations of Black feminists by providing them with a sense of continuity and connection to their predecessors. Seeing the documented struggles and successes of past Black feminists serves as a powerful reminder of Black women's resilience and agency, fostering a sense of pride and motivation to continue the fight for justice and equality. This transnational perspective on archival practices underscores the global interconnectedness of Black feminist activism and the importance of preserving its rich, diverse history.

Black feminist archival practices are essential for capturing and celebrating the multifaceted lives of Black women. Engaging with these archives through embodied knowing and emotional connection ensures their stories are preserved and their legacies honoured for generations. In my exploration of Black feminist archival practices, including my work on Amy Ashwood Garvey, I integrate autoethnography alongside traditional archival research to document and elevate the narratives of Black women. This approach is rooted in the understanding that personal experiences are inherently political, demanding a conscious, emotional and reflexive engagement with one's identity and beliefs. By intertwining personal reflections with scholarly inquiry, I seek to deepen our understanding of how race, gender, class, sexuality and other identities intersect to shape the experiences of Black women. This methodological framework challenges dominant narratives, amplifies marginalised perspectives and offers alternative insights that contribute to the liberation of Black women from systemic oppression.[28]

I draw upon the legacy of pioneering Black feminist anthropologists like Zora Neale Hurston and Eslanda Robeson, who innovatively blended personal experience with ethnographic inquiry, to inform my study of Amy Ashwood Garvey's life and work. Trained as an anthropologist in the late 1920s, Hurston spent several years in Florida, where she was born and raised, collecting and performing Black American folksongs for the Federal Writers Project. Hurston's groundbreaking work, which utilised techniques such as sound recordings, photography and filmmaking alongside autoethnographic essays and fiction writing, exemplifies an interdisciplinary and holistic approach to documenting cultural and social realities. Her exploration of everyday life, often drawing on personal memories and family histories, transcended conventional boundaries, enriching our understanding of Black diasporic experiences. Eslanda Robeson, trained as an anthropologist in the 1930s, used her scholarly background to challenge and reshape US public discourse on race and racism in the 1940s. Through her 1945 travel narrative *African Journey*, photography and public lectures, she constructed alternative, positive representations of Africa and its people, promoting Pan-Africanist activism and fostering political and cultural connections among people of African descent.[29]

Building on Hurston and Robeson's methodological daring, my approach to anthropology centres on Black feminist and Black diasporic epistemologies – ways of knowing, thinking, writing, and speaking that arise from and speak to the experiences of Black communities globally. This perspective challenges traditional archival practices that often overlook or marginalise Black women's contributions and experiences, including those of Amy Ashwood Garvey. Instead of merely seeking inclusion in existing archives, like Yula and Ego I advocate for creating and curating new archival spaces that prioritise Black feminist thought and activism.

Moreover, my methodology embraces Tina Campt's modality of refusal,[30] rejecting approaches that merely seek recognition within state-sanctioned archives. Instead, I aim to cultivate an archive of affect – a repository exploring how Black women of the African diaspora navigate their ambitions and desires amidst multiple oppressions and violence.[31] This practice-based, collaborative approach encourages what Alexis Pauline Gumbs describes as an interactive and immersive engagement with archival materials not just as historical artefacts but as prompts for imagining new futures and possibilities.[32] In this way, my research intersects with broader movements within Black feminist scholarship and activism to preserve and amplify Black women's histories that inform contemporary struggles for social justice and inspire future generations of Black feminists.

CURATORIAL FABULATIONS: EXPERIMENTS WITH THE ARCHIVE

Gail Lewis writes that Black feminist curation presents an assemblage of artefacts that together become material and intellectual objects (books articles, and exhibitions) which further Black feminism as political praxis, artistic creation, academic research and pedagogy.[33] For Yula Burin and Ego Ahaiwe Sowinski, Black feminist archival practice makes visible Black feminist histories and narratives without reifying what already exists in the archive. It is a mode of Black feminist curation that expands on existing knowledges about Black women's lives by capturing and preserving new histories and archives.

In her writing on Black women's histories and the archive, Saidiya Hartman employs critical fabulation in her exploration of Black women's histories and archival practices, merging Black feminist theory with historical research, critical theory and fictional narrative. Drawing inspiration from the creative expressions of Black artists and writers, Hartman's approach challenges the traditional boundaries between theory and art, and history and fiction. Her method seeks to address the archival 'silence' surrounding Black women's experiences, especially during the Middle Passage, by critiquing both the gaps and the inherent violence within archival records that often reduce Black women to mere commodities or victims. Critical fabulation, as Hartman defines it, involves speculative reimagining to disrupt accepted narratives, proposing alternative histories, dialogues and actions that have been marginalised or erased.

Inspired by Hartman's method, Lewis's theory of Black feminist curation, and Burin and Sowinski's articulation of a Black feminist archival practice, I present a biographic sketch of Amy

Ashwood Garvey's life. The writing does not follow a linear narrative; rather, each chapter presents a series of curatorial fabulations, which I theorise as a Black feminist archival practice that blurs the lines between research and the imagination, challenging conventional distinctions between academic scholarship and artistic creation.

My conceptualisation of curatorial fabulations is also deeply influenced by a collaborative project with Sula Douglas-Folkes, a Black feminist researcher and film programmer with a profound commitment to archival reimagination. During our time at the Institute of Contemporary Arts London, where I served as Curator of Learning and later Curator of Talks and Research, and Sula pursued her MA at Birkbeck University of London while working in the front of house, we embarked on an ambitious project aimed at expanding Black feminist curatorship through critical fabulation. Though primarily conducted online during the COVID-19 pandemic, our collaboration – ultimately shelved due to a lack of institutional support – had a significant impact on my approach to research and curation.

This book tells a story about Ashwood Garvey's life through an imagined biography based on historical research in archives, libraries and museums. It offers a critical engagement with the research process, which has involved attending to the conceptual challenges of working with dispersed and fragmentary archives through autoethnography, in the form of creative writing, photography, and moving image making. I also employ what Burin and Sowinski call 'black feminist archival consciousness' to curate a visual archive of Amy Ashwood Garvey's life and activism.[34]

Amy Ashwood Garvey's identity as a Black Jamaican woman, the descendent of enslaved Africans, born and raised in a British colony, is reflected in her visual archive. Using photographs from archival collections, and photographs taken during my autoethnographic research, I present a curated selection of images that depict Ashwood Garvey's life and activism, including her early years in Jamaica, her time in the various cities she called home in the US and Britain, and her travels throughout West Africa and the Caribbean. Through an analysis of the photographs and how I relate to them, I theorise how photographs function as archival texts that preserve Black feminist histories and visual narratives for future generations.

My experience researching Amy and working with her visual archive is interwoven throughout the narrative, juxtaposed with images from 'becoming with the archive' – an ongoing visual exploration of how my identity as a Black woman, a Black feminist researcher, and a woman of Jamaican heritage, born and raised in the US and now living in Britain, has evolved through my engagement with Black feminist archives. This curated and created archive of images is presented centrally within the book, illustrating the transformative power of archival research in reshaping personal and collective histories.

The chapters in this book are titled according to the archival fragments which I draw on and together they demonstrate the different registers through which I theorise Black feminist archives. In this way, this book experiments with archives and archival practice,[35] showing that the art of archiving has never solely belonged to the professional archivist. In *Auto/Biography as Archival Activism* (Chapter One), I use autoethnography, historical research, and the work of Black feminist biographers to expand upon how the biographies by Lionel Yard and Tony Martin have shaped what we know about Amy Ashwood Garvey's life and activism. This chapter reflects my experience of encountering two versions of Amy's life in these biographies, one that reads her as 'Mrs. Marcus Garvey Number 1', the other a 'biography of ... [the] Co-founder of the Universal Negro Improvement Association' written from the perspective of a close friend. These biographies contain the most information about Amy's childhood in Panama and Jamaica, so I use them as a starting point to imagine how those experiences shaped her becoming as a Black woman and Pan-African feminist.

The City as a Living Archive (Chapter Two) explores the social and political landscapes Ashwood Garvey navigated in the cities she frequented, beginning with her move to Harlem, where she strolled the city streets mobilising the local Black community to join the UNIA, before settling in London during the 1930s, where she immersed herself in a vibrant community of African and Caribbean migrants united in the struggle against racism and colonial rule. Responding to the community's needs in London, she established spaces like a social club and restaurant on Carnaby Street named after Florence Mills, a renowned advocate for Black American rights. Her venues became gathering spots for local and international Black luminaries, fostering dialogue among Pan-African activists, writers and future postcolonial leaders. Later, she converted her Bassett Road home into the Afro People's Centre, initially exclusive to women but eventually encompassing all Black people (and others). These diasporic hubs nurtured a shared sense of identity, community and belonging. This chapter uses archival mediations, autoethnographic vignettes and photographs to read the city as a living archive of Black diaspora.

In *Towards a Visual Archive of the African Diaspora* (Chapter Three), I use visual analysis to engage photographs of Amy Ashwood Garvey by herself or with political allies and friends. As demonstrated by the many photographs that make up the bulk of her archive, Ashwood Garvey was incredibly photogenic and liked to be photographed, especially in kente, a tradition she embraced after her first trip to the region in West Africa now known as Ghana, and continued for the rest of her life. I argue that these images reflect more than just Ashwood Garvey's style of dress. By presenting these images, I want show how Amy Ashwood Garvey used portrait photography to express her diasporic identity and consciousness through Pan-African iconography and aesthetics. Additionally, the chapter draws on photographs Ashwood Garvey took during her travels in West Africa, positioning her as an early Black feminist ethnographer and theorising autoethnography as a Black feminist archival practice

Chapter Four draws on the work of contemporary Black feminist researchers, archivists and artists, as well as my own artist research practice, to animate the process of creating and curating Amy Ashwood Garvey's archive. Through this chapter, I recover Ashwood Garvey's life and work as a significant political activist, artist and archivist in her own right. Revisiting the conditions of her fragmented archive, I detail my approaches to accessing this material and the methods I employed to narrate the story of this renowned Black woman activist. Returning to the book's overarching themes, I reflect on the challenges encountered in piecing together her scattered archive, offering insights into the future of Black feminist archival research. The fragmented nature of Ashwood Garvey's archive underscores the limitations of academia, the art world, and traditional archives in encapsulating Black feminist histories and their potential archival futures. This chapter argues that drawing on stories like these to expand upon what we recover from archives is a critical method that defines the future of Black feminist archives.

NOTES

1. Amy Ashwood Garvey, typewritten letter dated 1 January 1969, Lionel M Yard Papers.
2. Ibid.
3. Leigh Raiford, 'Notes toward a Photographic Practice of Diaspora', *English Language Notes*, 44, No 2, 1 September 2006, p212.
4. Lionel M Yard, *Biography of Amy Ashwood Garvey: 1897-1969: Co-Founder of the United Negro Improvement Association*, Associated Publishers Inc: New York, 1980, p213.
5. My thinking here is informed by Carole Boyce Davies, *Black Women, Writing, and Identity: Migrations of the Subject*, Routledge: London, 1994, p1.
6. They were also used in the biography by Tony Martin, which is how I first came to know about Amy and her archive. I purchased Tony Martin's biography of Amy Ashwood Garvey directly from his independent publishing website. In the preface, Martin recounts his serendipitous encounter with Lionel Yard, a lifelong Garveyite and great fan of *Race First: The Ideological and Organisational Struggles of Marcus Garvey and the Universal Negro Improvement Association*, one of Martin's earliest publications. Martin describes how Yard informed him about rescuing Amy Ashwood Garvey's private papers from destruction. Martin's visit to Yard's Brooklyn brownstone turned into an intense research trip, where he worked around the clock, deeply engrossed in Amy's manuscripts, memorabilia, and other materials in Yard's well-appointed library. Martin realised that the material Yard had was invaluable historical information that no other professional historian had accessed. Yard had already drafted his own biography of Amy Ashwood Garvey, which he published around 1988. Despite potential concerns of duplicating efforts, Martin decided to withhold his own work from publication until Yard's biography was released, which contributed to the delay in his own publication. During his

stay, Martin experienced the unique opportunity of sleeping in the same bed that Amy occupied during her stay with the Yard family in 1968 and having many discussions with the Yards about Amy's life. See Tony Martin, *Amy Ashwood Garvey: Pan-Africanist, Feminist and Mrs Marcus Garvey Number 1, or, A Tale of Two Armies*, Majority Press: Dover, Mass., 2008, ppix–xv.

7 See 'The Facts Behind the Story' in Yard, op cit, pp227-230.
8 Hakim Adi and Marika Sherwood, *Pan-African History: Political Figures from Africa and the Diaspora since 1787*, Routledge: London, 2003.
9 P Gabrielle Foreman, 'Sankofa Imperatives: Black Women, Digital Methods, and the Archival Turn', *A/b: Auto/Biography Studies*, 38, No 2, 4 May 2023: pp423-435, https://doi.org/10.1080/08989575.2023.2221941.
10 Thandeka Nomvele, 'Remembering Amy Ashwood-Garvey: A Pan-African Pioneer', *Jamaica Gleaner*, 27 November 2021, https://jamaica-gleaner.com/article/commentary/20211127/thandeka-nomvele-remembering-amy-ashwood-garvey-pan-african-pioneer.
11 Ashley Everson, 'Tracing the Pan-African Foundations of Transnational Black Feminism - AAIHS', 28 November 2022, https://www.aaihs.org/tracing-the-pan-african-foundations-of-transnational-black-feminism.
12 For more information about Women in Print, see https://womeninprint.co.uk/projects/women-in-print.
13 The Showroom, 'Women on Aeroplanes: Lungiswa Gqunta, Pamela Phatsimo Sunstrum and Emma Wolukau-Wanambwa', https://theshowroom.org/exhibitions/women-on-aeroplanes, accessed 28 June 2024.
14 Rhone Fraser, 'The Original Mrs. Garvey', A Gathering Together, 2018, https://www.agatheringtogether.com.
15 Rhone Fraser, 'Where is the grave of Amy Ashwood Garvey', *Jamaica Observer*, 28 October 2020, https://www.jamaicaobserver.com/2020/10/28/where-is-the-grave-of-amy-ashwood-garvey.
16 Yazzi Gokcemen, 'Beyond The Bassline Celebrates Centuries of Black British Music', *Notion*, 3 May 2024, https://notion.online/beyond-the-bassline-celebrates-centuries-of-black-british-music.
17 Mollie Godfrey and Seán McCarthy, 'Race, Space and Celebrating Simms: Mapping Strategies for Black Feminist Biographical Recovery' in *A/b: Auto/Biography Studies*, op cit, pp487-506.
18 Foluke Taylor, *Unruly Therapeutic: Black Feminist Writings and Practices in Living Room*, W W Norton & Co: New York, 2023, p2.
19 Holly A Smith, '"Wholeness Is No Trifling Matter"', *The Black Scholar*, 52, No 2, 3 April 2022, pp16-27, https://doi.org/10.1080

/00064246.2022.2042764; Tonia Sutherland and Zakiya Collier, 'Introduction: The Promise and Possibility of Black Archival Practice', ibid, pp1-6; Zakiya Collier and Tonia Sutherland, 'Witnessing, Testimony, and Transformation as Genres of Black Archival Practice', ibid, pp7-15.
20 Smith, op cit.
21 Tracy S Drake, Aisha Conner-Gaten, and Steven D Booth, 'Archiving Black Movements: Shifting Power and Exploring a Community-Centered Approach', *Journal of Critical Library and Information Studies* 4, No 1, 5 August 2022, https://doi.org/10.24242/jclis.v4i1.170.
22 Beverley Bryan, Stella Dadzie and Suzanne Scafe, *Heart of the Race: Black Women's Lives in Britain*, Virago: London, 1985; Black Cultural Archives, 'Oral Histories of the Black Women's Movement: The Heart of the Race, 2009-2010', accessed 24 June 2024, https://collections.blackculturalarchives.org/repositories/2/archival_objects/1716.
23 For more about the Black Cultural Archives, see Hannah Ishmael et al, 'Locating the Black Archive', in Andrew Prescott, Daniel Mutibwa and Simon Popple (eds), *Communities, Archives and New Collaborative Practices*, Bristol University Press, 2020, pp207-218, https://doi.org/10.46692/9781447341932.017.
24 For more information about BCA's collections and this inaugural exhibition, see the archives' website: https://blackculturalarchives.org.
25 Lopez de la Torre, 'Remembering Olive Collective', 30 September 2008, https://rememberolivemorris.wordpress.com/olive-morris-group.
26 This work originated from Longley's essay, 'Olive and Me in the Archive: A Black British woman in an archival space', in *Feminist Review* 129, No 1, 1 November 2021, https://doi.org/10.1177/01417789211041898, and a commission for Current Transmissions, a collaboration project between the BBC and the ICA.
27 Yula Burin and Ego Ahaiwe Sowinski, 'Sister to Sister: Developing a Black British Feminist Archival Consciousness', *Feminist Review* 108, No 1, 2014, pp112-9.
28 Burin and Sowinski, op cit; Longley, op cit, pp123-137.
29 Maureen Mahon, 'Eslanda Goode Robeson's African Journey: The Politics of Identification and Representation in the African Diaspora,' *Souls*, 1 September 2006, https://www.tandfonline.com/doi/full/10.1080/10999940600882830; Barbara Ransby, *Eslanda: The Large and Unconventional Life of Mrs. Paul Robeson*, Yale University Press: New Haven, 2014.
30 Tina Campt, *Listening to Images*, Duke University Press: Durham, 2017, p4.
31 Gayle Wald, *It's Been Beautiful: Soul! And Black Power Television*,

Duke University Press: Durham; London, 2015; Deborah A Thomas, *Political Life in the Wake of the Plantation: Sovereignty, Witnessing, Repair*, illustrated edition, Duke University Press: Durham, 2019.

32 Alexis Pauline Gumbs, 'Seek the Roots: An Immersive and Interactive Archive of Black Feminist Practice', *Feminist Collections: A Quarterly of Women's Studies Resources* 32, No 1, 1 January 2011, pp17-21; Alexis Pauline Gumbs, *M Archive: After the End of the World*, Duke University Press: Durham, 2018; Alexis Pauline Gumbs, 'Dread Archive: Audre Lorde and What We Are Afraid to Want', *The Black Scholar* 52, No 2, 3 April 2022, pp28-37, https://doi.org/10.1080/00064246.2022.2042765.

33 Gail Lewis, 'Once More with My Sistren: Black Feminism and the Challenge of Object Use', *Feminist Review*, 126 (1), 2020, pp1-18.

34 Burin and Sowinski, op cit, pp112-9.

35 Nydia A Swaby and Chandra Frank, 'Archival Experiments, Notes and (Dis)Orientations', *Feminist Review*, 125 (1), 2020, pp4-16.

1

Auto/Biography as Archival Activism

FROM REVOLUTIONARY WOMAN TO PAN-AFRICAN FEMINIST

In the first semester of my master's degree at Sarah Lawrence College, I enrolled in a course called Revolutionary Women. Taught by Priscilla Murolo, then director of the Women's History Program, this year-long seminar examined women's roles in revolutions that have shaped the modern world. While the syllabus focused primarily on the US, we also delved into women's involvement in political movements in other nations, including Guatemala, Russia, South Africa and the UK. Topics ranged from the revolutionary work of well-known figures like Harriet Tubman, Rigoberta Menchú, Mamphela Ramphele and Aleksandra Kollontai, to the unsung women heroes whose names we would never have otherwise known. We also looked into the emergence of internationally renowned women's organisations, including Southall Black Sisters and the Combahee River Collective, and scrutinised how movements have addressed, or failed to address, women's demands for equality and self-determination.

Alongside historical scholarship, my classmates and I read political treatises, memoirs, works of fiction and biographies, and we met for two hours on Tuesday evenings to discuss the assigned reading. Priscilla required two forms of assessment: a mid-term essay – mine was a response to a biography of Elaine Brown highlighting her involvement with the Black Panther Party – and a final essay, where I initiated my biographical work on Amy Ashwood Garvey.

Black feminist scholars specialising in Black women's political activism have powerfully illuminated their role in liberation movements across Africa and the diaspora. Much of this research takes a biographical approach, providing an in-depth examination of an individual Black woman activist's life.[1] A complementary body of work explores the collective efforts of many Black women who nurtured and sustained the vision of freedom from racism, gender discrimination and colonial oppression.[2]

Building on Black feminist scholarship on Black women's activism, the primary aim of my final essay for Revolutionary Women was to sketch a biography of Amy's political life, drawing on what I categorised at the time as secondary sources – journal articles, textbooks, histories and biographies. I also sought to underscore that Black women were leaders of groundbreaking political movements in the early twentieth century and beyond.

Determined to capture the essence of Amy's life and activism, I immersed myself in extensive reading about her and the political spaces she occupied. My goal was to write an essay that explored how she mobilised what I called 'Pan-African feminism'. In a meeting with Priscilla to discuss my paper's direction, she suggested that my research on Amy could evolve into a master's dissertation but stressed the necessity of engaging with primary sources. Reflecting on my notes from that time, I recall that she also recommended conducting research in London, with potential funding for travel, accommodation, food and research expenses from the Women's History Department and the Sarah Lawrence College Graduate Student Association. All I had to do was apply, specifying how I planned to use the money to support research for my MA dissertation.

When I presented this idea to my second supervisor, Mary Dillard, she shared my enthusiasm. A specialist in the history of science in Africa and the social history of West Africa, Mary would soon succeed Priscilla as the director of the Women's History Program. As we sat together in her office, Mary painted an evocative picture of me poring over dusty documents in London's historic archives, piecing together the fragments of Amy's life. She also reminisced about her own research, something she would often do during our meetings, and promised to connect me with her esteemed colleague, fellow West African studies scholar Hakim Adi.

I submitted a proposal to do research for my MA dissertation on 'The Political Life of Pan-African Feminist Amy Ashwood Garvey,' with glowing letters from both Priscilla and Mary. My elation peaked in May 2010 when I received crucial funding, the sole financial support for my research on Amy until May 2021, when Jumanah Younis commissioned this book for the Radical Black Women Series.

In August 2010 I arrived in London, where I immersed myself in archives during the day and strolled the city's lonely streets in the evenings. Over the course of the week, I spent countless hours at the Black Cultural Archives, Lambeth Archives, the National Archives, the Local Studies Archive at Kensington Central Library, and the British Newspaper Library at Colindale, hoping to uncover materials that would help me craft a coherent biography. What I found in the archive, juxtaposed with what I felt and experienced in London, engendered a profound connection to Amy that expanded my understanding of her life and fundamentally shaped my approach to archival research.

The experience also inspired me to relocate to London, where I completed my PhD at the Centre for Gender Studies at SOAS University of London, found a nurturing Black feminist community, and built enduring relationships with colleagues and friends. I also met my partner, Kobna, and welcomed our child, Adali, into the world. I still reside in London now, and my research on Amy continues to shape my life and work.

BIOGRAPHICAL WRITING BY BLACK FEMINIST SCHOLARS

The biographies of Amy's life by Tony Martin and Lionel M Yard were my initial sparks of inspiration for this research. I vividly recall the thrill of reading Yard's narrative of recovering Amy's archive from her home in London. Equally captivating was Martin's inclusion of excerpts from Amy's writings and other documents from her archive in the appendix of his book. Even now, years later, these moments of engagement with Amy's archive continue to fuel my exploration.

A Caribbean Studies scholar and lifelong Garveyite, Yard published his biography in 1988 with the Association for the Study of African American Life and Culture (ASALH).[3] In 2007, Martin released his biographical account of Amy's life through his independent publishing company, The Majority Press, which he also used to publish several works on Marcus Garvey.[4] As companion volumes, these biographies shed light on various details of Amy's life, from her middle-class upbringing and education to her activism in the US, the UK, Africa and the Caribbean. Historian Rhone Fraser observes that while Martin focuses on the history of Amy's political activism, Yard is more preoccupied with her emotional experience.[5] However, what is missing from both of these biographies is an analysis of how Amy's activism was informed by the lived experience of being a Black woman.

*

Biographical work on Amy's contemporaries enriches my understanding of her activism, her archive, and my work as a Black feminist biographer, recognising and honouring a Black woman's life. When writing on Amy, I am writing with Ula Y Taylor's analysis of *The Life & Times of Amy Jacques Garvey*, which illustrates how her activism intersects with various historical moments and political movements around the world,[6] and Carole Boyce Davies's exploration of *The Political Life of Black Communist Claudia Jones*, which underscores the intersection of race, class, gender and diaspora in shaping Jones's community building, writing, cultural and political activism.[7]

Two books by Barbara Ransby, one on Ella Baker, the other on Eslanda Robeson, also highlight the intersectionality of Black women's lived experiences and activism, set against the backdrop of the historical moments that informed their politics and shaped their lives.[8] Ransby's reflections on biographical writing in the introduction to both books underscore the deeply personal nature of the genre and the profound admiration that drives the research process, which resonates with me as I navigate the complexities of researching and writing about Amy. Ashley D Farmer's work on Queen Mother Moore adds to this discussion, with a specific focus on how Moore's identity as a working class Black American woman has resulted in the 'disorder distribution' of her archive and, ultimately, what we can know about her and other Black women activists like Amy, whose archives are dispersed and fragmentary.[9]

Each of these works offers a unique perspective that informs my approach to Amy's narrative and contributes to a broader understanding of Black women's lives, their activism, and their archives. Therefore, each serves as an invaluable resource that I have drawn on in piecing together a biography that extends beyond the surface to touch on the political and emotional aspects of Amy's biography.

I see myself as part of a tradition of biographical writing by Black feminist scholars who are deeply invested in and inspired by their subjects. From the abolition of slavery through anti-colonial, civil rights and Black empowerment movements, Black women have utilised biographical writing as a tool of activism, challenging dominant narratives about Black women and asserting their own identities within a society bent on silencing them.

Black feminist scholars like Carole Boyce Davies, Barbara Ransby, Ula Taylor and Ashley D Farmer exemplify this tradition, each contributing to the rich tapestry of Black feminist biography. Through meticulous research and analysis, their works recover the contributions of Black women activists who have been marginalised or overlooked in mainstream narratives of Black empowerment. By exploring the complexities of race, class, gender, migration, and diaspora, these scholars create compelling biographies that highlight Black women's lived experiences and contribute to our understanding of Black liberation movements.

By reclaiming their narratives in the form of autobiography and biography, Black women engage in a form of archival activism. Autobiographies and biographies offer invaluable firsthand accounts and nuanced analyses that enrich our understanding of Black women's lives, activism, and cultural contributions, and ensure the preservation and celebration of their stories for generations to come. These works not only preserve and celebrate their stories but also embody acts of Black feminist resistance, self-definition, and community-building, reflecting a commitment to Black feminist archiving. It is in this sense that I theorise Black women's auto/biography as a form of Black feminist archival activism.[10]

In expanding the existing biographies of Amy Ashwood Garvey by Lionel M Yard and Tony Martin, I aim to contribute to this tradition of Black feminist biography. By uncovering and presenting the rich details of Amy's political life and activism, this chapter seeks to ensure that her contributions are recognised and celebrated within the broader context of the global Black freedom struggle. I aim not only to highlight Amy's contributions but also to underscore the broader significance of documenting and analysing the lives of Black women activists. In doing so, I hope to honour her legacy and ensure that her story resonates for future generations.

'WHAT DO YOU KNOW ABOUT YOURSELF?': AMY ASHWOOD GARVEY'S AUTO/BIOGRAPHY

Much like her archive, Amy Ashwood Garvey's autobiography is dispersed and fragmentary. Through my research, I uncovered handwritten journal entries and unpublished autobiographical notes within the collections of Lionel M Yard and the Robert A Hill Collection. During a visit to Yard's family home in New York, I found unfinished manuscripts chronicling Amy's early life and the foundational period of the UNIA. These drafts, interwoven with reflections on her first meeting with Marcus Garvey and the formative days of the UNIA, offer a unique window into her life. Additionally, Amy's story unfolds through letters to friends, newspaper articles and autobiographical statements dispersed across archives in the US, the UK and the Caribbean. When pieced together, they form a compelling narrative that provides deep insights into Black feminist archives and the intricate nature of archival research.

In a brief but enlightening autobiographical account among Yard's research papers, Amy writes that she 'was born in the eastern tip of Jamaica in the most ancient and popular town of Port Antonio in the Parish of Portland'. She names her father as 'Michael

Delbert Ashwood' and her mother as 'Maudriana Ashwood (née Thompson)', citing her date of birth as 'the year 1895 on the 18th day of January'. This aligns with a registration on Ancestry.com for Amy Adina Ashwood, born in Port Antonio, Jamaica, to parents named Michael Ashwood and Maudrianna Strowfun.[11]

Passenger ship records catalogued on MyHeritage.com for arrivals in New York between 1910 and 1931 list varying birth years for Amy circa 1893, 1898, 1892, 1897 and 1899.[12] Her parents are consistently named Michael and Maud, while she appears as Amy Ashwood, Amy A Garvey, or Amy Garvey.[13] In an application to the American Consular Service in Port of Spain, Trinidad, on 14 October 1929, Amy noted, 'I am a British subject, having been born on the 10th day of January 1897.'[14] This date was printed on a US Immigration Identification Card, both of which are held in the Robert A Hill Collection. The document bears Amy's recognisable cursive signature and a passport-sized portrait of her styled in post-Victorian middle-class respectability. This date is also typed on registration forms Amy mailed to the US Department of Justice Immigration and Nationalization Service in March 1944. It has become the birthday most widely attributed to Amy.

In a 1946 interview for the *Ashanti Pioneer*, reflecting on her time in West Africa, Amy cited 1899 as her birth year.[15] When asked her age during a 1968 *New York Times* interview, she declined to disclose that information, remarking, 'Only in America can I see people looking into my face and asking themselves, 'How old is this old lady?'[16]

I first learned of inconsistencies in Amy's birthdate through Tony Martin's biography, which casts doubt on her autobiographical accounts. Although Martin's biography is well-researched, including the most extensive survey of archival collections and numerous primary sources, the text itself is imbued with sexist undertones. In the introduction, Martin describes Amy's autobiography as 'problematical', suggesting a lack of reliability in her stories and questioning the accuracy of her recollections about her personal life, relationships, and business activities.[17] This reflects a broader tendency to scrutinise and discredit women's narratives – especially those of Black women – as unreliable, eroding Amy's agency and diminishing her authority over her own life story.

Carole Boyce Davies reminds us that all autobiographical writing involves deliberate acts of curation, where authors choose aspects of their lives to highlight, strategically unveiling certain details while concealing others.[18] This selective storytelling allows Black women like Amy to construct a narrative that aligns with their desired themes, messages and purposes, offering readers a partial glimpse into their lives. By carefully curating their autobiographies, they assert agency over their own narratives, presenting themselves in a manner that reflects their self-perception and the image they wish to convey.

For Black women, the lived experience of race, class, gender and other social categories profoundly shapes what they choose to share in their autobiographical writing. When Black women feel unable to control their image in the public sphere or their bodies in private spaces, they develop strategies for maintaining the sanctity of their inner lives.[19] Navigating a society that oppresses or marginalises them, Black women may choose to keep certain aspects of their lives private as an act of resistance and empowerment. This decision to withhold personal information complicates efforts to find primary source material on the personal aspects of Black women's lives.[20]

I have often wondered about the reasons behind these discrepancies. Could Amy, like many Black women of her time, have strategically manipulated details of her personal history to navigate a hostile world? Presenting oneself as younger or older depending on the situation resonates with many Black women's experiences, who have had to adapt to societal expectations while asserting their agency. Historical records, particularly those concerning Black women, often contain discrepancies shaped by histories of enslavement and colonisation.

As a researcher, I must navigate what it means to present an 'accurate' portrayal of Amy's life. While cross-referencing with census records may offer some clarity, the wide variation in potential birthdates reminds us of the importance of approaching historical research with humility and an awareness of the limitations and inherent biases of available sources. The inconsistencies in Black women's writing, whether intentional or not, highlight the complexities of their lived experiences, shaped by a complex system of oppression, and the need for a nuanced understanding of their stories and the mechanisms by which we can research them.

*

Amy Ashwood Garvey's birth in the late nineteenth century places her within a period of significant social change in Jamaica and the wider Caribbean. Jamaica, a British colony since 1655, had an economy primarily based on agriculture, with sugarcane and banana plantations dominating the landscape. The labour force was largely composed of enslaved Africans who toiled under brutal conditions for generations. Although the slave trade was abolished in 1807, nearly 2 million enslaved Africans had already been traded to Jamaica, with tens of thousands dying on slave ships during the Middle Passage between West Africa and the Caribbean. After nearly 250 years of rebellion and resistance, emancipation was finally won in 1838. However, the descendants of enslaved Africans continued to face economic and social hardships, challenges that resonate in Jamaica today.

The post-emancipation period saw increased opportunities for education and economic advancement and the emergence of a Black middle class. Black professionals, entrepreneurs, and landowners began to assert greater influence in both local and national affairs. Economic activities, particularly in port towns like Port Antonio, flourished due to the booming banana trade and other agricultural exports, driven largely by the labour of Black workers. However, this economic growth was accompanied by deep-seated racial and class tensions. The burgeoning Black middle class often faced societal obstacles rooted in racist colonial hierarchies that favoured lighter-skin, while the Black working class found themselves shut out from the wealth accumulating in the new professional class.

This evolving socioeconomic landscape shaped the lives and aspirations of many Jamaicans, including families like Amy's, who navigated these complexities to achieve economic stability and social mobility. An article published in the *Jamaica Gleaner* in April 1939 describes the Ashwood family as 'highly respected' members of a burgeoning middle class in Port Antonio, buoyed by economic opportunities for urban Black Jamaicans.[21]

Located on the northeast coast of Jamaica, Port Antonio transformed from a modest settlement into a bustling port in the eighteenth and nineteenth centuries, driven by the export of bananas and coconuts. This economic boom attracted merchants and workers of different ethnic backgrounds, contributing to Port Antonio's growth. In Amy's account of her family history published in Yard's biography, she explains that her father, Michael, was already running several businesses when she was born.[22] Michael is described as a well-known businessman who worked as a baker and provided funeral services to the poor under contract with the local government,[23] reflecting the economic stability and upward mobility characteristic of the Black middle class in Port Antonio during this period.

Amy also describes her ethnic background, which highlights the complex interplay of historical and social forces shaping Jamaica at the time. Her father was a descendant of enslaved Africans, and his grandmother, who was born in Africa and was shipped to Jamaica as an enslaved African, was still alive. Her mother, Maudrina, was born in Jamaica to a mixed-heritage Haitian woman named Zelle Chantrelle, who had migrated to Jamaica along with her sister Gene Mendez during the expulsion of people with European heritage from Santo Domingo.[24]

In the late 1800s, a wave of migration saw Black and mixed-heritage Haitians moving from Haiti to Jamaica, driven by a combination of political, economic and social factors. Haiti, having achieved independence through a revolution that ended in 1804, experienced ongoing political instability and economic hardship, prompting many Haitians to seek better opportunities elsewhere. Jamaica, with its emerging economy and relative stability under British rule, became an attractive destination. The influx of Haitian migrants, particularly those of mixed heritage, added to the island's complex social fabric, where, under the racial politics of British colonialism, there was already an interplay between colour and class. These new arrivals often brought with them diverse skills and cultural practices, enriching Jamaican society. They integrated into various sectors, including agriculture, trade, and artesanal crafts, contributing to the economic and cultural development of their new home. This migration also highlighted the fluidity and interconnectedness of Caribbean societies, where movements of people, ideas and cultures continuously shaped the region's identity and social dynamics.[25]

Some of these new migrants also brought with them deeply entrenched racial ideas that placed them above people with darker skin. Amy's mother had this mixture of class and racial superiority ingrained in her. This created tension with Amy who, favouring her darker-skinned father, found herself at odds with her mother's views. This differing perspective would emerge as a key theme that shaped her future activism and commitment to Pan-Africanism and the global Black empowerment movement.

Amy was the middle child, with an older brother named Claudius and a younger brother named Michael. In her fragments of writing recovered by Lionel M Yard, Amy recounts how, soon after Michael's birth, the Ashwood family uprooted to Panama, drawn by the opportunities catalysed by the construction of the Panama Canal. By the canal's opening in 1914, approximately 70,000 Jamaicans, 45,000 Barbadians, and thousands from Martinique, Guadeloupe, the Dutch colonies, and elsewhere in the Caribbean had moved to Panama.[26] 'I found myself on the Isthmus of Panama at an early age, and my first school was a Spanish one where not a word of English was spoken', Amy recalled.[27] This marked the beginning of Amy's multifaceted upbringing, shaped by broader historical currents, which exposed her to diverse languages and cultures.

The Ashwood family settled in Colon, a burgeoning city in the midst of the canal's construction, where her father established a bakery and diner on the canal's banks. Amy's family also attended the local Methodist Church. Conveniently located across from 'D' Street where the family lived, the church played a central role in their community life. Amy's account of these days paints a vivid picture of Colon:

> Thousands of people were migrating from many islands in the Caribbean and pretty soon Colon where my parents lived became a living, flourishing city. Marriages were easily contracted, concubinage and prostitution followed in its wake. It was a new world and one where a cargo load came

into the harbor with women to be used either for domestic work or prostitution which was legal. When things reached this pinnacle, my mother was worried about me as I began to ask why men and women went to bed all day on Sundays and seemed happy in the evenings.[28]

Bustling with migrants and labourers from across the Caribbean and Europe, Colon faced challenges typical of growing urban centres. The presence of a significant male workforce involved in the construction of the Panama Canal contributed to a morally fraught environment for Amy's mother; her religious and cultural background emphasised the virtue of virginity in girls, so the surroundings posed serious questions about Amy's upbringing and future. Recognising the need for guidance, she consulted with the pastor of the local Methodist Church to navigate these sensitive issues. Together, they made the decision to send Amy to school in Jamaica, specifically to the prestigious Westwood High School in Stewart Town, Trelawny, ensuring she received a more stable and, in her mother's eyes, morally 'upright' education, away from the complexities of Colon's burgeoning urban life.[29]

Amy enrolled at Westwood in 1908, which she described as a 'refreshing change from any Spanish school in Colon'.[30] Founded in January 1882 by Baptist Minister Reverend William Menzie Webb, Westwood was known for its rigorous academic curriculum and focus on developing young women as leaders. Established with just six students, the school aimed to provide unsegregated education for girls, countering the prevailing colourism of the time. Reflecting its commitment to inclusivity, Westwood catered to students regardless of class, colour or creed, with most attendees being underprivileged Black girls.[31] The curriculum included geography, literature, history, mathematics, natural science, scripture and homemaking arts and crafts.[32] The teachers, who were predominantly white, instilled in their students an appreciation for women's intellectual capabilities. The academic environment at Westwood fostered Amy's intellectual curiosity and provided her with the tools to critically analyse social and political issues.

At a time when most secondary schools on the island refused children with dark skin, Westwood accepted girls of all skin complexions.[33] However, Amy's mother assumed herself superior to her dark-skinned neighbours, safeguarding a race-class privilege that Amy did not appreciate or understand.[34] Maudriana prevented Amy from developing relationships with darker-skinned or less affluent children in their neighbourhood.[35] But Amy's experiences at Westwood prompted her to reject the racialised class distinctions that separated the family from working class Black Jamaicans.

Despite Westwood's education and Amy's early political perspective, she was unaware of her African heritage, the legacies of slavery and the colonial history of the island. In Yard's biography, Amy recalled:

> At the age of twelve, when on a visit to the wife of the founder of my school, Mrs. W. N. Webb, a white lady, she inquired as to the amount raised for the mission fund. I told her the amount and she remarked that it was a pity it was not going to my people. I lapsed into silence believing she was making pointed reference to my parents. Seeing I was a trifle put out, she made haste to inform me that in Africa, a land faraway, my people lived in heathen darkness and in sore need of Christian religion, yet the money collected for the missions that year would be sent to India.
>
> Up to that time, I had no idea that I was an African or that my people had been slaves. She proceeded to tell me of the slave trade and of human beings brought along the middle passage to the Americas. 'Who brought them from their land?' I asked, and Mrs, Webb truthfully and diffidently answered that it was her English forbearers. I sprang away from her as from a deadly foe and ran as friend thousand devils were on my heels. On that very day consciousness of race stirred to life within me. A burning desire to know something of the land of my fathers seized me. The land that saw the beginning of things.
>
> I was restless. I wrote to my father, 'What is your name? What do you know about yourself?' My father was startled, and he came to Jamaica and took me to meet my great grandmother, Boahimaa, in the mountains of Manchester, who told me she came from the land of Ashanti and had

been kidnapped and taken into slavery after the abolition. My name was Dabas, meaning iron or strong wall. My ancestors were a virile, powerful, fighting tribe. Paramount rulers, princes, and kings were in my family.[36]

Like all children who went to school in a British colonial territory, Amy's education completely ignored the local history, culture and the ethnic composition of the population.[37] The experiences of Black people in Jamaica, let alone their connection to Africa or how they got to the island, was excluded from the curriculum, except for when it was necessary to discuss their relationship to the history of British conquest. Hearing her great-grandmother boast of an African heritage had a tremendous impact on Amy. It was a pivotal turning point in her political consciousness that changed the way she identified with other people of African descent. 'I was proud of myself [and] proud of my ancestry' she later recalled. I went back to school with a feeling of innate pride. I had a country; I had a name. I could hark back to my genealogy.'[38]

A popular student and leader among her peers, Amy shared what she had learned to her classmates, many of whom had no idea they were also connected to Africa. From that point forward, Amy was committed to empowering other Black people to take pride in their African heritage. 'I suddenly knew the meaning of race and felt the power of Blood. From this time onwards I nursed a passion in my heart for Africa. I dreamt dreams and built castles in the air.'[39]

*

Like her contemporary Amy Jacques, education emerges as a cornerstone of Amy Ashwood Garvey's upbringing, which is indicative of changing values in Jamaica in the context of an evolving, globalised economy. Religion, social activities and political awareness further shaped her worldview and values. These factors were significantly influenced by class. Her father, Michael Ashwood, was a successful businessman, and her mother, Maudriana Ashwood, was a homemaker. This relatively privileged background allowed Amy to receive a good education, which was uncommon for many Black Jamaicans at the time. Growing up in this environment, Amy was inadvertently exposed to ideas of Black pride and self-determination from an early age. Her parents encouraged her education and critical thinking about the world, shaping her future activism and leadership.

Understanding the historical context of Amy's birth and early life provides valuable insights into the forces that shaped her worldview and activism. Born into a period of colonial rule and racial inequality, yet nurtured in an environment that valued education and critical thinking, Amy emerged as a pioneering figure in the struggle for Black liberation and women's rights. Her early experiences in Jamaica laid the foundation for her lifelong commitment to social justice and equality. These formative years, marked by both privilege and the harsh realities of colonialism, equipped Amy with the tools and perspectives that would fuel her activism and influence in the global Pan-African movement.

'PORTRAIT OF A LIBERATOR': AMY'S FIRST ENCOUNTER WITH MARCUS

In the early weeks of August 2018, I received an email from Emma Wolukau-Wanambwa inviting me to participate in the *Women on Aeroplanes* artist research project at the Showroom Gallery in London. Curated by the Otolith Group, a collaborative effort between Kodwo Eshun and Anjalika Sagar, the London iteration of *Women on Aeroplanes* aimed to spotlight women's engagement in transatlantic networks and their significant contributions to revolutionary anti-colonial movements. Featuring newly commissioned artworks by Lungiswa Gqunta, Pamela Phatsimo Sunstrum and Emma herself, the project encompassed an exhibition and a public programme. Emma's exploration of anti-colonial organisations in the UK led her to my research. After reading my MA dissertation Emma asked me to join the project as her research interlocutor, sparking a collaborative effort between us.

Throughout the summer our meetings were frequent, taking place at various locations such as the Showroom Gallery and cosy cafes, restaurants and parks nestled between our homes in South

London. However, it was after Emma's return from her research journey to the US, the Caribbean and beyond that our discussions reached a new depth. Emma's visits to the iconic Schomburg Center for Research in Black Culture in Harlem, New York, along with stops at the Alma Jordan Library at the University of the West Indies in St Augustine, Trinidad, and The National Library of Jamaica, enriched our conversations as she shared insights gleaned from her research materials. The most significant for me were the research papers of Garvey scholar Robert A Hill papers, which are stored at the John Hope Franklin Research Center at Duke University in Durham, North Carolina. This collection includes more of Amy's autobiographical writing, providing additional details about her early life and how she came to know Marcus.

*

Reading Amy Ashwood Garvey's autobiographical drafts has helped me imagine and speculate on the possibilities of her intellectual and political development during her early life. During her teenage years, Amy Ashwood Garvey likely became increasingly aware of the racial and social disparities deeply entrenched in Jamaican society. It is plausible that she would have learned about the heroic efforts of Nanny of the Maroons, the eighteenth-century leader who guided the Windward Maroons in their guerrilla war against British authorities. She may have also come across the story of Samuel Sharpe, the leader of the 1831-2 Baptist War slave rebellion, which played a crucial role in the fight against slavery in Jamaica. Her voracious appetite for knowledge might have led her to immerse herself in the biographical works and speeches of influential Black male leaders such as Fredrick Douglass, Booker T Washington and W E B Du Bois. She may have found inspiration in Washington's *Up from Slavery*, which detailed his journey from enslavement to educational advocacy, particularly in establishing vocational schools for Black people.

Amy's burgeoning feminist consciousness could have drawn her to the writings of Anna Julia Cooper, a pioneering African-American scholar and activist. Cooper's essay on 'The Higher Education of Women' might have resonated deeply with Amy, emphasising the importance of intellectual empowerment and education for Black women. Born into slavery but completing a prestigious education, Cooper's achievements would have stood as a testament to what Black women could accomplish. Amy's exposure to these diverse perspectives within the broader context of racial and gender inequalities likely ignited her radical Black feminist perspective and set the stage for her lifelong commitment to Pan-Africanism and her relentless advocacy for the rights, education and empowerment of Black women globally.

After graduating from Westwood School for Girls, Amy moved to Kingston where, according to Lionel M Yard, she immersed herself in the vibrant cultural scene, participating in concerts and elocution contests.[40] Debating, a cherished pastime among middle-class Black Jamaicans, provided an avenue for social and intellectual expression. It was at a debate held in Kingston on 19 July 1914 that Amy crossed paths with Marcus Garvey. Her resounding victory in defending the notion that 'morality does not increase with civilization' caught Marcus's attention, setting the stage for their first encounter.[41]

In *Portrait of a Liberator: Biographical Sketch of Marcus Garvey*, an unpublished, undated monograph held in the Robert A Hill Collection, Amy vividly recounts the circumstances of her first encounter with Marcus. Edited by Lionel M Yard, the work describes how Marcus's magnetic presence and ardent admiration left an impression on Amy, paving the way for an immediate intellectual, political, and spiritual connection. Partial drafts are held in Yard's private research papers, excerpts of which are included in both Yard and Martin's biographies:

> I had just emerged triumphantly from the debate and filled with reasonable pride as a result of my forensic efforts. Just then a gentleman approached me. An undefinable something about him arrested my attention. I soon recognized him as my supporter in the debate. Without preamble he exclaimed: 'At last I have met the star of my destiny; I have found my Josephine.' Startled by his announcement, I was unaccountably thrilled and wafted up to blissful heights from which there was no desire to escape. I had so far got accustomed to

accepting as a matter of course, admiration and compliments from my contemporaries, but on this occasion I evinced a peculiar feeling of pleasure at the compliments of a stranger who had thus unexpectedly come forth to meet me in the glamorous moonlight.[42]

Although Amy was thrilled to hear the first words of admiration coming from Marcus, she 'restrained the desire to accept his offer' to see her home.[43] The next morning, she awoke to find the sun shining more brightly, the birds singing more sweetly. She was in love or, at least, she was infatuated. And so was Marcus.

The next afternoon, Marcus visited Amy at her home, and during their time together, Amy shared her story of self-discovery and pride in her African heritage. She recounted how, at the age of twelve, learning about the slave trade and meeting her great-grandmother, who spoke of their ancestral land, ignited her desire to find her roots. Amy promised her great-grandmother that she would one day reconnect with their homeland and family.

Marcus shared his story of emigrating to London in hopes of finding employment and befriending Duse Mohammed Ali, the Egyptian nationalist, Pan-Africanist and editor of *African Times and Orient Review*, who impressed upon Marcus the need for an anti-imperialist program for freeing Africa and Africans from white domination.[44] Marcus then told Amy his dream to launch an organisation that would emancipate Black people the world over and asked her to help to create it. 'Together we can educate our people,' he exclaimed. 'Together we can help to awaken the Black man to a sense of racial security'.[45] As they shared their personal narratives, Amy's pride in her African heritage resonated with Marcus's dream of emancipating Black people worldwide.

FOUNDING THE UNIA: 'ONE GOD, ONE AIM, ONE DESTINY'

Amy's partnership with Marcus was both personal and professional, deeply influencing her life's course. Together, they co-founded the Universal Negro Improvement Association (UNIA), which aimed to promote unity and self-reliance among people of African descent worldwide. Reflecting on their early days, Amy recalled,

> When we met to choose the name for our Association it took us a few days. It was very difficult to call it the Black Movement, for the word Black was an offensive word to the West Indies and even so in America. I can remember Marcus telling me a slogan used commonly among Negro people (as they then called themselves in America): 'When you're light (colored) you're right, when you're brown, stick around, but when you are Black stand back.' We couldn't call it colored, we were in a fix [sic]. However, we decided on the word Negro, then used with a common N which we capitalized. We then chose the word Universal to cover the whole Black World: the Universal Negro Improvement Association. We did not need to hesitate when it comes to Africa. Our name therefore became, UNIVERSAL NEGRO IMPROVEMENT ASSOCIATION and African Communities (Imperial) League.[46]

Marcus's inspiration to form the UNIA was significantly influenced by his reading *Up from Slavery*. The autobiography's portrayal of Washington as a 'self-made man' and its emphasis on economic self-reliance and vocational education resonated deeply with Garvey. Motivated by these ideals, Garvey envisioned an organisation that would uplift Black people globally. Marcus Garvey's admiration for Washington's principles extended to personal outreach; he contacted Washington in 1914-15 and planned to visit Tuskegee Institute, a trip that underscored his commitment to Washington's philosophy. Unfortunately, Washington's death in November 1915, just four months before Garvey's arrival in the US, prevented their meeting. Nonetheless, the influence of Washington's work on Garvey's vision for the UNIA remained profound, shaping the organisation's goals and strategies.[47]

The UNIA was deeply rooted in his working-class experiences and aspirations for Black economic empowerment and self-sufficiency. Marcus Garvey's upbringing and early career exposed him to the struggles of Jamaica's urban poor, shaping his advocacy for social and economic justice. Ashwood Garvey, in contrast, hailed from a more privileged background within Jamaica's emerging Black middle class. This contrast in their backgrounds provided Amy with a unique perspective on class dynamics within the Black community. While Marcus's activism was grounded in uplifting the working class, Amy's upbringing offered insights into the challenges and aspirations of a community striving for economic stability and social recognition. This intersection of their experiences within the broader context of Jamaica's socio-economic landscape influenced Amy's own understanding of class, contributing to her commitment to advancing the rights and opportunities of Black communities globally through her activism alongside Marcus in the UNIA. She played a crucial role in planning the inaugural meeting at Collegiate Hall in Kingston, diligently organising fund-raising activities to support the fledgling organisation.

Neither of Amy's parents particularly approved of her involvement in the UNIA, especially her mother, Maudriana. Initially, the UNIA's headquarters was a room at their home in Kingston, but the constant conflicts between Marcus and the executive board became too much for Maudriana. Disturbed by these quarrels, she threatened to shut down the entire operation. Her apprehension grew even more when Marcus began showing romantic interest in Amy and expressed his desire to marry her. Amy remembered these moments vividly:

> His love was something overmastering, searing, and elemental. I tried to remind him of our shared love for our motherland, but that could not satisfy the man's heart's hunger. He wanted to bind me to an engagement. My mother was furious and threatened to throw out the whole 'African Kingdom' if we persisted in carrying through such a suggestion. I was presented with a ring by my Romeo which he had obtained on approval from a local tradesman. It was to be worn when I was away from home as a sign of our betrothal.[48]

Marcus was determined to secure Amy's commitment to him, so they entered into a secret engagement. Given Maudriana's outright rejection of him, this was a mutual lovers' pact. The courtship was far from smooth; Amy, a free-spirited, loving, cheerful and sociable individual, was caught in a whirlwind of emotions. She later reflected, 'my courtship was riddled with conflicts. Marcus was jealous to the point of mania, attempting to restrict my freedom and even my smiles.'[49]

Marcus further sought to bind Amy to him with the slogan: 'One God, One Aim, One Destiny,' which eventually became the motto of their organisation. As Amy described, 'a popular slogan of the time was "Marcus Garvey, President; Amy Ashwood, Secretary; One God, One Aim, One Destiny."'[50]

According to Lionel M Yard, during their year-long secret engagement, Marcus Garvey's controlling nature began to surface. As co-founders of the UNIA and as lovers, they were constantly together, planning, discussing, contacting and meeting with potential members. Money was a significant issue, and as always, Amy took the initiative to organise fundraising activities. Despite these efforts, finances remained tight, leading to escalating conflicts between Marcus and Amy. Amy, naturally jovial and sociable but serious when necessary, prized her freedom. She noticed it gradually eroding under Garvey's jealousy and his demand for total control over her time, energy and person.[51]

Faced with an increasingly oppressive situation, Amy decided to return Marcus's ring and end the engagement. In her letter to him, she wrote, 'I cannot continue to accept your attentions. I wish for release from an engagement that promises nothing but unhappiness.' It was a difficult decision, but Amy saw it as crucial for regaining her autonomy. In reply, Garvey wrote a note to Amy declaring that life without her would be unbearable and even hinted at suicide, claiming he had gone to the beach to end his life.[52]

Yard suggests that this dramatic act was likely a ploy to garner Amy's sympathy. However, as a young, inexperienced woman, Amy was deeply alarmed upon receiving the note, breaking into tears and seeking solace from her mother. Maudriana saw through the ruse, while Amy felt overwhelmed with a sense of dread. Meanwhile, her father Michael, now residing in Colombia, South America, received an urgent call from his wife, summoning him to Jamaica. Despite managing a successful business in Panama, his daughter's well-being was his top priority. Amy reminisced, 'my father's sudden arrival shattered my sense of security. Unlike my stern, serious mother, he was a true son of Jamaica – gentle, soft-spoken, and kind-hearted.'[53]

However, Maudriana had prepared a list of grievances against Amy for her father, painting a lurid picture of Amy's behaviour that led her to lock herself in the bathroom. Amy recalled her mother's stance: 'She told my father he was too generous to permit an engagement with a man who did not even have a home to offer.'[54] Following this encounter, Amy's father gave her a strict ultimatum: she had six hours to pack for a boat trip to Panama. This sudden move was aimed at ending Amy's relationship with Marcus Garvey. Marcus was heartbroken by this quick separation. He accompanied Amy to the boat, reciting the Psalm of Life as a tribute to their parting.

> As we prepared to part, he presented me with a pledge thus, 'I, Marcus Garvey, promise to be faithful and true to you, Amy Ashwood, until death do us part, so help me God' Marcus signed it and gave me a copy to sign it. Love was binding and I signed as the boat was blowing for visitors to leave the ship. Being a doubtful and suspicious person, after he read it, he asked me to say it again and again. He stood by alert and tense and the visitors hustled past as I read it.[55]

The voyage from Jamaica to Panama was a sombre one for Amy. She suffered emotional shock and psychic distress, remaining in her cabin, disheartened and disillusioned. Her dream of marrying Marcus, and her commitments to cause of Black liberation, seemed to evaporate like the sea spray against the ship's hull, sparkling briefly in daylight before fading into the vast ocean.[56]

*

Amy resided in the heart of Panama City, overlooking Central Avenue. Living on the main thoroughfare, Amy found herself at the centre of community life, engaging in various local activities. She soon joined the Democratic Club, a platform for young people dedicated to discussing current social and political issues. Among its members were Panama's brightest minds: Charles Moulton, a future poet, priest, teacher, and executive secretary; Carl Elliott Ifill, poet, journalist, and educator; Beresford Jemmot, a fervent Garveyite and labour union organiser; and Edmund Headly, a journalist and family friend of the Ashwoods. The Democratic Club hosted debates and symposiums, fostering a lively cultural and intellectual environment. One member, Allan Cumberbatch, a local businessman, was particularly taken with Amy, but she remained devoted to her engagement to Garvey.[57]

During her initial months in Panama, Amy received little news from Marcus. The separation deeply saddened her, and just as despair began to set in, a letter from Marcus rekindled their correspondence. Marcus wrote diligently for six months before abruptly stopping. Amy later discovered that someone had falsely informed him of her death. Thankfully, a mutual friend, Mr Parker, corrected the misinformation upon meeting Amy, assuring Marcus that she was still alive. By then, Marcus had left Kingston and was living in Harlem.[58]

Yard suggests that Marcus's departure from Jamaica was not solely driven by new endeavours; it was prompted by his heartache over their separation. Amy was the linchpin balancing his ambitions. Life in Jamaica without her would have been bleak, deprived of her charm, smile, analytical mind, and organisational prowess. Amy rallied friends, hosted gatherings, and devised schemes to raise funds for the organisation. She set the stage for Garvey's appearances by reciting poetry, boosting meeting attendance, and bridging communication gaps with the conservative middle class. Without her, Garvey was merely another face in the crowd.[59]

In the spring of 1919, Amy's father travelled to the US and invited her to join him in Philadelphia. Eager to reconnect with Marcus, Amy arrived in New York that spring. By this time, Michael Ashwood had come to appreciate the notion of a global program unifying Black people, even if he held reservations about Marcus Garvey's leadership. Despite these reservations, he supported Amy's involvement in the UNIA.[60]

Upon arriving in New York, Amy discovered Marcus in a dire financial state but still fuelled by ambition and a commitment to their shared dream. Marcus, eager to reassert his influence in

Amy's life, quickly proposed marriage. Now accustomed to more relaxed relationships, Amy hesitated to accept a traditional patriarchal marriage demanding her full submission. Yet, her deep love for Marcus and belief in his vision compelled her to say yes. Despite the challenges, their shared tenderness and passion for their goals kept her committed to their partnership.

Settling in Harlem, Amy quickly re-engaged with the UNIA, serving as the organisational secretary. In this role, she was instrumental in organising and mobilising members, contributing significantly to the UNIA's rapid growth. She planned and accompanied Marcus on speaking tours, secured a venue in Harlem that became the first Liberty Hall, and helped distribute the UNIA's *Negro World* newspaper. Together, they travelled across the country, tirelessly setting up UNIA branches and garnering support for the central office. Beyond these organisational efforts, Amy played a pivotal role in establishing the Black Star Line in 1919. This pioneering venture, aimed at promoting economic independence and unity among people of African descent worldwide, sought to facilitate trade and transportation between Africa and its diaspora. By empowering Black communities economically, the Black Star Line challenged racial discrimination and fostered pride in African heritage and identity.

The Black Star Line was part of Garvey's broader vision of Pan-Africanism, aiming to unite people of African descent globally and promote self-reliance amid colonial oppression and racial prejudice. The company aimed to provide affordable and reliable transportation for goods and people, reducing dependence on colonial powers and stimulating economic development in Africa and Black communities in the Americas. Despite its ambitious goals, the Black Star Line faced numerous challenges, including financial mismanagement, legal disputes and sabotage from political opponents. These setbacks ultimately led to the company's demise by the early 1920s. Yet, the Black Star Line remains a significant symbol of Black empowerment and economic self-determination during a critical period in African diasporic history. Although the company faced numerous challenges, Amy's contributions to its inception highlighted her dedication to economic empowerment for Black communities.

'THE FIRST AMY TELLS': RECLAIMING THE NARRATIVE

Preserved in folders labelled 'Amy Ashwood Garvey' within the larger collection focused on Marcus Garvey and the UNIA, the Robert A Hill Collection includes some of Lionel M Yard's research files. Among these records, I discovered brief drafts that appear to be Amy's attempts to write her autobiography. One particularly intriguing document is a 'Tentative Chapter Outline' for a book titled *The First Amy Tells: Biography of Amy Ashwood Garvey, First Wife of Marcus Garvey*. The document lists twenty-two chapter titles, each bulleted using Roman numerals, and the word 'tentative' is emphatically crossed out. Imagining what these chapters might have contained is an exercise in curatorial fabulation – speculating on the narrative that Amy might have woven about her life, relationships and activism.

Another document, beginning with a typed 'Contents' page, reflects Amy's deep passion for poetry and the written word, suggesting a narrative where each chapter could be punctuated by poems that amplify the themes she cherished – perseverance, wisdom and the transformative power of education. Titles like 'The Story of Undefeated Amy' hint at a narrative that would have showcased her determination, intellectual pursuits, emotional journey and lifelong dedication to the causes she championed. 'The Poems Which Inspired Her' further underscores her love for poetry, implying that her life story might have been interwoven with verses capturing the essence of her experiences and emotions. These drafts reveal that Amy was poised to tell her own story on her own terms, despite the immense challenges she faced. One poem in particular, whether authored by Amy or simply cherished by her, reads like an allegory of her principles:

I believe in boys and girls,
The sons and daughters of the great tomorrow,
That whatsoever the boy soweth, the man shall reap.
I believe in the curse of ignorance,
In the efficacy of schools,
In the dignity of teachers,
And the joy of serving others.

> I believe in wisdom as revealed in human lives,
> As well as the Press and in printed books.
> In lessons taught not so much by precepts as by example,
> In ability to work with the hands as well as the head.
> The golden glory of love's light
> Has never dawned on my way,
> My life has always led through night
> To some deserted byway.
> But though life's greatest joys I miss,
> My thoughts will always dwell on this,
> I HAVE BEEN WORTHY OF IT.[61]

This poem, whether a reflection of Amy's own thoughts or an expression of the ideals she held close, could have served as a cornerstone in her autobiography. Amy's words reveal a profound belief in the potential of future generations, the transformative power of education, and the significance of service and wisdom. Even when she acknowledges a life missing certain joys, she finds comfort and pride in her worthiness. This resilience perhaps mirrors her response to the broader cultural and political landscape she navigated, a world where Black individuals, especially women, had to fight relentlessly for recognition, equity and justice.

These drafts and fragments, though incomplete, offer a glimpse into the autobiography that Amy might have written. The significance of her calling it *The First Amy Tells* is profound – it suggests a narrative where she claims her identity and story, perhaps for the first time, in her own words. The title also serves as a pointed response to the fact that Marcus would later marry another woman named Amy – Amy Jacques – emphasizing her role as the 'first' Amy in his life. Imagining the circumstances under which these drafts were written, one can picture Amy, later in life, reflecting on her experiences with the clarity and passion of someone who had lived through a transformative era. Her circumstances, likely marked by the challenges of illness, isolation, and the lingering trauma of her relationship with Marcus, may have made the completion of this autobiography all the more urgent for her, yet tragically unfulfilled.

In these archival pieces, I catch more than just a glimpse of a woman whose life and work epitomise the resilience and complexity of Black feminist thought and activism. Amy's integration of poetry into her life story not only underscores her literary passion but also places her within a rich Black feminist tradition of using poetry as a means for social change and personal empowerment. Through these scattered fragments, a compelling, if incomplete, narrative of Amy's autobiography emerges.

*

Amy's impact within the UNIA was profound, particularly through her pioneering efforts in establishing the Women's Division of the Harlem Chapter. As its president, she mobilised women to view their homes and roles in child-rearing not just as domestic spheres but as crucial spaces for activism and leadership, equal in importance to traditional organisational tasks assigned to men. Amy also played a crucial role in securing positions for women on the UNIA's executive branches, ensuring their significant presence and influence.[62] Her advocacy boldly challenged societal norms that confined women solely to domestic roles, advocating instead for the equality of women's contributions within the broader movement. A gifted orator and writer, she used her platform within the UNIA to advocate passionately for women's rights. Her speeches and writings inspired numerous women to join the cause, amplifying their voices in political and social activism. The Women's Division later developed into the Black Cross Nurses, which provided healthcare to Black people and promoted overall well-being through their health manuals.[63]

Amy also dedicated herself to promoting African heritage and culture within the UNIA, organising events that celebrated African traditions, music and art. These initiatives fostered a renewed sense of pride and identity among people of African descent, challenging the prevailing narratives of cultural marginalisation. In addition to her advocacy and cultural contributions, Ashwood Garvey recognised education as a vital tool for liberation. She believed deeply in ensuring that Black children had access to quality education, leading efforts to establish schools and educational programs aimed at uplifting and empowering the Black community. Amy's multifaceted contributions within the UNIA not only expanded the role of women but also underscored their essential role in advancing the UNIA's broader mission of social and racial justice, leaving an enduring legacy in the history of Pan-Africanism.

Beyond her role as a feminist and cultural leader, Amy's commitment to Marcus Garvey was rooted in a shared vision of Black unity and empowerment. She aspired not only to be his wife and homemaker but also his partner and co-leader within the organisation, championing their joint efforts towards racial and economic justice. Her bravery was evident when she intervened to save Marcus Garvey's life from an assassin's bullet in 1919. The incident unfolded in October when George Tyler, reportedly sent by an unknown assailant, entered the UNIA office with intent to kill Marcus. Armed with a .38-calibre revolver, Tyler fired four shots at Marcus Garvey, striking him twice in the right leg and scalp. Despite the wounds, he miraculously survived the attack. Amy's swift action and courageous defense of Marcus during this perilous moment underscored her commitment to their cause and her profound dedication to protecting his life.

On 25 December 1919, Amy married Marcus in a highly publicised and grand ceremony in New York City. Reflecting on the event, Amy described it as 'a spectacular affair.'[64] Being a Catholic, Garvey had the ceremony performed in a Catholic church at 138th Street in Harlem. This was followed by a public ceremony at Liberty Hall, where the second marriage ceremony took place. Here they were joined together by Dr J W Brodie, a Baptist Minister and a member of the organisation. A large reception was held immediately following the wedding with 3,000 people attending. Other celebrations were held simultaneously in many UNIA branches throughout the US who, Amy says, 'had come to associate me with Marcus while we were building branches in the various States'.[65] The couple received an overwhelming number of gifts, although, as Amy noted, 'because of the volume and the events that followed, their utility was limited.'[66] For their honeymoon they travelled to Montreal, Canada, accompanied by an entourage of officers and dignitaries of the UNIA.

Despite the grandeur of their wedding and initial joy, their marriage was fraught with challenges. Amy recounted,

Our marriage was short and stormy. Unfortunately, Marcus' personality and temperament were not geared to the intimate companionship that marriage demands. My extroversion piqued his jealousy and wounded his vanity. He could play the role of a co-operative partner for a brief time but unless one's attention was monopolized by him and his problems, he became irritable and sullen. Further, his psychosexual development and orientation, while appropriate in a West Indian milieu of that period, was outmoded in an American social climate where a wedding ring is not the symbol of total possession.[67]

After six years of political partnership and an off-and-on romantic relationship – and less than three months of marriage – Amy Ashwood Garvey and Marcus Garvey separated in 1920. No one knows what caused the end of their marriage and it seems that UNIA members split into warring factions over who was to blame. There was speculation that Marcus Garvey had begun a relationship with Amy Jacques.

Marcus countered by publicly accusing Amy Ashwood of alcoholism, infidelity and theft, and even denied her role in developing the UNIA. Several members of the organisation seconded his accusations that Ashwood Garvey's conduct was unbecoming of a wife and undermined her credibility.[68] In retort, Amy claimed that she had been a 'true, kind, loving, and dutiful wife' who had done everything possible to maintain a happy home.[69] She asserted that despite all the support she had offered him over the years, Garvey was 'a changed man from the glowing visionary' she had met in Jamaica and was now too 'caught up in the machinery of a growing Mass Movement.'[70] According to Ashwood Garvey he had become such a 'servant of that machinery' that his ego prevented him from effectively leading the organisation they had started together:[71]

> Garvey's difficulties as a leader and a husband were rooted in his own personality. I could not respond to his jealousy, suspicions and accusations without demeaning myself as a human being. This attempt to dominate me having failed he sought refuge in escape rather than trying to find some adjustable solution to our marital problems. Since the egocentric person-

ality appears to feel no sense of guilt in disregarding social conventions, Marcus peremptorily transferred his affections to the next in line – my maid of honor in the wedding. Her closeness to me was such that continued relation between us was impossible. In 1920 when I was hospitalized, he went a step further. With typical Garveyan impetuosity, he removed his belongings from our home and established a new domicile with his paramour. This outrageous behavior, this coup de pied, caused me much mental anguish but at no time did I attempt to retaliate by siding with his enemies. Garvey on the other hand, believing that the best defense is an attack sued for divorce on legally flimsy grounds and in April 1920 he dropped the suit. Members of the U.N.I.A. knew how hard I had worked to establish the organization and they were opposed to his action. For the next six years there followed a series of court actions which finally culminated on Dec. 11, 1926, when judge Hatting of the Supreme Court in New York City denied our motions for divorce.[72]

From her perspective, fortune and fame had become more important to Marcus than empowering the people. Politics aside, rumors of Marcus's sexual relationship with Amy Jacques, her dear friend, must have deeply hurt Amy. The man who once called her 'his Josephine' had betrayed her trust and caused her much embarrassment among their colleagues and friends. The two would battle it out in court for years, with the proceedings becoming a public spectacle. Ultimately, a jury found both Marcus and Amy guilty of misconduct: Marcus for committing adultery with Amy Jacques, and Amy for her affair with a man named Joseph Frazer.[73]

The trial also revealed an unfortunate situation involving Dr Hubert H Harrison, the principal editor of the *Negro World*. During the proceedings, a passionate love letter, allegedly written by Ashwood Garvey to Harrison, expressing her desire to leave Marcus Garvey and envisioning a future where they could lead the UNIA together, was read into the record. This revelation added another layer of scandal and complexity to the case. Despite the allegations and denials from both Harrison and Amy, the court found that

Amy Ashwood was Marcus's legal wife. Nevertheless, Marcus and Amy Jacques proceeded to assert the legitimacy of their marriage, and sought to erase Amy Ashwood from the history of the UNIA.[74]

Ula Taylor's analysis of Amy Ashwood and Amy Jacques's relationship reveals the complex dynamics of friendship, rivalry and influence within the UNIA. According to Amy Ashwood, she and Amy Jacques became friends in Jamaica before emigrating to Harlem. Ashwood Garvey recounts that in October 1918, upon learning that Amy Jacques needed a place to stay, she invited her to share the apartment she had with her father on Lenox Avenue. At that time, Amy Ashwood alleges Jacques showed little interest in the UNIA or any Black political movements. However, as Amy Ashwood's responsibilities with the UNIA and the planning of her elaborate wedding to Marcus Garvey in December 1919 began to weigh heavily on her, she offered Amy Jacques the role of her personal assistant, valuing her secretarial capabilities. Ashwood's intention was for Jacques to succeed her as one of the UNIA associate secretaries following her wedding. However, according to Taylor, the specifics of Jacques's entry into the UNIA remain somewhat murky. Amy Jacques herself denied knowing Amy Ashwood in Jamaica and minimised Ashwood's influence on her decision to attend a UNIA meeting.[75]

The animosity that later brewed between the two Amys complicates any attempt to accurately piece together their early interactions. Nonetheless, as Taylor explains, their relationship played a pivotal role in shaping the expectations for women's roles within the movement and underscored the consequences of challenging these predefined roles. Though there is no conclusive evidence that Amy Jacques lived with Amy Ashwood prior to attending her first UNIA meeting, it is significant to note that Jacques served as Ashwood's maid of honour at her wedding to Marcus. Despite the eventual estrangement, Amy Jacques's prominent role at Amy Ashwood's wedding indicates that their bond was once quite strong, adding layers to the political and personal tensions that emerged later.[76]

Although Amy carried feelings of resentment towards Marcus and Amy Jacques – a theme that appears at different points throughout her life – she still held fast to the ultimate aims of the UNIA, even as she moved away from the core principles of Garveyism. Her split from Marcus and the UNIA did not lead her to abandon what had brought them together. As her subsequent activism shows, Amy Ashwood Garvey was an active Pan-Africanist in her own right, not just in relation to her partnership with Marcus. Her work continued to emphasise the importance of Black empowerment and solidarity.

*

Piecing together Amy's life through a biography of archival images and documents has become a guiding principle for my research. Traditionally, archives have been seen as repositories of objective truths. However, Black feminist scholars have long understood them as sites of power and contention. The act of inclusion within archives is inherently political. Crafting a biography about a Black woman like Amy Ashwood Garvey becomes an act of defiance against the erasure of Black women's narratives from mainstream history. This intersection of Black feminism and archiving fuels 'archival activism,' an active process of searching for and preserving the stories of Black women's activism. Creating a biography about Amy is my participation in this activism, ensuring that her story, and by extension, those of countless other Black women, are heard and remembered.

Through this lens, the process of biographical recovery for Black women is deeply connected to archival activism. By reclaiming and amplifying marginalised voices, these biographies offer invaluable firsthand accounts, nuanced analyses, and critical insights into Black women's lived experiences. This approach enriches our understanding of their agency, activism, and cultural contributions, ensuring the preservation and celebration of their stories for future generations. My dedication to writing about Amy's archive, life, and activism is part of this broader tradition, contributing to the effort to recognise and honour Black women's lives.

NOTES

1 In this work, I most closely engage with biographies written about Amy Ashwood Garvey's contemporaries – Amy Jacques Garvey, Claudia

Jones, and Eslanda Robeson – because Amy knew them all in some way. However, this work is also inspired by other biographies that have shaped my approach, such as A'Lelia Bundles, *On Her Own Ground: The Life and Times of Madam C.J. Walker*, Scribner: New York, 2002; and Paula J Giddings, *Ida: A Sword Among Lions: Ida B. Wells and the Campaign Against Lynching*, Harper Collins: New York, 2009, considering that Amy had met both Walker and Wells in Harlem, and Delia Jarrett-Macauley, *The Life of Una Marson, 1905-65*, illustrated edn, Manchester University Press: Manchester, 2010, because Amy knew Marson in London. Farah Jasmine Griffin's *Harlem Nocturne: Women Artists and Progressive Politics During World War II*, Basic Books: New York, 2013, informed my thinking about Amy's life in Harlem, as discussed in the next chapter. Nell Irvin Painter's *Sojourner Truth: A Life, A Symbol*, W W Norton: New York, 1997, speaks to the way Black women used photography to assert their presence and agency, going back to the earliest days of the genre, which informed my thinking in Chapter Three. Additionally, Lynnée Denise's *Why Willie Mae Thornton Matters*, University of Texas Press: Austin, 2023, reminded me of the power of writing Black feminist biography from an embodied place, a theme that frames my writing throughout the text, but particularly in Chapter Four.

2   For examples, see Beverley Bryan, Stella Dadzie, and Suzanne Scafe, *Heart of the Race: Black Women's Lives in Britain*, Virago: London, 1985; Erik S McDuffie, *Sojourning for Freedom: Black Women, American Communism, and the Making of Black Left Feminism,* Duke University Press: Durham, NC, 2011; Ashley D Farmer, *Remaking Black Power: How Black Women Transformed an Era*, UNC Press Books, 2017; Milo Miller (ed), *Speak Out!: The Brixton Black Women's Group*, Verso, 2023.

3   Lionel M Yard, *Biography of Amy Ashwood Garvey, 1897-1969: Co-Founder of the United Negro Improvement Association*, The Associated Publishers Inc: New York, 1988.

4   Tony Martin, *Amy Ashwood Garvey: Pan-Africanist, Feminist and Mrs Marcus Garvey Number 1, or, A Tale of Two Armies*, Majority Press: Dover, Mass.; London, 2008.

5   Rhone Fraser, 'Amy Ashwood Garvey: A Bibliographic Essay', The Advocate, 18 October 2016, https://gcadvocate.com/2016/10/18/amy-ashwood-garvey-bibliographic-essay.

6   Ula Yvette Taylor, *The Veiled Garvey: The Life and Times of Amy Jacques Garvey*, University of North Carolina Press, 2003.

7   Carole Boyce Davies, *Left of Karl Marx: The Political Life of Black Communist Claudia Jones*, Duke University Press: Durham, NC, 2007.

8   Barbara Ransby, *Ella Baker and the Black Freedom Movement: A Radical Democratic Vision*, The University of North Carolina Press,

2005; Barbara Ransby, *Eslanda: The Large and Unconventional Life of Mrs. Paul Robeson*, Yale University Press: New Haven, 2014.

9   Ashley D Farmer, 'Disorderly Distribution: The Dispersal of Queen Mother Audley Moore's Archives and the Illegibility of Black Women Intellectuals', *The Black Scholar* 52, No 4, 2 October 2022, pp5-15, https://doi.org/10.1080/00064246.2022.2111648.

10 I am thinking here with the book *Mirror Reflecting Darkly: The Rita Keegan Archive*, which surveys the artist's life and work through her extensive archive. This book stands as a testament to Black feminist archival activism, combining autobiography with critical history to map Keegan's artistic journey – from her exhibitions at major institutions to her pioneering curatorship of the Women of Colour Index. By documenting her experiences within the Black British Art movement and her life as a Black female artist, *Mirror Reflecting Darkly* underscores the power of self-archiving in preserving marginalised histories and highlights archiving as an act of resistance and empowerment. For more information, see Rita Keegan and Matthew Harle, *Mirror Reflecting Darkly: The Rita Keegan Archive*, Goldsmiths, University of London, 2021.

11 'Amy Adinia Ashwood: Jamaica, Civil Registration Birth, Marriage, and Death Records, 1878-1995', accessed 3 July 2024, https://www.ancestry.co.uk.

12 Amy Ashwood In Ellis Island and Other New York Passenger Lists, 1820-1957, Birth circa 1983, Birth Circa 1898, Ellis Island and Other New York Passenger Lists, 1820-1957, digital image, www.MyHeritage.com.

13 Port Of New York, Index to Discharged or Deserted Crew, 1917-1957, digital image, www.MyHeritage.com; Manifest SS Independence, Arrival New York, NY 9 March 1921, A Ashwood age 29, Birth Circa 1893; Ellis Island and Other New York Passenger Lists, 1820-1957, digital image, www.MyHeritage.com; Manifest SS Caronia sailing from Liverpool, 5 April 1910, arrival in New York, NY 14, April 1910, List 9, Line 8, Amy Ashwood age 17, Birth Circa 1893; Ellis Island and Other New York Passenger Lists, 1820-1957, digital image, www.MyHeritage.com; Manifest SS General George W. Goethals, Cristobal, Canal Zone, 3 October 1918, arrival in New York, NY 14, April 1910, List 9, Line 8, Amy Ashwood age 20, Birth circa 1898; Ellis Island and Other New York Passenger Lists, 1820-1957, digital image, www.MyHeritage.com; Manifest SS American Legion sailing from Hamilton Bermuda, 10 May 1931, arrival in New York, NY 12 May 1931, List 11, Line 1, Amy A Garvey age 32, Birth Circa 1899; Ellis Island and Other New York Passenger Lists, 1820-1957, digital

image, www.MyHeritage.com; Manifest SS Bermuda sailing from Hamilton Bermuda, 21 October 1930, arrival in New York, NY 23 October 1930, List 1A, Line 11, Amy Garvey age 33, Birth Circa 1897.
14 Garvey Era Materials, Robert A Hill Collection, David M Rubenstein Rare Book & Manuscript Library, Duke University.
15 'An Interview with Mrs. Amy Ashwood Garvey', *Ashanti Pioneer*, December 1946.
16 C Gerlad Fraser, 'Widow of Marcus Garvey, "Black Moses", Revisits Harlem', *The New York Times*, 17 August 1968, ProQuest Historical Newspapers.
17 Martin, op cit, p18.
18 Boyce Davies, op cit, p201.
19 Shanna Greene Benjamin, 'Black Women and the Biographical Method: Undergraduate Research and Life Writing,' *A/b: Auto/Biography Studies*, 2 January 2017, https://www.tandfonline.com/doi/abs/10.1080/08989575.2017.1240397.
20 Deborah Gray White, 'Mining the Forgotten: Manuscript Sources for Black Women's History', *Journal of American History* 74, No 1, June 1987, pp237-242, https://doi.org/10.2307/1908622; Benjamin, op cit.
21 *Jamaica Gleaner*, 6 April 1939, p21.
22 Yard 1988, op cit, p2.
23 Ibid.
24 Unpublished handwritten biography of Amy Ashwood Garvey, Lionel M Yard Papers. Also in Yard 1988, op cit, p4; Martin, op cit, p16.
25 Michael J Smith, *Liberty, Fraternity, and Exile: Haiti and Jamaica After Emancipation*, University of North Carolina Press, 2014.
26 James Ferguson, *Migration in the Caribbean: Haiti, the Dominican Republic and Beyond*, Minority Rights Group International, 2003, p6. For a contemporary Black feminist history of Caribbean migration to Panama, see Kaysha Corinealdi, *Panama in Black: Afro-Caribbean World Making in the Twentieth Century*, Duke University Press, Durham, NC, 2022.
27 Lionel M Yard Papers, op cit. Also in Yard 1988, op cit, p4.
28 Ibid.
29 Yard 1988, op cit, p5.
30 Ibid.
31 Adewale McLaughlin, 'Hats off to Westwood! Trelawny School Rises from Humble Beginnings to Take Place Among Jamaica's Best', *The Gleaner*, 28 July 2014, https://jamaica-gleaner.com/article/lead-stories/20140728/hats-westwood-trelawny-school-rises-humble-beginnings-take-place-among.
32 Yard 1988, op cit, p8.

33 Iris G Edwards, 'Early History of Westwood High School and Tribute to its Founder Reverend William Menzie Webb,' *The 100th Anniversary of Westwood High School, 1882-1982,* 1982, quoted in Tony Martin, *The New Marcus Garvey Library, vol 4, Amy Ashwood Garvey: Pan-Africanist, Feminist, and Wife No. 1.* Majority Press: Dover, Massachusetts, 2000, p17.
34 Amy Ashwood Garvey, unpublished manuscript, quoted in Yard 1988, op cit, p4 (hereafter 'unpublished manuscript').
35 Yard 1988, op cit, p3.
36 Ibid.
37 Ibid, p6.
38 Ashwood Garvey, unpublished manuscript, op cit, p8.
39 Amy Ashwood Garvey, unpublished manuscript, Lionel M Yard Papers.
40 Amy Ashwood Garvey, unpublished manuscript, nd, Yard Collection, quoted in Yard 1988 op cit, p10; and Amy Ashwood Garvey, unpublished manuscript, *Portrait of a Liberator: Biographical Sketch of Marcus Garvey,* no date, Garvey Era Materials, Robert A Hill Collection, David M Rubenstein Rare Book & Manuscript Library, Duke University.
41 Yard 1988, op cit, p9.
42 Ashwood Garvey, unpublished manuscript, op cit, p10; and Amy Ashwood Garvey, unpublished manuscript, *Portrait of a Liberator: Biographical Sketch of Marcus Garvey,* nd, Garvey Era Materials, Robert A Hill Collection, David M Rubenstein Rare Book & Manuscript Library, Duke University.
43 Ibid.
44 Yard 1988, op cit, pp13-15.
45 Ashwood Garvey, Unpublished Manuscript, Lionel M Yard Papers.
46 Ibid.
47 For more information on Marcus Garvey and his influences, see Tony Martin, *Race First: The Ideological and Organizational Struggles of Marcus Garvey and the Universal Negro Improvement Association,* Majority Press, 1986; Marcus Garvey, Amy Jacques Garvey, and Tony Martin, *The Philosophy and Opinions of Marcus Garvey, or, Africa for the Africans,* centennial ed, Majority Press, 1986; Colin Grant, *Negro with a Hat: The Rise and Fall of Marcus Garvey,* Oxford University Press, 2010; John Henrik Clarke, Amy Jacques Garvey, and Runoko Rashidi, *Marcus Garvey and the Vision of Africa,* Black Classic Press: Baltimore, 2011.
48 Ashwood Garvey, Unpublished Manuscript, Lionel M Yard Papers, quoted in Yard 1988, op cit, p25.
49 Ibid, p26.
50 Ibid.

51. Ibid.
52. Ibid.
53. Ibid.
54. Ibid, p28
55. Ibid, p29.
56. Ibid.
57. Ibid, p31.
58. Ibid, p32.
59. Ibid, p33.
60. Ibid, p37.
61. Amy Ashwood Garvey, 'CONTENTS', Unpublished Manuscript, nd, Garvey Era Materials, Robert A. Hill Collection, David M. Rubenstein Rare Book & Manuscript Library, Duke University.
62. Thandeka Nomvele, 'Remembering Amy Ashwood-Garvey: A Pan-African Pioneer,' 27 November 2021, https://jamaica-gleaner.com/article/commentary/20211127/thandeka-nomvele-remembering-amy-ashwood-garvey-pan-african-pioneer; Rhoda Reddock, 'The First Mrs Garvey: Pan-Africanism and Feminism in the Early 20th Century British Colonial Caribbean,' *Feminist Africa*, 1 January 2014, pp58-77.
63. Nomvele, op cit.
64. Amy Ashwood Garvey op cit, Unpublished Manuscript, *The Wedding*, nd, Garvey Era Materials, Robert A Hill Collection.
65. Ibid.
66. Ibid.
67. Ibid.
68. Martin discusses the complaints Marcus Garvey made about Amy Ashwood Garvey as well as UNIA members' allegations about her alleged indiscretions in Martin, op cit, pp46-53.
69. 'Summons with Notice: Action for Separation', 4 June 1921, Amy Garvey vs Marcus Garvey, Supreme Court, New York County, No 22524/1921 quoted in Martin, op cit, p71.
70. Ashwood Garvey, Lionel M Yard Papers, op cit.
71. Ibid.
72. Ashwood Garvey, *The Wedding*, op cit.
73. 'Both Garveys Found Guilty; H H Harrison Denies Mrs. Garvey Wrote', *The Pittsburgh Courier*, 18 December 1926, ProQuest Historical Newspapers.
74. Ibid.
75. Taylor, op cit, pp26-7.
76. Ibid, p27.

2

The City as a Living Archive

HARLEM WORLD: A PLACE OF IMPORTANCE FOR BLACK WOMEN

When I moved to Harlem in the weeks before I started my master's degree at Sarah Lawrence College, I did not know about Amy. I knew that Harlem had been the headquarters of the UNIA and I had seen photographs of Marcus Garvey, the Black Cross Nurses, and other UNIA members dressed in their uniforms at the iconic 1920 UNIA parade in Harlem. But I was not yet familiar with Amy, her relationship to Harlem, or her role in the formation of the organisation. I moved to Harlem because most of my friends lived in Brooklyn neighbourhoods like 'Bed-Stuy', Fort Greene, Clinton Hill, and Crown Heights, where I had lived as a child before my family moved to Florida. So, I also wanted to live in one of the City's five boroughs, not too far away from my friends but with easy access to the college campus just north of the Bronx. After weeks searching through online listings, I found a room in a two-bedroom apartment on Adam Clayton Powell Jr Boulevard, just twenty-five minutes' walk from the commuter rail station to Bronxville. Although I had only seen pictures of the apartment something about it felt right – a sentiment that guided my decision to move to Harlem.

Originally inhabited by the Wecquaesgeek people indigenous to southern New York and western Connecticut, today Harlem is as a predominantly Black neighbourhood in Upper Manhattan. Its name originates from a city in the Netherlands that was adopted by Dutch immigrants who established a colonial settlement there in

1660. Harlem's Black community traces its roots back to the 1630s when it was a small, rural village populated by European farmers, traders, and people of African descent, both free and enslaved. However, the twentieth-century Great Migration brought a significant surge in the population as Black people from the south migrated north, seeking refuge from the racism and violence of Jim Crow. As they moved to the neighbourhood in greater numbers, Harlem's Black residents formed intentional communities, became politically active, and established themselves in public life. This pivotal period saw the rise of Harlem's Black churches, politicians, and political organisations – The National Association for the Advancement of Colored People (NAACP) established a chapter in Harlem in 1910 and a local branch of the UNIA was formed in 1916. Marcus Garvey purchased Liberty Hall, the site of UNIA meetings and the annual convention, in 1919. The Abyssinian Baptist Church was constructed next door in 1922 under the pastorship of Adam Clayton Powell Sr, whose son, Adam Clayton Powell Jr, was the first Black person from New York to be elected to Congress. Collectively, these activities solidified Harlem's reputation as the 'capital of Black America'.[1]

The 1920s and 1930s marked the height of Harlem's creative effervescence, with Black women artists, activists, and scholars contributing to the emergence of the Harlem Renaissance. Known first as the 'New Negro Movement', the Harlem Renaissance was a cultural and intellectual movement encompassing Black American scholarship, literature, poetry, theatre, music, and visual arts. Both the UNIA and the NAACP provided the political backdrop for the Harlem Renaissance, highlighting the interplay between creativity and the politics of Black identity. During this period, the New Negro emerged as a symbol of Black self-determination, liberation, and sophistication, laying the foundation for the Black is Beautiful movement of the 1960s and 1970s that radically reshaped how Black individuals envisioned themselves and Black American culture. But the use of the Black experience as a foundation for creative and political expression transcended the geographical confines of Harlem and the US, permeating the culture and political activism of Black communities throughout the diaspora, especially in major global cities like London. Black women were at the forefront of this movement, and were among the most radical thinkers, using the arts to explore new ways of thinking about race, class, gender, and sexuality, with a focus on issues affecting the Black community.

Moving to Harlem in August 2009, it felt as though I was immersing myself in this profound legacy. On my inaugural commute to Sarah Lawrence, I followed the route my new roommate Joy had recommended. A Black woman writer and passionate educator, Joy Osborne was an English teacher at a local charter school and had lived in Harlem for years. We had connected the previous evening over cups of tea and a shared love for Zora Neale Hurston. Zora had lived in a brownstone at 108 West 131st Street when she studied anthropology at Barnard, where she was the first Black student. Zora published seven books in her lifetime, yet her writing rarely featured Harlem. Nevertheless, the Black pride and artistic legitimacy she discovered in Harlem contributed significantly to her sense of self. Harlem had also been central to my academic journey at Rollins College, a small liberal arts college in Winter Park, Florida where I minored in African American Studies and took a course called 'African American Literature: The Harlem Renaissance'. My work on the Zora Neale Hurston Oral History Project and the annual Zora Neale Hurston Arts and Humanities Festival in the neighbouring town of Eatonville, immortalized in Hurston's seminal text *Their Eyes Were Watching God*, further deepened my affection for Harlem as a place of importance for Black women artists, writers, and researchers.

As I made my way to the train station, I turned left from Adam Clayton Powell onto 139th Street, following Joy's directions to make a right onto Malcolm X Boulevard. I soon came across the Schomburg Center for Research in Black Culture on the corner of Malcolm X and 135th Street. A spontaneous decision to stow my Canon digital camera in my backpack just before leaving my apartment proved serendipitous, allowing me to capture images of the building and its surroundings. I resolved to secure a job there, unknowingly setting the stage for my future research into Amy's archive, life, and legacy.

AMY ASHWOOD GARVEY AT THE SCHOMBURG CENTER

Named in honour of historian and writer Arturo Alfonso Schomburg, a notable figure of the Harlem Renaissance, the Schomburg Center is an archive repository of the New York Public Library (NYPL) dedicated to researching, preserving, and exhibiting materials on African and African diasporic experiences. It dates back to 1926 when the Andrew Carnegie Foundation gave the NYPL a $10,000 grant to acquire Schomburg's private collection of archival material, forming the basis of the Negro Literature, History and Prints division at the 135th Street Branch – the sole library employing Black librarians at the time. Arturo Schomburg would work there as a curator, managing research access to the collection from 1932 until his death in 1938. The 135th Street Branch became 'The Schomburg Collection of Negro Literature, History and Prints' in 1940. It was renamed the 'Schomburg Center for Research in Black Culture' in 1972 and moved to its current location at 515 Malcolm X Boulevard in 1980. Over the years, it has transformed into the most extensive collection of African diasporic archives within any US public library, boasting more than 10 million objects distributed across five divisions.[2] A focal point of Harlem's cultural life, the Schomburg Center also sponsors programs and events that illustrate the richness of Black history and culture worldwide.[3]

After my meeting with Priscilla Murolo to discuss my final essay for the course Revolutionary Women, she suggested that my biographic work on Amy Ashwood Garvey could become the focus of my MA dissertation. Following her advice, I began searching online databases for primary sources to support my work. I first accessed archival collections at the Schomburg Center after that meeting. For our next meeting, I met with Priscilla at her office at Sarah Lawrence, where I shared a list of archival materials on Amy I had discovered through ArchiveGrid.

Launched in 2006 as part of the Online Computer Library Center subscription-based discovery service, ArchiveGrid is an online database housing over five million archival objects from various archives, libraries, museums, and historical societies in the US, Canada, Australia, and the UK. Funded by the Research

Libraries Group (RLG), a consortium comprising Columbia, Harvard, and Yale universities, and the New York Public Library, ArchiveGrid aims to facilitate the accessibility of archival collections and materials. Described as 'the ultimate destination for searching through family histories, political papers, and historical records held in archives around the world', it played a pivotal role in my research.[4]

I explained to Priscilla that a late-night search on ArchiveGrid, conducted from the comfort of my bed in my Harlem apartment, directed me to the New York Public Library's online catalogue. The majority of the materials I had uncovered were housed at the Schomburg Center, right around the corner from my home. I could not believe my luck. By the following Wednesday, I found myself entering the Schomburg Center's modest vestibule, greeted by a receptionist who requested my sign-in. After adding my name to the list of registrants, I proceeded across the hall to stow my belongings in the cloakroom. Armed with my laptop, a notebook, pencils, wallet, and camera, I made my way to the elevators that would transport me upstairs to the Photographs and Prints Division.

Over the next three months, I found myself deeply immersed in the archives at the Schomburg Center, becoming a regular fixture there twice a week. Each visit was a journey through time, unravelling the layers of Amy Ashwood Garvey's life and legacy across all five divisions. My primary research site, the Photographs and Prints Division, housed the invaluable Amy Ashwood Garvey Portrait Collection and the Claudia Jones Memorial Photograph Collection, which also contained images of Amy.[5] In the Amy Ashwood Garvey Portrait Collection, I encountered portraits of Amy alone, exuding strength and grace, as well as group portraits that hinted at the close-knit community she fostered. Some images resembled family portraits, while others depicted West African people in cultural dress, capturing the Pan-African and African diasporic community Amy was part of. One particularly striking photograph showed Amy with two unidentified women on the steps of the Afro Women's Centre, while another group portrait from the 1960s featured Amy posing with fellow members of the Jamaica United Party. The banner behind them includes the political party's name and logo, and notes that it was 'founded 4th Dec 1966', indicating that Amy continued to be politically active later in life.

The Claudia Jones Memorial Photograph Collection added another layer to my understanding. The collection (1955-1964) vividly depicts Claudia Jones's political activities after her deportation from the United States to Great Britain. It includes individual portraits of Jones, views of her attending various political gatherings, and candid shots with friends and colleagues. Among these are photographs of Jones with Amy, intertwining their stories and highlighting their shared commitment to Black liberation, Pan-Africanism and feminism. The Manuscripts, Archives and Rare Books Division holds treasures like the West Indies National Council Collection (1922-1926), where Amy served on the board of directors. The Research and Reference Library contains the Proceedings on the Africa New Perspectives Conference, which Amy attended in April 1944.[6]

Each artefact that I encountered in the Schomburg Center brought me closer to Amy. It was an intimate, almost sacred process, piecing together these initial fragments to create a narrative of her life. The experience underscored the crucial role of Black and African diasporic archival institutions in preserving and retelling Black women's stories. Without ArchiveGrid pointing me to the Schomburg Center's collection, Amy's story might have remained elusive. This discovery not only guided my research but also inspired me to delve deeper into relevant collections at archives in London, enriching my understanding and appreciation of her impactful legacy. The future of Black feminist archives is contingent on the development and expansion of Black women's collections within these spaces. The importance of cultivating not only Black archival institutions but also specific Black herstory archives, as envisioned by Black feminist researchers Yula Burin and Ego Ahaiwe Sowinski, is paramount. These dedicated spaces ensure that the contributions, struggles, and triumphs of Black women are preserved and celebrated, providing a more comprehensive and inclusive historical narrative.

I started working at the Manuscripts, Archives and Rare Books Division (MARB) at the Schomburg Center in May 2010, a month after submitting my research paper and nine months after moving to Harlem. Engrossed in the research that would become the focus of my master's dissertation, I found that I was living in a neighbourhood Amy once called home. The street I lived on was named after Adam Clayton Powell Jr, her political ally and friend, and my workplace, the Schomburg Center, housed an archive deeply rooted in the radical politics and creativity of the Harlem Renaissance. This dual experience of living and working in Harlem, where both the archive and the neighbourhood were pivotal to my research, laid the groundwork for my exploration of cities as living archives of alternative histories and knowledge, which I use to attend to the gaps in Amy's archive.[7]

STREET STROLLING: URBAN SPACES AS ARCHIVES OF BLACK WOMEN'S LIVES

Historian Ula Taylor emphasises the significance of Harlem as a dynamic urban space where Black women artists, activists and intellectuals could encounter, gather and learn from each other.[8] Amy Ashwood Garvey was one of these women. She strolled through Harlem's streets, walking door to door to recruit new members for the UNIA and spread the message of Pan-Africanism. Amy recalled, 'from midnight until four in the morning, Marcus and I would trudge around the streets of Harlem, putting a slim copy of Negro World in people's doors.'[9] Taylor argues that through these strolls, Amy theorised Pan-African struggle by engaging with the people she met and the lessons she learned on Harlem's streets.

Taylor's concept of street strolling provides a unique perspective on understanding cities as living archives. Walking through urban spaces, observing, and interacting with the environment can yield rich insights into the history, culture, and experiences of the people who inhabit these spaces. In the context of the Black diaspora, street strolling becomes a method of uncovering and documenting traces of Black life and history embedded in the cityscape. From architectural styles and types of businesses to public art and graffiti, these physical manifestations tell the story of the Black diasporic experience. Taylor's theory also emphasises the subjective and experiential nature of understanding urban spaces. Street strolling is inherently personal, shaped by an individual's perceptions, interpretations, and interactions. This approach reframes the city as a dynamic and evolving repository of Black histories, communities and cultures, challenging traditional notions of what constitutes an archive.

To know Amy and imagine her life and activism, I often strolled the streets of Harlem. To write about her involvement in the early years of the UNIA, I needed to see the spaces she moved through and occupied when she was the General Secretary and founder of the Women's Division of the Harlem chapter. Whenever I had writer's block, I walked to the former location of the UNIA's headquarters on W 135th Street, where Amy edited the *Negro World* and helped launch the Black Star Line Steamship Company. Or I walked to the former site of Liberty Hall at 114 W 138th Street. These excursions, often taken during work breaks, became my moments for dissertation contemplation, note-taking, and capturing inspiration through photographs. Amy had secured both buildings and participated in the first meetings at Liberty Hall on 27 July, 1919, using her gift for public speaking to encourage women's involvement in the UNIA. This historic site was not only a meeting place but also a space where Amy encountered influential Black American women such as Ida B Wells, who spoke at a UNIA meeting in 1916, and Madame C J Walker, a UNIA donor who hosted Amy and Marcus in her Harlem residence. I also visited Amy's former apartment at 666 Nicholas Avenue and the locations of her various offices in Harlem, using addresses she included in newspaper articles and advertisements, on private letters, and on personal or organisational letterheads.

Cultivated in Harlem and inspired by my knowledge of the Harlem Renaissance, this approach has become central to how I conduct archival research. In addition to traditional archival work, my process involves using photography and later filmmaking to document the urban spaces where each repository is geographically located. On my first research trip to London in August 2010, I hoped to unearth fresh insights into Amy's activism and explore the spaces she owned and operated in the city.

Newspaper clippings at the British Newspaper Library referenced

Amy's involvement in 'social work' following the Notting Hill race riots. These articles painted a picture of a woman deeply involved in the fight for racial equality and social justice and provide a glimpse into the political climate of the time. Local records from the Westminster Library and the Local Studies Archive at Kensington Central Library offered a different perspective on Amy's life. These documents suggested that Amy was not just a political activist, but also a key figure in the local business community. My exploration extended to the National Archives, where I combed through several folders of police records, hoping to find discussions about Amy's involvement in community organising following the Notting Hill race riots. Within these official documents, where government officials monitored the political activities of Black radical organisers, I occasionally stumbled upon Amy's name. However, many of the official documents at The National Archives related to her political activities were redacted, making it difficult to gain a complete understanding of her role in these events.

I also consulted records at the Black Cultural Archives, where I first met Kelly Foster, an open knowledge advocate and public historian, working both online and 'on road' as a London Blue Badge Guide.[10] To situate Amy's activism in London within the broader context of Black women's activism in Britain, I asked Kelly, then BCA's operations manager, to suggest the best collections to explore. She recommended the papers of Stella Dadzie and Jan McKenley, founding members of the Organisation of Women of African and Asian Descent (OWAAD), the first national Black[11] women's organisation in the UK. After moving to London, I got to know Kelly and had the privilege of attending her walking tour of Black Women/Black Power in Brixton, which further shaped my approach to street strolling.

In London, as in Harlem, street strolling became a way to expand upon what I learned about Amy in the archives. I treat the city itself as an archival space where traces of Amy can be found and felt. This method allows me to connect with Amy's spirit and legacy, making the past come alive in the present through the streets she once walked. Street strolling can therefore be seen as a Black feminist archival method, a way of engaging with the city that allows for the recognition and documentation of often-overlooked aspects of Black women's lives. By walking through the city and observing its environment, we can uncover rich, layered stories about the lives of Black women and their contributions to the community.

Using street strolling as a Black feminist archival method not only allows for the discovery of hidden histories but also challenges conventional archival practices that often overlook the experiences and contributions of Black women. This approach emphasises the importance of everyday experiences, interactions, and the physical environment in shaping historical narratives. Additionally, as a Black feminist researcher, the feelings and emotions that emerged during these walks can also be valid storytelling tools. The streets evoke memories, invoke emotions, and provide a sensory dimension to historical research that often remains untapped. By acknowledging and incorporating my emotional responses, I can add depth to the stories of Black women's lives. As I walk the same streets that Amy once did, I honour her legacy and continue the work of documenting and preserving the vibrant, dynamic history of the Black diaspora. Walking through these historical spaces allows me to not only engage with the material aspects of Amy's life but also to feel a connection that bridges the past and the present, highlighting the intersections of history, affect and activism.

ON STAGE: AMY ASHWOOD GARVEY'S CONTRIBUTIONS TO THE HARLEM RENAISSANCE

As Amy's marriage to Marcus was reaching its end the Harlem Renaissance was just beginning, and Amy, a creative at heart, became an active part of this burgeoning cultural scene. The Harlem Renaissance was much more than an artistic explosion; it was a cultural revolution. It was a time when African American artists, writers and performers gathered in the New York neighbourhood to celebrate Black culture and assert their political presence. Even though Amy's name does not appear frequently in the historical record, her contributions to the Harlem Renaissance are undeniable. She not only drew inspiration from Harlem's creative realms but also left her own mark on the movement. Under

Amy's influence, the UNIA used music, drama and literary events to attract new members. Many of the Black artists who performed at Liberty Hall went on to become synonymous with the Harlem Renaissance, and some of its early writers, Zora Neale Hurston and Augusta Savage among them, first published in the *Negro World*.

The cultural and political activism Amy would undertake in the following years, particularly in London, was often informed by the people she admired, worked or connected with in Harlem. When *Shuffle Along*, the Broadway show credited with sparking the Harlem Renaissance, debuted in May 1921, Amy was inspired. Written and performed entirely by Black Americans, including actors Adelaide Hall, Josephine Baker, Paul Robeson and Florence Mills, *Shuffle Along* was widely attended by Black celebrities and political figures and was written about favourably by Harlem Renaissance thinkers like Claude McKay and W E B Du Bois. Amy loved the theatre, was a fan of Florence Mills, and would become friends with Paul Robeson. By the mid 1920s, Amy had also branched out into the world of theatre, staging three musical shows, *Brown Sugar*, *Hey! Hey!*, and *Black Magic* at the Lafayette Theater in Harlem.

Known locally as 'the House Beautiful' and located at 132nd Street and 7th Avenue, the Lafayette Theater was at the forefront of Black entertainment during the Harlem Renaissance. From its opening in 1912 until its conversion into the Williams Christian Methodist Episcopal Church in 1951, the Lafayette Theater played a crucial role in Black American theatre. It made significant history as the first major theatre to desegregate theatregoers, and was the home of The Lafayette Players, one of the most renowned Black acting companies, serving as both a training ground and a showcase for performers who later found success on Broadway and in films.[12]

A critical and box office success, *Hey! Hey!* debuted at the Lafayette on 8 November 1926. According to one reviewer, it depicted 'the pathetic fall of Marcus Garvey', providing an outlet for Amy to publicly criticise her ex-husband. *Brown Sugar* was a jazz musical examining race and class as factors in shaping the outcome of romantic relationships. It opened in August 1927, the same week as Marcus's birthday.[13] Keeping with the musical format, *Black*

Magic included 'beautiful dancing, hilarious comedy, sweet music, gorgeous costumes, and dazzling scenery'.[14] The plays received rave reviews from several Black periodicals, among them the Harlem-based newspaper the *New York Amsterdam News*, which reported: 'Mrs. Garvey's venture into the theatrical profession seems to be a success. If *Hey! Hey!* is as well received in its subsequent performances, and there is little doubt that it will be, the first wife of Marcus Garvey is well on her way to gain additional laurels.'[15] Taking a starring role in each one was Sam Manning (1898-1960), Amy's long-term on-off partner. Nevertheless, reviewers tended to focus on – and even speculate about – her relationship with her former husband instead.

*

Sam Manning was a celebrated Trinidadian calypso singer and actor, renowned for his vibrant musical style and charismatic performances. Manning's career took him from the Caribbean to the US in the 1920s, where he performed and recorded music that fused jazz and calypso rhythms and began acting in Broadway plays. His recordings and performances in Harlem's bustling nightlife scene, juxtaposed with his political activism, solidified his status as a cultural icon. It was likely during this period, amidst the thriving artistic and intellectual milieu of the Harlem Renaissance, that he and Amy crossed paths. Their shared passion for Pan-Africanism and cultural expression would have drawn them together, sparking a romance that flourished in the creative and politically charged atmosphere of the time.

Amy's relationship with Sam was a significant chapter in her life, marked by passion and complexity. Still healing from her tumultuous marriage to Marcus Garvey, Amy found solace and excitement in Sam's company. Unlike Marcus, Sam viewed Amy as an equal partner, valuing her opinions and supporting her endeavours. Their relationship, while deeply loving, was inevitably complicated. Amy's fierce independence and resistance to conventional roles often clashed with the traditional expectations of romantic partnerships. While Amy and Sam were touring the Caribbean in 1923, Sam married a woman in Barbados, mentioned in the archives only as 'Josephine'.[16] Then, in 1939, Sam married Melitta Schoittenberg, a Viennese baroness who worked in the entertainment industry, and they later had two children. Melitta had been Amy and Sam's travel companion in Jamaica while recruiting talent for a musical production in England. This situation mirrored the love triangle with Amy Jacques and Marcus twenty years earlier.[17] Yet, Sam's presence in her life brought a healing balm to Amy's wounded heart, making him one of the greatest loves of her life. Together, they navigated a love that respected Amy's unyielding spirit and desire for freedom, fostering a deeper friendship rooted in mutual respect and admiration.[18]

*

Amy's work, infused with the creative spirit of Harlem and a keen sense of political activism, sought to influence and change societal norms both in Harlem and beyond. Retelling her work on these plays seeks to place her at the centre of the Harlem Renaissance, recognising her significant yet often overlooked contributions. After their success at the Lafayette Theater, Amy and Sam took their productions on tour, attracting large crowds in Pittsburgh, Columbus, New Orleans and Chicago. Both productions were fairly successful, giving Amy and Sam a modicum of financial security. However, the economic downturn that developed into the Great Depression made it harder to find investors and paying audiences for Black theatre productions. Shortly after the US stock market crash of October 1929, Amy and Sam left New York. They travelled the Caribbean extensively, stopping in Trinidad where Sam was greeted with a front-page story in his honour. Their travels were motivated in part by a series of theatrical productions in which Sam was involved.

LONDON TOWN: 'THE HEADQUARTERS FOR NEGROES IN THE ENGLISH METROPOLIS'

By 1934, Amy and Sam set sail for London. Amidst the economic turmoil that affected virtually every country in the world, they laid plans for a new business venture aimed at the growing African and

Caribbean community in the UK. When Amy was in London a decade earlier she had met Nigerian law student Ladipo Solanke, after an article he had written in the journal *West Africa* struck a chord with her. The two formed a friendship and there were even indications that Solanke may have had romantic intentions.[19]

A member of the Union of Students of African Descent, Solanke was among a wave of West African students living in Britain who agitated against racism and colonialism – future political leaders who would shape the postcolonial transitions back home after independence. With Amy's encouragement, Solanke gathered twelve of his fellow students to create the Nigerian Progress Union (NPU). Their objectives were to promote the welfare of Nigerian students and research into Nigerian history and culture. They also aimed to raise funds to provide scholarships for young Nigerians to attend university, to maintain and grow the school network in Nigeria, and to open a hostel for Nigerian students in London. Most NPU members were studying law or medicine in London, but their concern was that in Nigeria there were no universities or colleges.[20] Through the NPU, members hoped to 'solve the social, industrial, economic, and commercial problems of Nigeria' via the platform of increasing access to education.[21]

Amy introduced NPU members to her philosophies on education, emphasising its role in Black self-determination and as a crucial part of the anti-colonial struggle. She pledged to do whatever she could to support the organisation. During its early stages, she held informal meetings with some NPU members. In a meeting in early August 1924, the NPU decided to bestow upon Amy the name 'Iyolade,' a title granted to women of honour by the Yoruba and Solanke would later recall that the NPU was 'conceived, born, and mothered by' her.[22]

Amy returned to the US soon afterwards while Solanke stayed in London. In 1925 he co-founded the West African Students' Union (WASU), along with Sierra Leonian Doctor Herbert Bankole-Bright. Adopting some of the policies of the NPU regarding provision of student accommodation, WASU opened up a hostel at 62 Camden Road in northwest London. Serving as both a residence and a space for political and social activities,

WASU's hostel was a sanctuary for many students, offering a space where they could share experiences, engage in intellectual discussions, and organise efforts toward decolonisation and civil rights. WASU played a crucial role in nurturing future leaders who would go on to shape the political landscapes of their home countries. The hostel on Camden Road was more than just accommodation; it was a crucible for the ideas and activism that would drive the fight for independence and equality across the African continent.

Amy's involvement in these organisations, along with her reputation as co-founder of the UNIA, meant that by the time she moved to London she was already a prominent figure within the African and Caribbean community. Amy's first venture in London, the International Afro Restaurant, launched around 1935 at 62 New Oxford Street, in the basement of her building. This space quickly became a vibrant hub for writers, artists, students and academics from the African diaspora, where 'the only good food in town was served and if you were lucky, the 78s of Trinidadian Sam Manning, Amy's partner, spun late into the night.'[23] Among her regulars were notable figures like Una Marson, a fellow Jamaican who was just beginning her career at the BBC; the Trinidadian writer and historian C L R James, and the journalist George Padmore. The restaurant also attracted young intellectuals such as Jomo Kenyatta, a student of anthropology at the London School of Economics who would later lead Kenya, and Eric Williams, an Oxford history scholar who would become the first Prime Minister of Trinidad and Tobago. Learie Constantine, destined to be the first Black member of the House of Lords, and Paul Robeson, a by then a West End star celebrated for his roles in *Showboat* and *Othello*, were also frequent visitors.[24]

In 1936, Amy expanded her entrepreneurial efforts by opening a nightclub, the Florence Mills Restaurant and Social Parlour, at 50 Carnaby Street.[25] This new venture further solidified her status as a central figure in London's cultural and social scene. Located in Soho, an area renowned for its rich cultural life, the Florence Mills Social Parlour was one of the few nightclubs in London that catered almost exclusively to a Black clientele.[26] On any given night, Sam and his orchestra filled the air with Caribbean melodies, and after a brief intermission a comedy team would take over. Following the live performances, the floor was cleared so patrons could spend the rest of the night dancing to everything from calypso to the foxtrot.[27] Local and international celebrities often visited the club, among them American athlete Jesse Owens, American jazz musicians Fatts Waller, Benny Carter, Ike Hatch, and Reginald Forsythe, who was described as the 'Duke Ellington' of Britain.[28]

Amy's nightclub was a diasporic space that facilitated social, cultural and political interaction between people from Africa and the diaspora visiting London and the local Black community. Certainly, this explains how it earned the mythic reputation recalled by Pan-Africanists and recorded by journalists.[29] On 25 July 1936, the *New York Amsterdam News* reported that the Florence Mills was 'the headquarters for Negroes in the English metropolis.'[30] Meanwhile, a journalist for the *London Sunday Express* proclaimed that the Florence Mills was where '[race] intellectuals from all parts of the world where wont to gather.'[31]

In an interview with Tony Martin, C L R James further emphasised the significance of the Florence Mills, describing it as 'very important' and 'the center [sic] of a good deal of West Indian agitation.'[32] The Florence Mills was one of the few places in Britain where members of the Pan-African community regularly encountered each other, making it a hub for a wide range of political activities. It was not unusual to see prominent political leaders, Ashwood Garvey among them, engaged in heated ideological discussions while enjoying the venue's menu and ambiance.[33] T Ras Makonnen, another notable Pan-African thinker, frequented Amy's nightclub and restaurant. Like James, Makonnen remembered the social spaces Ashwood Garvey created with great affection, noting that the Florence Mills was '[one] of the most famous' London venues that welcomed people of African descent. He recalled, '[you] could go there after you'd be slugging it out for two or three hours at Hyde Park or some meeting and get a lovely meal, dance, and enjoy yourself.'[34]

As a setting for social interaction and political expression, the Florence Mills was also central to Pan-African organisations. James remembered that the International African Friends of Abyssinia (IAFA), an organisation established in response to Italy's invasion of Ethiopia in 1935, was formed at the Florence Mills, and that it also served as its meeting place. The primary function of IAFA was to solicit sympathy and support and to 'assist by all means in their power' in the maintenance of Ethiopia's 'territorial integrity and political independence.'[35] The IAFA thus took advantage of every opportunity to gain the British public's support and criticised Britain and its allies for not taking a stand against fascist aggression in Ethiopia.

By 1937, the IAFA was replaced by the International African Service Bureau (IASB), whose leadership also included Ashwood Garvey, James and Padmore. Similar in design to the IAFA, the IASB also aimed to alert the British public to the social and political problems on the African continent. However, instead of drawing attention to Italy's invasion of Ethiopia, the IASB focused on the deplorable conditions in the British colonies throughout West Africa. To do this, the IASB published a series of short-lived but important journals: *Africa and the World* (July-September 1937), *African Sentinel* (October 1937-April 1938), and *International African Opinion* (July 1938-March 1939). Ashwood Garvey was instrumental in putting together this organisation and again, the Florence Mills was its meeting place.

*

A spontaneous outing to 50 Carnaby Street in November 2023 marked the first time that I attempted to photograph the former location of the Florence Mills. During a writing session, I googled the phrase 'Amy Ashwood Garvey and the Florence Mills', which revealed a Wikipedia page listing an address previously unknown to me. A few days later and I am standing in front of the entryway of Nobody's Child, the fashion brand which occupies the retail space that once was a vibrant diasporic social space owned and operated by Amy, which would go on to become the site of several music venues. Home to the Florence Mills Social Parlour in 1936 and the Blue Lagoon Club in the 1940s, 50 Carnaby Street became Club Eleven and Sunset Club in the early 1950s, the Roaring Twenties nightclub from 1961, before adopting the name Columbo's in the 1970s. Each transformation reflected the evolution of Soho's music scene, from jazz and bebop to pop rock, reggae and R&B. I stood there for a while, trying to imagine how the building had changed over time, as people passed by unaware of 50 Carnaby Street's significance in London's Black history.

Surroundings that felt like home, good food, music and dance fostered much-needed conversation, which evolved into political organising and social networks for the African and Caribbean diaspora in Britain. However, since few records of either of Amy's establishments exist, we can only imagine the atmosphere they created, both socially and politically, and infer their significance from the testaments of those who frequented them. Still, because there were so few places like these at the time in London, and given that Black people were not welcomed in mainstream establishments, it is safe to say that the International Afro-Restaurant and the Florence Mills Social Parlour operated as de facto community centres for African and Caribbean migrants needing a reprieve from the strain of living in Britain. The people who frequented these establishments were not just customers, diners, or regulars; they were Sam Selvon's Lonely Londoners, longing to feel connected to some sense of home again.

The International Afro-Restaurant must have been where Black people went when they were feeling homesick, where migrants stopped by after a hard day at work to eat an affordable meal. The Florence Mills may have been where students gathered to celebrate a birthday, or to listen to jazz music and dance among friends. Or maybe the students assembled there to talk about issues concerning their experience at university. What we do know is that the International Afro-Restaurant and Florence Mills were pivotal to the people who frequented them and, with time, these establishments became much-needed gathering places for a burgeoning generation of political leaders and activists who would go on to spearhead anti-colonial struggles 'back home' as well as anti-racist and social justice initiatives in Britain.

1 BASSETT ROAD: BRITAIN'S FIRST BLACK WOMEN'S CENTRE

The Black communities in London that Amy had worked with before the Second World War were fairly small and largely comprised of West African students and Pan-African intellectuals. The postwar years vastly expanded Britain's African and African Caribbean population, changed its class composition and created new social, economic and political challenges, which Amy was determined to meet. To some extent this required a shift in focus from facilitating social interaction between Pan-African leaders as a means of supporting anti-colonial struggles in Africa and the Caribbean, to addressing the situation of Commonwealth migrants who were settling in Britain.

In 1934 Amy moved to a large Victorian home at 1 Bassett Road in Ladbroke Grove. A West London neighbourhood in the Royal Borough of Kensington and Chelsea, at that time Ladbroke Grove was one of the few areas in the city where migrants could find affordable housing – and landlords willing to rent to them.[36] A large number of migrants from West Africa and the Caribbean began settling in the area, joining existing migrants from Ireland, Poland and other countries in Europe. Yet, because of discriminatory housing policies, disillusionment and disappointment was an everyday experience. Although the British 'colour bar' was not government sanctioned or supported by legislation, it was a harsh reality that made it difficult, if not impossible, for African and Caribbean migrants to find adequate housing. At this time, there were no state agencies where one could find settlement assistance.[37] With its substantial African and Caribbean migrant population and the obvious need for community support services, Ladbroke Grove was the perfect place for Amy to live and work.

Shortly after moving to the area, Amy's friend and colleague Eva Saunders introduced her to Sir Hamilton Kerr, a local Member of Parliament who had publicly expressed his sympathy towards Britain's growing 'black community.'[38] During their meeting Amy addressed her dissatisfaction with social and housing conditions in Ladbroke Grove and insisted on the need for a community centre that would offer guidance on how to get established in London. What Amy envisioned was a centre that, with support from local authorities, would offer resettlement advice and services as well as short-term accommodation. Sir Hamilton Kerr gave Amy £10,000 to support this venture, and in 1954 she established a residential and community centre in her home.[39]

The Afro Women's Centre & Residential Club was the first Black women's centre in Britain. According to an advertisement donated to the Alma Jordan Library by Thelma Rogers, a Pan-African feminist comrade Amy met in Trinidad, the purpose of the Afro Women's Centre & Residential Club was to 'promote the welfare of women of colour' and 'answer the long-felt need of the coloured woman for spiritual, cultural, social, and political advancement.'[40] Amy's goal in establishing the centre was to create an atmosphere where women could express their talents and aspirations.[41] She hoped to foster an appreciation for the arts and literature, as well as for the study of the social sciences and politics. The centre would eventually become a restaurant, a boarding house, a welfare agency and the headquarters of several small business ventures.[42]

Women of African descent from different parts of the world became political allies and friends at the Afro Women's Centre. Despite its name, Amy hoped that the centre would promote a better understanding among women of all backgrounds, encouraging a spirit of solidarity between them.[43] Although the majority of the Afro Women's Centre's clientele were Black, Ashwood Garvey dreamed of running a multicultural establishment. In a letter describing her plans for the centre, Amy shared that she wanted to 'create among women a multiracial society,' for she had come to realise that 'one cannot fight segregation and practice it at the same time.'[44] By July 1954, there were two white English women living at the centre and Amy had invited two Indian women to live there as well.[45] Reflecting on the evolving inclusivity of the Centre, Amy noted, 'We experienced a difficult year establishing the Centre, but events pointed the way to a new order of things as the Centre became a "Peoples" Centre, rather than a "Womens" [sic]. We have been taking men here for 9 months, and I must confess that their conduct has been quite superior to that of the women.' In 1955, she renamed it the Afro People's Centre to better represent its gender inclusiveness and the reality of male boarders.[46]

*

All of the social spaces Amy Ashwood Garvey created were established with the intention of offering a meeting place for social connection and political organisation. Living in London at the time, George Padmore frequented the centre and distinguished Black people visiting London often entertained there. Most of the centre's boarders were students, and in some cases parents formally placed their children in Amy's care.[47] While the centre's primary purpose was to offer settlement assistance to students and labour migrants, providing an entry point into British society, the safe and nurturing environment that Amy engendered offered much more.

Centrally located on a tree-lined block the Afro People's Centre was a networking hub that gave those who were struggling to acclimate to life in Britain a place to freely express their frustrations and to maintain their cultural identities, as well as forge a new one as part of the diaspora. At the centre, visitors could participate in a range of recreational activities and Amy planned to offer vocational training, which she hoped would make it easier for those who enrolled to gain meaningful employment.[48] Although clearly there were economic benefits to these ventures for Amy, she never lost sight of her commitment to uniting the community she aimed to serve.

As more and more African and Caribbean migrants settled and obtained work in the area, the social and political climate became increasingly tense. The white working-class community was particularly hostile to Black working-class families, claiming that their presence threatened job stability and housing in the area. The situation was exploited by Sir Oswald Mosley's Union Movement[49] and other fascist groups, who urged dissatisfied white residents to 'Keep England White'.[50] Supporters of Mosley and other fascist groups harassed newly arrived migrants, making it difficult for them to gain employment or find accommodation. In many parts of Britain at this time, it was not only unpleasant but also unsafe for a person of African descent to walk the streets, especially at night.[51] Those who ventured out often met with hostile stares and racial epithets, and sometimes suffered unprovoked physical assaults.[52] White youths, commonly known as 'Teddy Boys', engaged in racially motivated violence, attacking unsuspecting Black people who in many cases were not able to defend themselves.[53]

On Saturday, 23 August 1958, a group of Teddy Boys went on a rampage in Nottingham with the intended purpose of assaulting African and African Caribbean migrants. By the following week, racist riots had also broken out in Notting Hill, which neighbours Ladbroke Grove, while similar occurrences involving 300-400 white youth were also taking place in other parts of London. Black people were attacked in the streets, their homes set on fire, and Black-owned business were ransacked and looted.[54] Several Black people were arrested and issued fines for resisting violence.

Though it was initially launched as a social centre and housing institution, due to the increased racial hostility in the area, the Afro People's Centre became the home of several anti-racist and grassroots organisations. One such organisation was the Association for the Advancement of Coloured People (AACP) which, like its American namesake, advocated for the civil rights of the African diaspora in Britain. Claudia Jones, a close friend of Amy, served as the AACP's general secretary. The two were already familiar with each other in Harlem and maintained their connection as they both moved to London. Together, the two women established a Defence Committee, which provided advice on dealing with racial discrimination and legal services for those arrested or fined for defending themselves.[55] To support this effort, Claudia organised a Caribbean Carnival, held on 30 January 1959 at St Pancras Town Hall, which Amy attended. This event, a precursor to the Notting Hill Carnival, aimed to raise funds to improve race relations and also to pay the fines of those arrested during the Notting Hill Race Riots.[56] According to Claude Ramsey, a Barbados-born migrant who became active in the anti-racist political scene in London, the Defence Committee 'was able to give invaluable support to West Indians at a time when the courts were handing out stiff penalties for those found guilty of public order offences.'[57] In addition to providing legal services, the AACP offered workshops to train Black people to serve as social welfare workers in the community. Articles that appeared in local newspapers promoted the AACP's many activities, calling Ashwood Garvey 'a well-known energetic social worker amongst the coloured people' who had been 'fighting a lone battle for racial tolerance during her twenty-five years in Britain.'[58]

Arriving at The British Newspaper Library at Colindale with the aim of examining Amy's activism during the Notting Hill Race Riots, I focused on area-specific newspapers from that turbulent period. My research began by poring over editions of *The Kensington News and West London Times* from August 1958 to July 1959. Through this, I learned that Amy had been selected by the local government to take part in a committee formed to examine race relations in the area and to investigate the causes of the riots.

The most revealing article was in the 19 September 1958 edition, which noted that 'Coloured delegates to the Coordinating Committee are being selected by a group under the chairmanship of Mrs. Garvey, a well-known coloured welfare worker.' This committee was tasked with addressing the racial tensions that had escalated into the riots, making it a critical effort to foster understanding and propose solutions for the community.

On 26 September 1958, an article titled 'Mayor's Committee Chosen' listed Amy Ashwood as the only woman of colour on the panel and described her as 'a woman who has been fighting a lone battle for racial tolerance during the 25 years she has lived in London.' This committee was not just a symbolic gesture; it was an active attempt by the local government to include diverse voices in the conversation about race relations and to directly address the issues that had led to such unrest. More insights came from the 17 October 1958 piece, 'Mayor's Race Committee Criticised', revealing criticisms of the committee chaired by Amy. These discoveries underscored Amy Ashwood Garvey's tireless efforts and her pivotal role in advocating for legal reforms during a crucial chapter in London's history.[59] Her involvement in the committee was a testament to her lifelong commitment to social justice and her influential presence in shaping the discourse on race relations in Britain.

By forging a site where African and Caribbean migrants could interact with one another, as well as access needs-based services, Amy created a social space that was emblematic of the community organising that would blossom and grow in the area in the years to come. Inspired by the Harlem Renaissance, Amy linked the cultural and social, as well as the economic and political interests of the African diaspora in Britain, Amy set into motion the radical politics that would come to define social institutions like Notting Hill Carnival and the London dub-poetry and reggae scene. Of course, both of these social practices have since garnered much recognition as key sites of contestation and resistance for the Black communities in London.

*

In November 2009 the Octavia Foundation, in partnership with the Nubian Jak Community Trust, unveiled a blue plaque commemorating the life and achievements of Amy Ashwood Garvey. The unveiling ceremony, which was conducted by former Jamaican High Commissioner Burchell Whiteman and ex-Mayor of the Royal Borough of Kensington and Chelsea, Timothy Coleridge, and attended by a host of community activists and local historians, was followed by a reception with Caribbean food, calypso music and speeches from people who knew Amy and her work. Since that time, the Octavia Foundation has produced an hour-long documentary, *Hidden Herstories: Women of Change*, which focuses on the lives of four women, among them Ashwood Garvey, Claudia Jones, Octavia Hill and Jayaben Desai. The building the plaque is mounted on features prominently in the film, and the segment on Amy concludes at the unveiling ceremony, with Whiteman stating that the blue plaque is significant because the community in which Amy Ashwood Garvey lived and worked 'needs to remember her and for those who don't know her, to learn about her, so that the present community can appreciate the history of the very community in which they live and the part she played in it.'[60]

When the idea of erecting 'memorial tablets' was first proposed in 1863 by William Ewart MP, it was hoped that the scheme would encourage the preservation of houses of historical interest, by paying tribute to the link between a person and a building. A significant tool in preserving the history of notable figures, the Blue Plaque Scheme serves as a public commemoration of the individuals who have made substantial contributions to London. Or in the words of a correspondent to *The Times*, the aim of the scheme was to 'make our houses their own biographies.' Mounted on a residential building that was Amy's home from 1934 until 1960, the blue plaque indeed transforms the building into a biography of sorts. The blue plaque not only commemorates her contributions as a feminist, human rights campaigner, and Pan-Africanist, but also serves as a reminder of the vibrant African-Caribbean community in London. It transforms the building into a living archive, connecting past and present, and inspiring the research of present and future generations.

Exiting Ladbroke Grove tube station in August 2010, camera in hand, I was eager to photograph the former site of the Afro People's Centre. As I turned left from the high street onto Bassett Road, three images lingered in my mind. In one of the images, Amy is dressed in kente, enjoying the company of unnamed guests. It is the only picture from inside the house I have ever found. The other two are pictures from the outside of the building; one can be found in the biography of Amy by Lionel M Yard, the other in the collection of images held at the Schomburg Center. In the latter, Amy is figured with two women standing on the steps in front of her home at 1 Bassett Road. The sign above reads 'Afro Women's Centre', and to their right, 'Residential Club'. It is unclear why the picture was taken, but they appear dressed up for an occasion, suggesting that the centre was a place of joy and celebration as well as a place of residence.

We might infer from these photographs that Amy was not only the owner but a resident, and an active participant in the Afro Women's/Afro People's Centre's activities. We also know from her archive that Amy was a central figure within the Black community in Ladbroke Grove. The image of her dressed in kente, a traditional West African fabric, indicates her appreciation for and connection to that culture, and may suggest that Amy was involved in Pan-African cultural preservation or education within the Afro-People's Centre. The photographs also raise questions about Amy's relationships within the centre. The guests in the photographs taken inside the centre, and the two women in the photograph taken outside it, could have been friends, employees, partners, or lodgers, or perhaps a combination of these. The photographs also provide a visual record of the Afro-People's Centre itself. The building, its signage, and its location in relation to the surrounding area all offer valuable context for understanding Amy's life and work.

Crossing the street towards the opposite row of houses, I delicately placed my camera on the tallest post of a concrete gate, then walked back. I had set my camera's timer for sixty seconds, with the intention of taking a portrait of myself against the backdrop of the Afro-People's Centre, channelling a connection to Amy and the women in the image from the Schomburg Center. Taking photos of myself embodying Amy and the people she is figured with would eventually become a critical part of my creative practice.

UNEARTHING THE HISTORY OF THE PAN-AFRICAN CONGRESS IN MANCHESTER

I arrived at the Working Class Movement Library (WCML) on a rainy morning in May 2022 with plans to review a collection related to the Fifth Pan-African Congress. Set in a redbrick Victorian building called Jubilee House, across the street from the Salford Museum and Art Gallery, WCML holds an impressive collection of objects from the trade union movement, the cooperative movement, and political parties and campaigns on the left, including books, periodicals, pamphlets, banners, badges, and other artefacts related to the history of working-class movements in Greater Manchester and beyond. The collection is also home to the papers of Manchester-born political activist Len Johnson, who attended the Fifth Pan-African Congress.[61] Amy was the only woman to chair a panel at the event, which was held in Manchester on 15-21 October 1945, and I went to WCML in search of material that would help me to understand the significance of her participation.

I am greeted at the door by Belinda Scarlett, the Library Manager,, who later tells me that she has only worked at WCML for a few weeks so she is still getting used to the catalogue system. I stand in the Victorian-style foyer, which the library uses as an exhibition space, pull out my phone and take a picture. Lindsey Cole, the Assistant Librarian, leads me to the Will Thorne Reading Room before taking me on a housekeeping tour. Lindsey explains the layout of the reading room, then guides me back to the foyer where she shows the 'hallway that leads to the loos' and the adjoining room where I can stretch my legs or eat lunch. 'We used to share the kitchen with researchers, but we've had to stop because of Covid. Visitors tend to eat lunch in the square when it's nice out', Lindsey says as she points towards a window on the far side of the Reading Room. 'But it's quite rainy out, so if you're here all day, feel free to take a break here.' I peer into the small but comfortable room and can tell immediately that it is where researchers listen to audio files, watch videos and films.

As we re-enter the foyer, I explain to Lindsey that I am writing a book on Amy Ashwood Garvey so I want to look at anything related to the Pan-African Congress, which Amy attended. Lindsey tells me that most of the material I requested is already in the reading room, but she wants to show me relevant items from Len Johnson's collection that are currently held in the exhibition cases. An active member of the Communist Party of Great Britain (CPGB), Johnson ran for Manchester City Council six times between 1947 and 1962. He was a founding member of the New International Society, a social club and anti-racist campaign organisation based in Moss Side, an area synonymous with Manchester's African and Caribbean communities. Johnson attended the Congress with fellow activists Wilf Charles and Pat Devine, whose names are written in blue ink on the copy of the 'Declarations and Resolutions adopted by the Fifth Pan-African Congress' that Johnson donated to WCML.[62] I lean towards the cabinets to take a closer look at the red badge worn by a delegate, possibly Johnson himself, and wonder if he met Amy there. Lindsey explains why the resolutions, the badge, and three sheets of paper with the signatures of some of the delegates, are featured in the exhibition space. 'It's important to us that anyone who visits the library can learn about the Congress. It's such an important part of Manchester's history, and we want to highlight that'.

I ask to look at the three scraps of paper and search for Amy's signature on them. Lindsey removes the items as I continue to peruse the exhibition. I turn the corner and see a photograph of Claudia Jones and a copy of the *West Indian Gazette and Afro-Asian News* – of course a library dedicated to archiving the political struggles of the working class would have files on Claudia Jones. I ask Lindsey if I can look at those items too, and anything else on Claudia Jones.

*

The idea for a Pan-African Congress was first conceived in 1893, when a group of Pan-Africanists convened in Chicago to mobilise a collective response to colonial threats in Africa. They condemned the partition of Africa by European nations and called for an end to colonisation on the continent and beyond. A second convening, the 'Pan-African Conference', was held in London in 1900. Called by Trinidadian barrister Henry Sylvester Williams under the auspices of the African Association, the meeting took place at Westminster Town Hall. Like most early Pan-African meetings hosted in Europe or the US, participants were drawn almost entirely from the diaspora. It was attended by thirty-seven delegates, among them the first Black mayor of London, John Archer, British composer and conductor Samuel Coleridge Taylor, and African American sociologist W E B DuBois.

The First Pan-African Congress was hosted in Paris in February 1919. It was organised by DuBois and his close friend Ida Gibbs Hunt, an African American feminist, educator and activist who was active in the French Red Cross during the First World War. DuBois and Hunt planned the congress in response to the Paris Peace Conference, with the intention of persuading political leaders of Britain, France, Italy, and the US that the principle of self-determination should also be applied to Africa.

With a continued focus on decolonisation and demands for self-rule, in 1921 the second congress convened in London, Paris and Brussels. It was attended by 110 delegates from countries in Africa and the diaspora, including Liberia, Nigeria, Sierra Leone, Martinique, Jamaica, Grenada, and observers from India, the Philippines, and Morocco. Planning for this meeting was also led by DuBois, who selected the delegates. Like earlier conferences, this meeting centred the voices of the most eminent and well-known activists, a point of contention for more radical Pan-Africanists, particularly Marcus Garvey, who criticised DuBois for his elitism in the *Negro World*.[63]

Hosted over two sessions in London and Lisbon in 1923, the third Pan-African Congress was not as well funded or organised as previous congresses. Planning for the meeting was beset by in-fighting between delegates who argued for the need to develop within colonisation and those who lobbied for self-determination. In an effort to salvage the congress and boost attendance, DuBois appealed to delegates to attend and called for the need to continue the fight for Black liberation in whatever form.[64]

After the fourth congress in New York in 1927, Pan-Africanism was subsumed by localised Black political struggles until its resurgence during the Second World War. The war had been fought in the name of freedom from rising fascism in Europe with the support of Black servicemen, when millions of people around the world still lived in colonies ruled by Britain, France, Holland and other European nations. During the war, renewed unity and calls for self-determination began to emerge among the diaspora, which resulted in formation of the Pan-African Federation (PAF), a multinational organisation founded in Manchester in 1944.

The fifth Pan-African Congress was conceived during the World Trade Union Movement Conference, which was held in London in February 1945. Representatives from African and Caribbean countries were invited to Manchester, where an informal meeting was hosted by members of the PAF. During the meeting, they exchanged information about the advances made by workers and discussed the link between labour movements and anti-colonial struggle. George Padmore suggested the idea of hosting another Pan-African Congress where these issues could be discussed in further detail with a wider audience. This suggestion was warmly received and the business of planning a congress in Manchester soon proceeded.[65]

Organised by Padmore and Kwame Nkrumah, and PAF leaders T Ras Makonnen and Dr Peter Millard, the Manchester Pan-African Congress was widely promoted in newspaper adverts in Britain, North America, Africa and the Caribbean. The theme of the congress was 'The Coloured Problem in Britain', which meant not only the problems facing Black people living in England, but also people of African descent in the British Commonwealth and its colonial territories.

Attended by some of the most well-known Pan-Africanists including Jomo Kenyatta, who would become the first Prime Minister of Kenya, Jaja Wachuku, the first Nigerian Ambassador to the United Nations, and W E B Du Bois, the fifth convention brought together representatives from independence movements in British colonies to discuss what they wanted for the future. Amy Ashwood Garvey was one of two women on the roster of panelists; the other was Alma La Badie, a representative of the UNIA of Jamaica who wrote articles for the radical Jamaican weekly *Public Opinion*. Sessions addressed the postwar struggles of Africa and the Caribbean, and for the first-time people from different colonies learned of each other's economic conditions and situations.[66] Earlier Pan-African Congresses had centered on the 'black vanguard', a small circle of intellectual elites who purported to champion the rights of the Black masses. But the Fifth Congress aimed to create a Pan-African movement based in the underprivileged sections of colonial populations. There were over 200 delegates and observers drawn from political, trade union and farmer's movements, as well as enthusiastic students, and alliances were formed that connected progressive intellectuals to the labouring classes.[67] The congress was held in at Chorlton-upon-Medlock Town Hall, which is now part of the new Arts and Humanities Building at Manchester Metropolitan University.

AMY ASHWOOD GARVEY AND THE BLACK WOMAN QUESTION

On the last day of my trip to Manchester I visited Chorlton-upon-Medlock Town Hall. Designed by Richard Lane in 1831, the neoclassical building is located on Cavendish Street, across from a large park that was filled with students when I visited. I took several photographs and a short video of the building's facade, capturing its grand architecture and the surrounding area. As I made my way through the park and across the cobblestone road, I stopped to photograph the red commemorative plaque mounted on the building. The plaque describes the congress as 'historic', attributing the liberation of African countries to decisions made there. As I entered through large doors to the left of the plaque, I continued to film the entrance and the plaque, feeling the building's historical resonance as a cultural anchor and political hub for West African students and an emerging generation of Pan-African thinkers dedicated to the fight against colonialism.

Continuing my journey from Chorlton-upon-Medlock Town Hall to Manchester Central Library, I passed the Oxford Road train station, where Amy would have arrived if she took the train from London. As I walked, I felt a profound connection with the city's energy, cultural richness, and historical significance. The streets, bustling with people from diverse walks of life, seemed to whisper stories of past struggles and triumphs. I imagined Amy's footsteps mingling with mine, a Black feminist archival practice that transformed my street strolling into a vivid reenactment of her experiences. Inside the library, I discovered another copy of the congress resolutions and a photograph of Amy alongside conference attendees. These documents were not just artefacts; they were vibrant threads in the tapestry of Amy's legacy. I also found a VHS recording of a 50th-anniversary event in 1995, organised by the Broad African Representative Council (BARC) in Manchester. The footage captured a remarkable celebration of the congress' legacy, featuring numerous women dressed in vibrant cultural attire that showcased their deep connections to Africa and the diaspora. The event, held at the Molden Gallery of Manchester Metropolitan University, highlighted the enduring impact of the Pan-African Congress and how Amy's work continued to resonate.

Reflecting on the flickering images, I was moved by the sight of these women proudly displaying their heritage, reinforcing the ongoing influence of the Pan-African movement. The interviews in the Resource Centre, conducted with attendees from 1945, provided further insights into the significance of the Congress and the community that emerged around it. The 50th-anniversary event demonstrated how Amy's contributions had galvanised new generations of activists and scholars, illustrating that her legacy is not confined to dusty archives but lives on in the cultural and political movements she inspired. It was clear to me then that Manchester is a city where Amy's legacy can both be discovered in archives and felt in the very fabric of the landscape, as her impact resonates through the city's streets and buildings.

*

On the fifth day of the congress, Amy participated in a panel that reported on the conditions of Black people in the Caribbean. Chaired by Dr Peter Milliard, a graduate of Howard University's medical school and founder of the International Brotherhood of Ethiopia, the panel comprised a range of intellectuals who specialised in investigating the social and economic conditions of the Black working class. Panellists included Alma La Badie, I T A Wallace Johnson, a reporter for the *Daily Times of Lagos* and co-founder of the African Workers Union, and W E B Du Bois.[68]

During the panel, La Badie stressed Jamaica's need for a proper system to channel water to farmlands and for storing water in preparation of an inevitable drought.[69] J A Linton, representing the St Kitts Workers' League and the St Kitts-Nevis Trades and Labour Union, read a memorandum from the Joint Advisory Committee of Labour that asked for changes to the St Kitts constitution to eliminate owning property as a prerequisite to manhood suffrage.[70] And W E B Du Bois addressed African people's right to self-governance.[71] Amy Ashwood Garvey, ever the advocate for women, criticised the treatment of Black women, who occupied the lowest position within the labour market:

> Very much has been written and spoken of the Negro, but for some reason very little has been said about the Black woman. She has been shunted to the social background to be a child bearer. This has been principally her lot ... The labouring class of women who work in the fields, take goods to the market, and so on, receive much less pay for the same work men do. I feel that the Negro men of Jamaica are largely responsible for this, as they do little to help the women to get improved wages.[72]

The Fifth Pan-African Congress' focus on mobilising the labouring class opened the door for Amy to address women's liberation because, as she pointed out, Black women made up a significant portion of this class. By criticising Black men for not supporting Black women's access to better wages, Amy introduced 'The Black Woman Question' into the Pan-African movement.[73] Tired of theories that focused on emancipating and empowering Black men without addressing Black women, Ashwood Garvey seized the opportunity to challenge this approach. She believed that women's full participation in the Pan-African movement was essential if women were to be liberated in the new, postcolonial world Pan-Africanists aimed to build. In order for women to participate fully, she knew that there had to be some form of social and economic improvement for Black women. Amy thus ensured that the predominantly male leaders of the Pan-African movement heard women's concerns and addressed their needs in a formal discussion.

At the end of the congress six resolutions were introduced that included women or specifically addressed gender equality – without a doubt a result of Ashwood Garvey's influence. One resolution called for 'full equality of rights for all citizens, without distinction of race, colour, and sex', and another called for the 'removal of all disabilities affecting the employment of women, e.g., removal of "marriage bar" for women employed by government services.'[74] Although the final resolutions outlined a plan that called for gender equality, in general Pan-African leaders lacked an effective program for mobilising women, let alone a program to truly liberate them from their triply oppressed status.[75] Unlike male leaders of the Pan-African movement, Amy's efforts to emancipate women did not end with crafting resolutions. Rather, she devised and implemented a series of feminist programs that would empower women to organise on behalf of themselves and other Black women living around the world.

*

Stepping out into the chill of a rainy March morning in 2024, I made my way to Harlem. With my camera slung over my shoulder and my laptop safely tucked into my bag, my goal was to capture the essence of Harlem's history and honour the legacy of Amy

Ashwood Garvey. Exiting the 145th Street station, memories flooded back. This was the stop for my old flat and Amy Ashwood Garvey's former home. The rhythmic tap of rain on my umbrella accompanied my journey to Nicholas Avenue. Remarkably untouched by gentrification, the neighbourhood's buildings stood as sentinels testifying to a bygone era, their facades weathered but full of stories to tell.

Nicholas Avenue was alive with history. I approached a building unchanged by remodeling, its exterior a snapshot of the early 1900s when Amy lived here. The entryway, marked by three arches and a sturdy black door, bore the numbers 666 glinting in gold. I raised my camera and took my first pictures, hoping to capture the essence of Amy's time. Across the street stood the Harlem School of the Arts at the Herb Alpert Center, a testament to Dorothy Maynor's visionary work. Founded by Maynor, an American soprano and concert singer, in 1964, HSA has nurtured countless young artists thanks to her unwavering dedication to the arts. Its programs are fuelled by the creativity generated by Amy Ashwood Garvey and other figures of the Harlem Renaissance.

As I walked further, I passed St James Presbyterian Church, an establishment deeply rooted in African American history. I paused to reflect on how Amy would have walked past this church every day, likely aware of its historical significance to the local Black community. Born from Shiloh Presbyterian Church, St James had been a part of the Underground Railroad, serving as a beacon of hope and faith for its congregation. I stared at the building and wondered if she attended services or Bible study here, or participated in the cultural events it hosted. The rain continued to fall, adding a sombre, reflective mood to my journey.

Continuing my walk, I arrived at St Nicholas Park. This spacious park, located at the intersection of St Nicholas Avenue, 127th Street, St Nicholas Terrace, and 141st Street, borders the Manhattan neighbourhoods of Hamilton Heights, Manhattanville, and Harlem. I imagined Amy walking past the house that once belonged to Alexander Hamilton, now the Hamilton Grange National Memorial. The park's greenery and open spaces must have offered her a moment of respite in her bustling life, a place to gather her thoughts or meet with friends.

Leaving the park, I headed towards the former location of Liberty Hall. Turning left on 138th Street, I entered Strivers' Row, a historic district that has been home to Black intellectuals and artists since 1919. Known initially as the King Model Houses, these homes earned their colloquial name from their ambitious residents. Walking these streets, I felt the presence of legends like Will Marion Cook, Eubie Blake, and Adam Clayton Powell Jr, whose contributions to culture and politics have shaped the neighbourhood's legacy. I recalled how, in 1944, Amy Ashwood Garvey dined at the home of Adam Clayton Powell. Upon returning to New York, she joined the West Indies National Council and the Council on African Affairs, campaigning for Powell, who would become the first African-American elected to Congress from New York.

Finally, I arrived at the site of Liberty Hall, now an empty lot. Standing there, I reflected on how this space once buzzed with the fervor of UNIA meetings. James Weldon Johnson's descriptions of Garvey's grand entrances, the solemn hymns and vibrant community gatherings played vividly in my mind.[76] On Sunday evenings, Liberty Hall hosted weekly UNIA meetings that resembled religious services, complete with prayers, the UNIA anthem, and musical programmes featuring the Liberty Choir and the Black Star Line Band. The gatherings were elaborate, with the African Legion and Black Nurses flanking the aisle, and Garvey's majestic march to the rostrum evoking awe. Liberty Hall had once been the beating heart of Harlem's cultural and political scene. It was a place where religious services, musical programmes, and Garvey's grand visions came to life. Yet, by 1930 this vibrant hub had transformed into apartments, a reflection of its financial highs and lows. The UNIA headquarters, and the offices of the Black Star Line, had been located first at 36 West 135th Street, in the Crescent Theater building, and from 1919 at 54-56 West 135th Street, next door to the Lincoln Theater. These locations were at the very heart of Black Harlem. Standing there, I could almost hear the resonant voices of the Liberty Choir and the melodies of the Black Star Line Band, echoing the legacy that was both created and diminished here. I took pictures of the empty lot, each click of the shutter a tribute to the historical significance of the place.

With my camera and my heart brimming with contemplation, I made my way to the Schomburg Center. The entire day had been a walk through history, each step deeply intertwined with Harlem's illustrious past and the unyielding spirit of Amy Ashwood Garvey. I was eager to delve into the archives, to uncover more narratives and images, and to continue exploring a history that had significantly shaped not just a community but a whole cultural movement.

*

Amy's transition from Harlem to London marked a significant evolution in her work and influence. In Harlem, she was deeply involved in the UNIA, and actively engaged in the theatrical arts, using performance as a means of cultural expression and political commentary. After moving to London, Amy shifted her focus to encompass a broader range of social, cultural, and political issues. The Afro-People's Centre, along with the Florence Mills Social Parlour, became hubs for Black intellectuals, activists and artists, fostering a sense of community and solidarity among the African diaspora. These spaces provided a platform for Amy to advocate for the rights of Black people, particularly Black women, and to promote Pan-Africanism. Her move to London allowed her to connect with a broader network of artists, activists and intellectuals, making her a prominent figure in the Pan-African movement and community organising. Engaging with international organisations and forums like the Fifth Pan-African Congress, Amy's voice and influence were amplified, enabling her to advocate for decolonisation and the rights of people of African descent on a global scale.

Amy's exposure to different cultural and political contexts in both Harlem and London enriched her understanding of the struggles faced by people of African descent worldwide. This informed her activism and writings, contributing to a transnational perspective on race, gender, and colonialism. Her experiences in both cities allowed her to develop a transnational perspective, which continues to resonate in contemporary discussions. Her deepened engagement with transnational solidarity and collaboration also informed her efforts to visit Africa, a lifelong dream realised in 1946 during a speaking tour in West Africa, where she continued advocating for women.

By tracing Amy Ashwood Garvey's steps through the streets of Harlem and later exploring her impact in London, I recognised the city itself as a living archive, its spaces and structures infused with legacy of historical figures. This exploration underscored the importance of remembering and documenting the past. Amy's legacy, preserved in the buildings, parks, and memories of Harlem and beyond, serves as a powerful reminder of the transformative power of community activism and dedication. By walking the streets she once walked, I engaged in a Black feminist archival practice that bridges past and present, transforming historical research into a living, breathing narrative. This method of street strolling as not only honours Amy's memory but also ensures that her legacy remains a dynamic and influential force in the ongoing struggle for Black liberation and social justice.

NOTES

1 For more on the history of Black communities in Harlem, see Claude McKay, *Harlem, Negro Metropolis*, 1st edn, Harcourt Brace Jovanovich, 1968; Gilbert Osofsky, *Harlem: The Making of a Ghetto : Negro New York, 1890-1930*, Ivan R Dee, 1996; John Jackson Jr, *Harlemworld: Doing Race and Class in Contemporary Black America*, University of Chicago Press: Chicago, IL, 2003, https://press.uchicago.edu/ucp/books/book/chicago/H/bo3643926.html; Jonathan Gill, *Harlem: The Four Hundred Year History from Dutch Village to Capital of Black America*, 1st edn, Grove Press: New York, 2011.

2 For more information on the history of the Schomburg Center and Arturo Schomburg's archive, see Hannah J M Ishmael, 'Reclaiming History: Arthur Schomburg', *Archives and Manuscripts* 46, No 3, 2 September 2018, pp269-288, https://doi.org/10.1080/01576895.2018.1559741; Vanessa K Valdés, *Diasporic Blackness: The Life and Times of Arturo Alfonso Schomburg*, illustrated edition, State University of New York Press, 2018.

3 'Schomburg Center for Research in Black Culture, The New York Public Library', accessed 20 July 2024, https://www.nypl.org/locations/schomburg; 'About the Schomburg Center for Research in Black Culture', The New York Public Library, accessed 20 July 2024, https://www.nypl.org/about/locations/schomburg.

4 Tony Martin, *Amy Ashwood Garvey: Pan-Africanist, Feminist and Mrs Marcus Garvey Number 1, or, A Tale of Two Armies*, Majority Press: Dover, Mass, 2008; 'ArchiveGrid', OCLC, 11 June 2024, https://www.oclc.org/research/areas/research-collections/archivegrid.html.
5 Schomburg Center for Research in Black Culture, Photographs and Prints Division, Sc Photo Garvey, Amy Ashwood and Sc Photo Claudia Jones Memorial Collection boxes 1 & 2.
6 Ibid, Sc MG 665 and Sc 960-C.
7 Alexander Vasudevan, 'The Autonomous City: Towards a Critical Geography of Occupation', *Progress in Human Geography* 39, No 3, 1 June 2015, pp316-337, https://doi.org/10.1177/0309132514531470; Samuel Burgum, 'This City Is An Archive: Squatting History and Urban Authority', *Journal of Urban History* 48, No 3, 1 May 2022, pp504-522, https://doi.org/10.1177/0096144220955165.
8 Ula Taylor, 'Women in the Documents: Thoughts on Uncovering the Personal, Political, and Professional, *Journal of Women's History* 20, No 1, 2008, pp187-196.
9 Martin, op cit, p37.
10 http://kellyfoster.co.uk, accessed 20 July 2024.
11 In this context Black referred to political Blackness.
12 Cary D Wintz, 'The Lafayette Theatre: Crucible of African-American Dramatic Arts', in *Early Race Filmmaking in America*, Routledge, 2016; 'The Lafayette Players: An Oral History', The Kennedy Center, accessed 21 July 2024, https://www.kennedy-center.org/education/resources-for-educators/classroom-resources/media-and-interactives/interactives/drop-me-off-in-harlem/theme-and-variations/the-lafayette-players; 'Lafayette Theatre Remembered as an Important Venue in Black History', 22 February 2017, https://blacktheatrematters.org/2017/02/22/lafayette-theatre-remembered-for-as-an-important-venue-to-black-theater.
13 Martin, op cit, p106.
14 Article in *West Indian American*, 2 November 1927, p17, quoted in Martin, op cit, p106.
15 'Mme. Garvey's Show a Hit at the Lafayette', *The New York Amsterdam News*, 10 November 1926, ProQuest Historical Newspapers.
16 Martin, op cit, pp64, 155, 163.
17 Ibid, p163.
18 Ibid, p115, pp158-163.
19 For more on this see Hakim Adi, *West Africans in Britain, 1900-1960: Nationalism, Pan-Africanism, and Communism*, Lawrence and Wishart: London, 1998.
20 Hakim Adi, 'Amy Ashwood Garvey and the Nigerian Progress Union', in *Gendering the African Diaspora: Women, Culture and Historical*

Change in the Caribbean and Nigerian Hinterland, Judith Byfield, LaRay Denzer, and Anthea Morrison (eds), Indiana University Press: Bloomington, 2010, pp205-6.
21. Ladipo Solanke, 'The Why of the Nigerian Progress Union' quoted in Adi, op cit, p204.
22. Ibid, p203.
23. Delia Jarrett-Macauley, *The Life of Una Marson, 1905-65*, illustrated edn, Manchester University Press: Manchester, 2010, p84.
24. Marc Matera, *Black London: The Imperial Metropolis and Decolonization in the Twentieth Century*, University of California Press, 2015, pp145-6; Lizzie B, 'Amy Ashwood Garvey (1897-1969)', *Women*, 31 October 2021, https://womenwhomeantbusiness.com/2021/10/31/amy-ashwood-garvey-1897-1969.
25. Martin, op cit, p139.
26. T Ras Makonnen, *Pan-Africanism from Within*, Oxford University Press, 1973, p130.
27. Lionel M Yard, *Biography of Amy Ashwood Garvey: Pan-Africanist, Feminist and Wife No. 1*, The Associated Publishers, Inc: New York, 1988, p108.
28. 'Britishers Get Flo Mills Club', *New York Amsterdam News*, 25 July 1936, ProQuest Historical Newspapers.
29. Ibid.
30. Ibid.
31. *London Sunday Express*, as quoted in Martin, op cit, p140.
32. Tony Martin, interview with C L R James, San Fernando, Trinidad, 1980, quoted in Martin, op cit, p141.
33. Yard, op cit, p109.
34. Makonnen, op cit, p130.
35. George Padmore, *Pan-Africanism or Communism?*, Double Day: New York, 1971, p123.
36. *Grove Roots*, DVD, dir Gabrielle Tierney, Octavia Foundation: London, 2009.
37. Yard, op cit, pp194-6.
38. Ibid, p194.
39. Ibid, p195.
40. Excerpt from an Afro Women's Centre advertisement, nd, Amy Ashwood Garvey Memorabilia, Main Library, University of the West Indies, St Augustine Campus, Trinidad & Tobago.
41. Ibid.
42. Ibid.
43. Martin, op cit, p256.
44. Amy Ashwood to C A Richardson, letter, nd, Lionel M Yard Papers.

45 Amy Ashwood Garvey to Thelma Rogers, 27 July 1954, Amy Ashwood Garvey Memorabilia Collection, University of the West Indies, St. Augustine, Trinidad.
46 Martin, op cit, p257; Amy Ashwood Garvey, 'My Dear Friends', 27 December 1955, in Amy Ashwood Garvey, The Alma Jordan Library, The University of the West Indies, St Augustine Campus, Trinidad and Tobago.
47 Martin, op cit, pp256-7.
48 Ibid, p256.
49 Sir Oswald Mosley (16 November 1896 – 3 December 1980) was a British politician who founded the British Union of Fascists. Mosley was vehemently opposed to immigration and launched a campaign to prevent West Indians and Africans from migrating to Britain.
50 In 1955, Prime Minister Winston Churchill suggested that the Conservatives fight the next election on the slogan 'Keep England White.' This phrase, and its variant 'Keep Britain White', has been a recurring theme in British politics, tracing its roots back to the racial hierarchies established during the British Empire. The slogan was notably propagated by figures such as Sir Oswald Mosley, leader of the British Union of Fascists, and later echoed in the rhetoric of politicians like Enoch Powell.
51 New Scotland Yard, *Special Branch Report # 4*, 10 November 1959, p3, *Special Branch Report # 3*, 21 July 1959, pp5-6, *Special Branch Report #2*, 17 June 1959 and Metropolitan Police, *Special Branch Report*, 28 May 1959, pp9-11, PRO: CO1031/2946, National Archive, London, UK.
52 Winston James, 'The Black Experience in Twentieth Century Britain', in *Black Experience and the Empire*, Philip D Morgan and Sean Hawkins (eds), Oxford University Press: Oxford, 2004, p375.
53 Edward Pilkington, *Beyond the Mother Country*, I B Tauris: London, 1988, p107.
54 Ibid, p119.
55 "The Windrush Legacy: Memoirs of Britain's post-War Caribbean Immigrants," Black Cultural Archives, 1998, p38.
56 Lola Olufemi, 'preface', in Marika Sherwood, *Claudia Jones: A Life in Exile*, 2nd edn, Lawrence Wishart: London, 2021.
57 Claude Ramsey in 'The Windrush Legacy', op cit, p38.
58 'Liaison Group Launched', *The Kensington News and West London Times,* 26 September 1958, and 'Split Over Mercy Plea', *The Kensington News and West London Times,* 12 December 1958.
59 Ibid.
60 Burchell Whiteman, *Hidden Herstories: Women of Change*, Octavia Foundation: London, 2009.

61 Len Johnson Collection, papers and documents related to the Pan-African Congress, Working-Class Movement Library, Salford, England.
62 Ibid.
63 Jake Hodder, 'The Elusive History of the Pan-African Congress, 1919-27', *History Workshop Journal*, Vol 91, 1, Spring 2021, pp113-131, https://doi.org/10.1093/hwj/dbaa032.
64 Hakim Adi and Marika Sherwood, *The 1945 Manchester Pan-African Congress revisited*, New Beacon Books Ltd: London, 1995 (includes a reprint of the report on the Congress).
65 'Declarations and Resolutions adopted by the Fifth Pan-African Congress: Manchester England, October 13-21, 1945', Len Johnson Collection, Working Class Movement Library, Shelfmark: AG Johnson, Len. See also George Padmore (ed), *Colonial and Coloured Unity: History of the Pan-African Congress,* The Hammersmith Bookshop Ltd: London and Sherwood and Adi, op cit.
66 Marika Sherwood, introduction to *The 1945 Manchester Pan-African Congress Revisited*, Hakim Adi and Marika Sherwood (eds), New Beacon Books, 1995, p9.
67 George Padmore (ed), *Colonial and Coloured Unity: History of the Pan-African Congress*, The Hammersmith Bookshop Ltd: London, and Sherwood and Adi, op cit, p139.
68 Sherwood and Adi, op cit, p98.
69 Ibid, p99
70 Ibid.
71 Ibid, pp100-1.
72 Ibid, pp98-9.
73 Hakim Adi also argues that Ashwood Garvey raised the 'question of the Black Woman' at the Fifth Pan-African Manchester Congress in 'Amy Ashwood Garvey and the Nigerian Progress Union', in *Gendering the African Diaspora: Women, Culture and Historical Change in the Caribbean and Nigerian Hinterland*, Judith Byfield, LaRay Denzer and Anthea Morrison (eds), Indiana University Press: Bloomington, 2010, p212.
74 'Declarations and Resolutions adopted by the Fifth Pan-African Congress: Manchester England, October 13-21, 1945', Len Johnson Collection, Working Class Movement Library, Shelfmark: AG Johnson, Len. See also George Padmore, op cit, and Sherwood and Adi, op cit.
75 Olufemi, op cit.
76 James Weldon Johnson, *Black Manhattan: Account of the Development of Harlem*, new edn, Da Capo Press Inc: New York, NY 1991, p255.

3

Towards a Visual Archive of Diaspora

THE SOCIAL LIFE OF THE PHOTOGRAPH

When I first saw the photograph of Amy Ashwood Garvey printed on the cover of Tony Martin's biography, where she is described as 'Pan-Africanist, Feminist, and Mrs. Marcus Garvey No. 1,' I was overcome by a desire to know the intimate details of her life. How old is she here?, I wondered. Was the photograph taken before or after she met Marcus Garvey? Had they already established the UNIA? What prompted her to sit for this portrait? What facets of her identity was she trying to convey – Pan-Africanist? Feminist? Mrs Marcus Garvey number one? I had just collected Martin's biography from the reference desk at the Esther Raushenbush Library at Sarah Lawrence College, where it had arrived via interlibrary loan the previous day. I cannot recall the name of the library that sent the book or how long I waited to receive it, but I vividly remember the impact of seeing Amy's likeness in this format for the very first time.

I stared at the portrait of Amy, running my hands over the smooth surface of the dust jacket. I opened the book and flipped through its pages, pausing to read phrases, sentences and paragraphs that caught my eye. I closed the book with a deep sigh and held it firmly in my hands. I was overcome by a wave of emotions that took me to a different place, a different moment in time. It was a feeling akin to what Brent Hayes Edwards describes as a 'taste of the archive', that 'sensation of encountering a past' through a photograph.[1] I understood this past to be intertwined with my own, this photograph and biography connected to my own family histories and archives. I stared again at the portrait of Amy dressed in a scarf and a hat, her hair pulled back, and looked into her eyes as if she were looking back.

*

What we see when we look at an old photograph is more than just a moment from the past – we are also observing a record of choices. Analysing a photograph as a record of choices often involves questioning the intentions of both the photographer and the subject and offering insights into their motivations and desires.[2] Engaging in such speculative analysis enriches our interpretation, moving beyond surface impressions to uncover a deeper significance embedded within the visual narrative.

Tina Campt's concept of the 'social life of the photograph' has been particularly useful to my analysis of Amy's photographic archive, providing a framework for interpreting the diasporic dimensions embedded within an image.[3] This concept refers not only to the content and visible elements but also to the broader context in which the photograph exists. By exploring the social life of an image, as Campt suggests, we can uncover the interplay between broader social, cultural and historical dynamics and the construction of Black diasporas. In portraiture, this analysis allows us to untangle complexities of intention, representation and agency, shedding light on the diverse Black diasporic identities and experiences captured within and beyond the frame.

Since my initial encounter with this portrait, I have actively collected images of Amy. I have examined the social life of each photograph, speculating about the possible intentions of both the photographer and the subjects portrayed. Often I find myself struck by the diasporic connections that draw my family and me into the frame. The first images I collected were scans from Lionel M Yard's collection, which are prominently featured in his biography. Among them is the portrait of Ashwood Garvey on the cover of Tony Martin's book, which Yard included in the third chapter of his biography.[4] According to Yard, this portrait dates back to 1924, after Amy's marriage to Marcus ended and as she embarked on a new phase of her life marked by international travel, which she actively documented through writing and photography.

Amy's archive does not disclose her reasons for sitting for this portrait, nor does it credit the photographers. We cannot know her intentions. Yet, in these photographs of Amy, I perceive the roots of what Campt, in her analysis of postwar African Caribbean migrants to Britain, describes as 'the gendering of diasporic aspiration.'[5] Dressed in their finest attire, these individuals posed for portraits sent to loved ones in the Caribbean or displayed in their homes in England. Each photograph captures histories of colonialism, migration and settlement, reshaping the postwar culture of the Black Atlantic.[6] For Campt, these images serve as 'sites of diasporic articulation and aspiration,' expressing personal and social statements about how individuals envisioned their sense of self, subjectivity and social status. These images preserve specific articulations for both the present and future.[7]

So, I have come to view photographs of Amy as part of an archive of Black diasporic becoming in that the images evoke forms of subjectivity and identification I now recognise as constitutive of 'the African diaspora'.[8] As a Black woman of the African diaspora, these images resonate deeply in that I associate the subject of the photo, Amy, with myself and my family. And I am touched by the image. Even now, whenever I look at this photo of Amy, I feel moved.

This portrait of Amy reminds me of my Great-Grandmother Theressa Pinnock, who posed for a similar portrait around the same period. Born into middle-class Black Jamaican families between the late 1890s and early 1900s, both women embody the 'quiet and meditative quality' that Deborah Willis describes as a hallmark of the era's Black photography.[9] Their poised postures and confident gazes reflect a shared sense of grace and assurance, with studio settings emphasising the intentional nature of their portrayals. Unlike many Black Jamaican women photographed in studios before them – often depicted as 'types' or 'character studies' – these women chose to be documented on their own terms.[10]

I have not seen that portrait of my Great-Grandmother Theressa Huie in more than a decade, but I vividly recall the photo's framing and its placement on the wall in the front room at my Great-Aunt Gloria's house. My Aunt Gloria, the daughter of Theressa and the sister of my mother Grace's father, was the archivist for the Huie side of my family tree – a role she intended to pass on to me. So, in moments of reflection, I think about the weeks after my Aunt Gloria's passing in August 2018 and the realisation that because of tensions in that side of my family I would never see that photograph again, and how it felt like another loss I had to grieve. Then I am reminded of another portrait of my Great-Grandmother Theressa that was smaller in size, in a tarnished silver frame among perfumes and jewellery boxes on her dressing table. During my last visit to her home in Gary, Indiana, Aunt Gloria gifted me a copy of that photograph, along with an original copy of a travel document granting Theressa the right to emigrate from Jamaica to Guatemala to meet her husband, my Great-Grandfather Ivan Huie. That photograph is now in a frame on my writing desk in London.

After sharing my work on Amy with my grandmother Iris Sinclair – my father Neville Swaby's mother – and explaining who she was, she told me that her parents, Arlethia Wheeler and Henry Plummer, were members of the UNIA in Jamaica and had invested in the Black Star Line, the steamship company founded by Marcus and directed by Amy. Sometimes, when I look through the photographs I have collected, I think about the great-grandparents that I never knew and wonder if they knew about Amy and her pivotal role in the organisation's creation. I use the concept of the social life of the photo to embrace the inherent subjectivity of my interpretations, imagining Amy's inner world through an autoethnography of personal history, identity, emotions and affect. These photographs help me navigate the intricate web of personal and collective memory, weaving together past, present and future within a visual archive of Amy's social life and political activism that I am also curating. This, I think, is the visual practice of diaspora, whereby photography shapes diasporic imaginings of individual and collective Black selves.[11]

A VISUAL TESTAMENT TO A REMARKABLE LIFE

Amy Ashwood Garvey's visual archive is a testament to her remarkable life, illustrating her connection to pivotal moments and movements across Africa and the diaspora. Spanning the early 1900s to the late 1960s, this rich collection of still and moving images primarily comprises portrait photography of Amy, figured by herself and alongside her political allies, mentees, adopted children, partners and friends. Additionally, it includes evocative photographs of landscapes taken during her travels in West Africa and the Caribbean.

Many of these invaluable photographs were recovered by Lionel M Yard when he visited Ashwood Garvey's former home in London. Some remained in the possession of his daughter and grandson, Patricia and Phillip Maillard, when I conducted my research at their home in Brooklyn in August 2009. By August 2018, during artist Emma Wolukua-Wanambwa's research for her exhibition at the Showroom Gallery, Patricia still held several images. However, by the winter of 2020, when our colleague Adisa Vera Beatty connected with Yard's family, several photographs, manuscripts, and letters had gone missing. Born and raised in Brooklyn, Adisa was a doctoral candidate in African Diaspora History at Howard University. She would become quite close with Patricia and Phil, as did Emma, who was always good at maintaining connections, which is why she excelled at facilitating collaborations.

An exciting portion of Amy's visual archive is housed at the John Hope Franklin Research Center at Duke University in Durham, North Carolina. Emma initially informed me of this collection, sharing a reference photograph she took during her research trip archives in the US and the Caribbean. Although I have not yet seen the collection in person, the high-resolution files I purchased for $566 through the Duke University Library website hold a cherished space on my laptop. Named in honour of the esteemed historian John Hope Franklin, the centre was created to continue his groundbreaking work on the Black American experience. Since its inception, the centre has been dedicated to collecting, preserving and providing access to materials that document the lives, struggles and achievements of Black Americans, from the colonial era to the present day.

Acquired at auction for $1,140 in March 2013, this collection comprises sixty small, black-and-white photographs dating from the 1930s to the 1950s.[12] It includes portraits of Amy's diverse circle of friends and acquaintances in West Africa, encompassing politicians, heads of state, lawyers, and students. It also features ethnographic and travel photography that captures the landscapes and people Amy encountered throughout her West African journeys. These photographs depict significant gatherings such as meetings, funerals, vibrant street market scenes and other historical events. While the collection provides extensive details, many images remain unnamed, inviting curiosity and speculation about the lives they encapsulate. Although Amy likely took many of these photos, some were sent to her by others, and several candid shots of Amy were captured by unidentified photographers.

Another valuable part of Amy's visual archive resides at the Schomburg Center in Harlem, New York.[13] This collection spans the early 1900s to the late 1960s and includes portraits of Amy both alone and in group settings with unidentified individuals. Some group portraits resemble family photos, while others depict West African individuals in cultural attire. The collection also includes an image of Amy with two unidentified women on the steps of the Afro Women's Centre sometime in the mid-1950s. There are also two video recordings of Amy being interviewed by Gil Noble on *Like It Is*, a TV programme that aired on ABC from 1968 to 2011, focusing on issues relevant to the Black American community.

Beyond these primary archives, Getty Images holds significant footage and photographs of Amy.[14] This includes three clips of Amy being interviewed in front of her Afro People's Centre in London in 1956, as part of a segment about immigration from the Caribbean for the British Broadcasting Company (BBC), and four images of Amy from the 1945 Pan-African Congress in Manchester, England. There are photographs of Amy at the Alma Jordan Library, in St Augustine Trinidad at the National Library of Jamaica in Kingston, and I am certain there are more photographs out there in institutional archives and private collections.

My curation and study of Amy's visual archive continues to enrich my understanding of her personal life and activism. As new images surface and existing ones are re-examined, they highlight the significance of visual archives in reconstructing historical narratives that might otherwise be lost or forgotten, ensuring that her contributions are remembered and celebrated.

BLACK PHOTOGRAPHY: A SENSE OF PURPOSE AND PRIDE

Amy Ashwood Garvey visual archive offers an important contribution to the rich canon of Black twentieth-century studio portraiture and vernacular photography. During the height of the Harlem Renaissance, studio portraiture played a pivotal role in shaping and celebrating Black identity and culture. Visionary photographer James Van Der Zee, celebrated for his iconic images of Marcus Garvey and the UNIA, captured the essence of the Harlem Renaissance, depicting the diverse Black identities and communities that emerged from the movement. His Guaranteed Photo Studio was renowned among Harlemites for producing beautiful and technically well composed photographs. Conveniently situated next to a 135th Street branch of the New York Public Library, which would become the Schomburg Center for Research in Black Culture, and just across Lenox Avenue from the UNIA headquarters, Van Der Zee was perfectly positioned to document the vibrancy of Harlem's social, cultural and political life, in his studio and on the streets.[15] Since I have been unable to find images of Amy from this time, Van Der Zee's iconic photographs of UNIA members at the historic UNIA parade in Harlem are the ones I see in my mind whenever I think about Amy and her role in curating cultural and social events during the early days of the UNIA. When photographs of Amy relevant to a specific period or event do not exist, I juxtapose Black photography from that era with existing portraits of Amy to position her and her activism within the broader historical narrative of the Harlem Renaissance and the UNIA.

Much like Van Der Zee immortalised Marcus Garvey and the UNIA, conferring legitimacy to the leader and his movement,

Amy's photographs offer a glimpse into her role as a pioneering Pan-African feminist and advocate for social justice.[16] Through her portraits, Amy becomes not only a subject but also a symbol of resilience and empowerment in the face of colonial and racial oppression. These visual archives underscore the profound connections Amy had to the continent and its diaspora, and they highlight the multifaceted nature of her legacy. But they are more than just documentation. Collectively, these images constitute significant contributions to what I consider a visual archive of the Black diaspora. My thinking here builds on the work of Tina Campt and Leigh Raiford and the rich body of scholarship that offers innovative approaches to studying the photographic practice of the African diaspora across time and space, showing how Black identities are forged and remade through diasporic visual encounters.[17] They have demonstrated how Black communities in North America, Europe and the Caribbean have used various sub-genres of photography, from family snapshots to studio portraiture and the selfie, to engage in Black diasporic articulation, embodiment and self-fashioning. Furthermore, they have highlighted how Black intellectuals, activists and artists have employed photography to underscore their connection to the global Black world.[18] My work on Amy consolidates these approaches, using my personal experiences as a Black woman of Jamaican heritage and as a Black feminist researcher to piece together fragments of Amy's visual narrative.

What strikes me most about Amy's portraits is their ability to convey complex narratives about her life, her work and her identity. In each image, she presents herself with a sense of purpose and pride, using her clothing, props and poses to reinforce her connection to Africa and the diaspora. In photographs from Amy's early life, she is always depicted in the style that highlights her gendered respectability, in a similar way to the postwar African-Caribbean migrant women who are captured in their 'Sunday Best' in photographs analysed by Tina Campt.[19] In a portrait from the 1940s held at the Schomburg Center, Amy appears to be wearing a well-made, dark-coloured blazer or dress, her ears and neck adorned with pearls, and her hair pressed with a hot comb or relaxed, most likely at the salon of Madam C J Walker, whom Amy befriended when she lived in Harlem.[20]

Amy in the early years of her activism, 1924. Courtesy of Patricia and Phillip Maillard.

A photograph from Amy's travel documents, c. late 1920s. Courtesy of David M. Rubenstein Rare Book & Manuscript Library, Duke University.

Amy dressed in the kente cloth given to her during her time in the Ashanti Region, c. late 1940s. Courtesy of The National Library of Jamaica.

The Afro Women's Centre in London, England, c. 1954. Courtesy of Patricia and Phillip Maillard.

Amy entertains at the Afro Women's Centre, c. 1954. Courtesy of Patricia and Phillip Maillard.

Amy and two residents on the steps of the Afro Women's Centre, c. 1954. Courtesy of the Schomburg Center for Research in Black Culture, The New York Public Library.

My first research trip to the former location of the Afro Women's / People's Centre, 2010. Photograph by the author.

Snapshots from Amy's journey to West Africa, 1946-1949. Amy is pictured wearing kente, engaged in a gathering with Ashanti King Prempeh II, and addressing an audience with her characteristic poise. Courtesy of Patricia and Phillip Maillard.

A portrait of Amy that belonged to her friend Thelma Rogers, c. 1955. Courtesy of Alma Jordan Library, University of the West Indies, St Augustine, Trinidad.

Amy at the funeral of Sam Manning, Accra, Ghana, 1961. Courtesy of David M. Rubenstein Rare Book & Manuscript Library, Duke University.

Amy and the sons of Dr Asseo Martin, Ethiopian Minister to the London League of Nations, at a demonstration in Trafalgar Square organized by the International Friends of Abyssinia, c. 1935 © Getty Images.

Amy with Thelma Rogers, and an unnamed man, c. 1955. Courtesy of Alma Jordan Library, University of the West Indies, St Augustine, Trinidad & Tobago.

Amy with members of the Jamaica United Party, 1967.
Courtesy of Schomburg Center for Research in Black Culture,
New York Public Library.

Amy with Claudia Jones, Eslanda and Paul Robeson, c. 1960.
The Mayor of Lambeth, Alderman J.W. Calder, is also posed with
his wife. Courtesy of Schomburg Center for Research in Black
Culture, The New York Public Library.

Unnamed, undated photographs of in Amy's archive that offer a glimpse into the intimate connections and relationships central to her life and activism, c. 1940-60. Courtesy of David M. Rubenstein Rare Book & Manuscript Library, Duke University.

Photographs from Amy's travels in West Africa offers a glimpse into the diverse landscapes she encountered, c. 1946-9. Presented here with images take during my research trip to Kumasi, 2021. Courtesy David M. Rubenstein Rare Book & Manuscript Library, Duke University and the author.

Amy at the Fifth Pan-African Congress in Manchester, England, 1945 © Getty Images.

Plaque commemorating the Fifth Pan-African Congress, Manchester School of Art, 2022. Photograph by the author.

Amy on stage at the Fifth Pan-African Congress, 1945 © Getty Images.

Amy with the chief of Juaben Nana Yaw Sarpong II, the Queen Mother, and dignitaries from Darman in the weeks before her lineage ceremony, 1947. Courtesy of the Schomburg Center for Research in Black Culture, The New York Public Library.

Me in Adanwomase with chief of the traditional council, Nana Kwadwo Ntlamo Panin II, the Queen Mother, Nana Korama Brimpomaa, and other leaders following my naming ceremony, 2021. Photograph by the author.

Amy poses with a bouquet of tropical flowers.. Taken after her naming ceremony, the image highlights a celebratory moment, c. 1947. Courtesy of Patricia and Phillip Maillard.

Amy seated in a chair c. late 1960s. The photograph is undated, but I like to imagine that it is the 'very last picture taken in Africa' that Amy references in her 1 January 1969 letter to Lionel M Yard. Courtesy of Patricia and Phillip Maillard.

Photographs and stills from *Amy and Me in the Archive* (2024), an artist film inspired by my exploration of Amy Ashwood Garvey's archive, life, and activism. These images represent a dialogue between the past and present, as I reimagine iconic photographs of Amy in the kente cloth she acquired during her time in the Ashanti Region.

A portrait of Amy featured in the exhibition at the 3rd annual Kwame Nkrumah Pan-African Intellectual and Cultural Festival at the University of Ghana, Legon, 2021. Photograph by the author.

Amy being interviewed by Gil Noble for an episode of Like It Is, 1960. The image appears on a TV screen in the Moving Images and Recorded Sound division at the Schomburg Center, 2019. Courtesy of the author.

In another collection of portraits that appear to be taken in studio settings, which I gathered from multiple sources, Amy is dressed in kente, a different fabric in each photograph. The fabric is sometimes tied high at her waist, in others it is thrown over her shoulder. In some images she wears a wrap on her head, or she is posing with flowers, or in front of plants. These images are rich with objects symbolising her heritage and a sustained connection to her African roots and Pan-African ideology. Capturing moments that spanned continents, the content in these photographs artfully showcases a Black diasporic subject in becoming.

Beyond her personal presentation in studio spaces, many of Amy's photographs capture cultural events or places steeped in global Black history and culture. Each photograph serves not just as a personal memento but as a visual narration of her global journey as a Pan-Africanist. In one striking photograph from a protest held by the International African Friends of Abyssinia (IAFA) in Trafalgar Square, London in 1935, Ashwood Garvey is seen standing alongside IAFA co-founder C L R James, and the two sons of Dr Asseo Martin, Ethiopian Minister to the London League of Nations.[21] The demonstration was organised to protest against Italy's policy in its dispute with Ethiopia and to demand the lifting of the British arms embargo against Ethiopia. Amy, dressed in a dignified manner, stands with poise and determination, while James and Dr Martin's sons, dressed in light trousers, embody the serious yet hopeful spirit of the event. I first encountered this photograph in an installation curated by David Bailey at Tate Britain in 2023, which focused on Black political organising in the UK. The image, along with others from key moments in the history of Pan-Africanism, is available for purchase through Getty Images, where it can be accessed online. These images symbolise the transnational nature, historical and cultural interconnectedness of African diasporic experiences, capturing the essence of Amy's identity and her enduring commitment to anti-racist and anti-colonial activism.

In another powerful image preserved by the Schomburg Center, Amy stands proudly with fellow members of the Jamaica United Party, a political party that contested the national elections in 1967 but failed to win a seat.[22] The party was not involved in any further elections, but this image confirms its existence and Amy's involvement. Seated front and centre among a group of men and women of varying ages, she is wearing kente cloth and stares directly into the camera. The choice to wear this attire in this setting further underscores her deep connection to her diasporic identity and African heritage.

One of the photographs, published in the biography by Lionel M Yard, captures a lively and intimate event held at the Afro Women's Centre, likely after it transitioned to the Afro People's Centre due to the presence of both men and women in the image.[23] The scene depicts a gathering of seven individuals, with Amy Ashwood Garvey prominently positioned in the foreground, standing and engaging in conversation. Amy is elegantly dressed in another kente wrap, exuding a sense of grace and warmth as she interacts with a man seated beside her, who is also dressed in cultural l attire. The background reveals a cosy indoor setting, with patterned curtains and comfortable furniture suggesting a welcoming and homely atmosphere. Four men are seated on chairs and a sofa, dressed in a mix of formal and semi-formal attire, including suits and ties. Their postures range from relaxed to attentive, indicating a comfortable yet engaged presence. Among them, one man appears to be deep in thought, while another is caught in the midst of speaking. Two women are also present, one standing beside Amy and another seated, both dressed in stylish yet modest clothing. The woman who is standing, likely a guest or a member of the centre, appears to be smiling, adding to the congenial mood of the gathering. This photograph not only documents an event at the Afro People's Centre but also highlights the inclusive and collaborative spirit of the centre. It showcases the diverse community that Amy fostered, emphasising her commitment to creating spaces for dialogue, cultural exchange and solidarity among people of African descent.

Complicating this visual narrative is a photograph affixed to the wall in the background of Prince Phillip the Duke of Edinburgh dressed in British military uniform. The presence of this photograph within this space evokes the legacy of imperial socialisation, which ingrained in colonial subjects a sense of deference to figures of British authority and the Royal Family. This practice of displaying portraits of British royals and other colonial figures within homes in the colonies was a subtle yet pervasive way of reinforcing imperial loyalty. The socialisation process encouraged a symbolic allegiance to the Crown, often manifested through the placement of images of the Royal Family in prominent locations within one's home. I am reminded of the framed portrait of a young Queen Elizabeth II that hung on the wall of my Aunt Gloria's house, next to a portrait of her mother, Theressa Pinnock, a portrait of my mom, Grace Huie, and a portrait of me from when I was about three. These images, placed side by side, reflect the complexities of diasporic identity for Britain's colonial and postcolonial subjects, where personal and familial pride coexisted with the remnants of colonial influence.

In this context, the photograph of Prince Phillip on the wall at the Afro People's Centre serves as a visual reminder of the deep-seated legacy of British imperialism, a legacy that shaped the social and cultural practices of colonial subjects in the colonies and the metropolis. It highlights how these visual representations were not just passive decorations but active agents in the maintenance of colonial power structures, subtly reinforcing the authority of the British Empire within the intimate spaces of everyday life. Meanwhile, Amy's presence alongside other Black intellectuals, activists and artists underscores her active participation in Pan-African and anti-colonial movements and her role in shaping Black identities and consciousness. I see this in the way she documented her time in West Africa, capturing photographs of historical events, such as mourners gathered around the grave of Herbert Macaulay, often regarded as the father of Nigerian nationalism,[24] as well as the way she preserved images of herself posing alongside her friends and comrades such as Claudia Jones, Eslanda and Paul Robeson.[25] By documenting her involvement in cultural, political and social events related to the African diaspora, Amy's photographs offer a view of the historical and social contexts in which she lived, contributing to a broader visual record of the African diaspora's evolution and resilience. In addition to their aesthetic appeal, Amy's portraits serve as crucial historical documents, offering insights into the social, political, and cultural milieu of the time. Each image is a piece of a larger puzzle, providing valuable context for understanding the complexities of Amy's activism and the broader Pan-African movement. Whether documenting her camaraderie with fellow activists or capturing the fervent atmosphere of protests and rallies, these portraits offer a window into Black life during this transformative period in history.

By curating a visual archive of Amy's life and activism within this book, I blend multiple approaches to show the evolution of Amy's diasporic identity. Through curated photographs, I dissect how Amy's lived experiences as a member of the diaspora profoundly shaped her social life and political activism. My camera becomes an archival and autoethnographic tool, meticulously documenting Amy's role in various movements while also providing rich, layered insights into her personal life and the broader historical contexts she navigated. Utilising autoethnography, I engage deeply with these images, allowing self-portraiture, personal narrative and scholarly analysis to intersect. This approach uncovers facets of Amy's life and legacy that are both personally and historically significant.

'WOMEN OF THE WORLD MUST UNITE'

In a 1944 interview with the *New York Amsterdam News,* Amy Ashwood Garvey discussed her plans to publish an international women's magazine. She had been living in Jamaica since the start of the Second World War, where she wrote an unpublished manuscript, *The Black Woman in the Post-War World*.[26] Now she was back in the US for the first time in a decade. In Jamaica, Amy had co-founded the J A G Smith Political Party. She had also forged an adult education programme for working-class Black Jamaican women. Amy had also lived in London, where she opened the Florence Mills Social Parlour and Restaurant, named in honour of the cabaret singer and dancer who used her fame to advocate for Black Americans. C L R James and George Padmore were among Ashwood Garvey's many regulars, and you could find them engaged in political exchanges with fellow Pan-African thinkers there; the International African Friends of Abyssinia was formed in response to Italy's invasion of Ethiopia during one of these discussions. Indeed, transnational and anti-imperialist thinking and activism was the heart and soul of the Florence Mills and Amy was always at the centre of it.

When Amy returned to Harlem, it was with an expanded view of the world. In London, she had developed an internationalist perspective that transformed how she imagined herself in relation to people of African descent around the world. This deepened her engagement with transnational solidarity and collaboration, and she was excited to share what she had learned with other Black women. To announce her new magazine, Ashwood Garvey held a press conference in Harlem and invited potential collaborators 'here and abroad' to write to her office with expressions of interest. Ashwood Garvey said its mission would be to:

> Bring together the women, especially those of darker races, so that they may work for the betterment of all [...] There must be a revolution of thought among women. They must realize their importance in the post-war world [...] In the post-war world there must be unity. Women of the world must unite.[27]

Amy explained that although Black women in the US had made excellent strides towards economic and social independence during the war, women of colour in other parts of the world had much to lose when the war was over. She therefore believed that women in countries with a more progressive view on women's rights should help to improve the conditions for all.

In the photograph accompanying her announcement, Amy is captured looking thoughtful and serious. The black-and-white headshot shows her in a reflective pose, her gaze directed slightly downward as if in contemplation. Her hair, neatly styled with soft curls framing her face, is gently lit, emphasising her strong features. Amy's strategic use of photography here connects seamlessly with the themes of her announcement. The contemplative nature of the photograph contrasts with the dynamic vision she has for the magazine, aiming to unite women of the African diaspora and promote understanding and progress in a postwar world. Choosing a headshot highlights her personal commitment and leadership in this endeavour, making her the relatable and inspiring face of the movement.

Amy envisioned the magazine as a platform to bring together women from 'the Americas, Indo-China, and the West Indies', fostering a global sisterhood.[28] Her poised and reflective demeanour in the image provides a visual representation of her as a thoughtful leader dedicated to her cause. Amy's serious expression conveys a deep awareness of the challenges ahead and a determination to overcome them. This photograph is more than just a personal portrait; it is a powerful symbol of Amy's mission. It captures the essence of her leadership and the gravity of her commitment to creating an international network of women dedicated to mutual support, education and cultural exchange. Through this image, Amy communicates both her personal involvement in the project and the broader importance of the magazine as a tool for global unity and empowerment among women of colour.

As a step towards fostering greater internationalism, Ashwood Garvey sought to publish a magazine that would increase Black women's awareness of the interconnectedness of their struggles with broader movements for women's rights and social justice. The magazine would examine the experiences of women of color around the world. Articles would highlight the progression of women's rights in different nations and the activities of local women's organisations. There is no evidence that this magazine ever came to fruition, but Amy was working on other ways of creating a transnational network of politically engaged Black women. For example, in the spring of 1945 she formed the Afro Women's International Alliance, a charity that offered women's health services, childcare and adult education, in Harlem and beyond. It also shipped clothing to women's charities in Jamaica and solicited books for a library in Liberia.[29]

THE FACT OF BLACKNESS: VISUALIZING DIASPORIC FEMINIST SOLIDARITY

Amy Ashwood Garvey was a fervent believer in the power of international feminist networks. This belief drove her to embark on a lecture tour of the Caribbean during the summer of 1953. Her journey took her to Aruba, Antigua, Barbados, Guyana, Trinidad and Tobago, Suriname and Dominica.[30] With support from her feminist comrades in the Universal Negro Improvement Association (UNIA), she met Black women across these nations, engaging in discussions about their roles in local anti-imperialist movements and the broader global Black freedom struggle. Ashwood Garvey's engagements were not limited to women of African descent; she also connected with Caribbean women from diverse ethnic and social backgrounds, reflecting her conviction that solidarities should be forged around gender as well as nation, class or colour.[31]

While in Barbados, Ashwood Garvey worked to mobilise political solidarities by bringing together various women's organisations, resulting in the formation of the Barbados Women's Alliance. This group aimed to educate women about the island's political and economic affairs, encouraging their active participation.[32] In Trinidad, she developed relationships with leaders of the Women's Federation, who invited her to share her insights from Africa. Her visit included a three-day lecture series, with one notable presentation titled 'Women as Leaders of World Thought.' Additionally, she was honoured at a dinner hosted by the Coterie of Social Workers, one of Trinidad's most influential women's organisations.[33]

Led by Audrey Jeffers, the Coterie of Social Workers was established in 1921 to provide free lunches to underprivileged school children. The first breakfast club was established in 1926, and by 1927 the organisation began celebrating Mother's Day to honour the vital role of motherhood and educate the public about its importance. The Coterie also established a Junior Coterie to engage young women, reflecting its broad scope and commitment to fostering youth involvement in sociopolitical causes. During these events, the Coterie invited distinguished figures from the African diaspora, including Amy Ashwood Garvey. Jeffers, who became Trinidad's first female City Councillor in 1936, may have extended the invitation to Amy during her tenure, recognising the significance of her contributions. Amy's activism and leadership were later chronicled by her nephew Tony Martin, who would have been in a teenager when Amy visited Trinidad.

Amy's impact resonated strongly with the younger women who attended her presentations. Her relationship with Thelma Rogers, a member of the Coterie Social Workers, exemplifies how she mentored young women to engage in activism. Reflecting on Ashwood Garvey's presentations in a letter to friends, Thelma Rogers recalled that she was an excellent public speaker who kept 'the crowds spellbound at her knowledge of the history of Africa.'[34] Thelma and Amy's friendship blossomed into a lifelong bond, with Thelma often reflecting on how profoundly Ashwood Garvey's inspirational presence transformed her life. This connection spurred Thelma to engage in various community service projects and to dedicate herself to empowering other women. As a tribute to their enduring friendship and shared activism, Thelma generously donated an invaluable collection of Amy Ashwood Garvey memorabilia to The Alma Jordan Library, which contains some of my favourite photographs of Amy.

The Alma Jordan Library at the St Augustine Campus of The University of the West Indies in Trinidad and Tobago has a rich collection that stretches back to 1898. Initially part of the Imperial College of Tropical Agriculture (ICTA), the library's collections expanded significantly when ICTA merged with the University of the West Indies in 1960. Originally known as the John F Kennedy Library and later as the Main Library, it was officially renamed The Alma Jordan Library in 2011 to honour its first Campus Librarian. Dr Alma Jordan, who served from 1960 to 1989, including as University Librarian from 1982 until her retirement, led the library's transformation into a significant repository of knowledge. It now houses a vast array of print and online resources, along with prestigious special collections on notable national figures such as Eric Williams, Derek Walcott, and C L R James.[35]

Thelma Rogers's donation of Amy Ashwood Garvey's memorabilia to the library might have been influenced by Dr Alma Jordan's efforts to preserve Caribbean women's history and culture. This collection not only underscores the deep personal connection between Thelma and Amy but also highlights their continued activism. The collection is rich with historical artefacts, including a wide range of correspondence and memorabilia, such as letters and telegrams spanning from 3 July 1954 to 14 December 1967. These documents detail Amy's communications with Thelma and her sister Laurie and outline the activities of the Afro Women's Centre. Other notable items include Sylvia Pankhurst's preview of Amy's unpublished work *Liberia Land of Promise*.

The collection also includes an extended-play vinyl record titled *Up You Mighty Race: Memorial to Marcus Garvey*, which features Ashwood Garvey's reflections on her former husband, accompanied by music from Thelma Massy and Lord Obstinate, with The Tony Thomas Orchestra. Preserved in the audio-visual collection of the Alma Jordan Library and the Moving Image and Recorded Sound Division at the Schomburg Center, this record offers a rare and intimate opportunity to hear Amy's voice. The back of the record presents a striking portrait of Amy, holding a bouquet beside a large vase of tropical flowers, above a photograph of Reverend George Weston, the president of the Marcus Garvey Foundation. Ashwood Garvey is adorned in kente cloth, a fabric that reappears throughout her visual archive, symbolising her deep connection to West African culture and the legacy of the UNIA.

The record is more than just a historical artefact; it is a part of the visual and auditory archive of the African diaspora, preserved within the broader context of Black feminist archival practices. After my most recent research trip to the Schomburg Center in May 2024, I listened to the record from beginning to end for the first time and felt a profound connection to Amy's legacy. I later purchased a copy online through Discogs Marketplace from a record shop in Winter Park, Florida, less than a mile from where I grew up. Now, this record holds a special place in mine and my partner's extensive collection in the front room of our home in London, serving both as a personal keepsake and a testament to Ashwood Garvey's lasting influence in the visual and sonic archive of Black diaspora.

Accompanying these treasures are eighteen photographs, some capturing intimate moments with Amy, Thelma and friends in London and Harlem. One striking photograph depicts Ashwood Garvey in profile, dressed in the style of the mid twentieth century. She is adorned in a black-and-white, Mandarin collared ensemble with pearl earring, her hair neatly pulled back, elegant and poised. Another photograph features Amy, Thelma, and an unnamed man, all impeccably dressed, seated at a table with teacups on saucers in front of them. Thelma is wearing a pill hat, the man is in a tie, and both women are adorned with brooches, holding purses in their laps. Embodying the style of the period, these images are more than just snapshots; they offer a window into a world where style and sophistication are celebrated, and where the act of being photographed becomes an assertion of presence and agency. In this sense, they reflect the broader visual practices within the Black diaspora, each photograph a testament to what Leigh Raiford describes as 'the fact of blackness' that makes visible racial, gendered and diasporic ways of being and becoming.[36]

AMY ASHWOOD GARVEY'S VIEW OF WEST AFRICA

It was Amy Ashwood Garvey's dream to travel to Africa. In March 1946 that dream came true when she boarded the *SS Gambia* in Liverpool, England bound for West Africa. Amy had learned of her African ancestry from her father's grandmother, Boahimaa, who at the age of sixteen was kidnapped and forcibly taken to Jamaica to work on a plantation. Boahimaa explained that she was born in Darman, a village in Juaben, an independent state in the Ashanti region. Boahimaa recounted whatever she could remember about their family, their customs and culture, which left Amy with a feeling of pride she had never experienced before. Ashwood Garvey would later write to Lionel M Yard about her time in Africa, sharing insights for what would become his biography of her life. She referred to herself as a 'very happy globe trotter', yet she also expressed an inner conflict. Amy's joy was tempered by her anger about the tragic histories that led to her grandmother's kidnapping and, consequently, her own displacement:

> No sooner had the boat sailed, and I was engulfed in emotion. Here I was returning to the land of my ancestors a detribalized African, relieved of every vestige of my Culture. I laid awake in my cabin unable to sleep. The Africa to which I

was returning had been dominated by nations of varying cultures: Portugal, Spain, England, France, Belgium, Italy, and Germany. They were primarily responsible for the destruction of the Black man's land, liberty, and life which was irremediably disrupted....There in my lonely cabin filled with the beautiful flowers dear friends had sent me, I faced the traducers. I called down vengeance on the heads of the slave masters and African collaborators.[37]

Amy's first glimpse of the continent was the Island of Gorée. Situated 3 km off the coast of Dakar, the capital of the Republic of Senegal, Gorée holds a significant place in history as one of the earliest sites of European colonisation in Africa. A small island measuring about 900 by 300 metres, Gorée was the epicentre of the African slave trade from the fifteenth to the nineteenth centuries. It was governed by various European powers and its landscape characterised by the juxtaposition between the austere buildings that contained enslaved Africans and the large colonial houses that belonged to European traders. Gorée was designated a historic site in 1944, two years before Amy's arrival. But it was only after Senegal gained its independence in 1960 that the government began to consider its restoration. The House of Slaves (*Maison des Esclaves*), a museum designed to honour the victims of this genocide, opened its doors in 1962. While historians continue to debate the exact number of enslaved Africans held here and Gorée Island's overall impact on the trans-Atlantic slave trade, it has since become a significant pilgrimage point for visitors from Africa and the diaspora. Gorée stands today not only as a haunting reminder of human exploitation but also as a space for reflection and remembrance.

Amy's arrival in West Africa preceded Goree's transformation into a tourist destination primarily targeting the descendants of enslaved Africans seeking to connect with their heritage. However, Ashwood Garvey was acutely aware of the island's historical significance. From her vantage point aboard the ship, she would have seen the remnants of former military forts and castles scattered along the coastline, tangible reminders of a harrowing past. As the vessel approached land, she likely experienced a surge of emotion, akin to the profound moment I encountered when I first went to Ghana in December 2014. The sight of people bearing a resemblance to her standing on the dock would have stirred deep feelings within Amy, much as it did for me upon stepping out of Kotoka International Airport into the sounds of a lively West African city, the warm evening air, and the aroma of dust in Accra. As Amy made her way down the gangplank, she might have wiped a tear from her face, just as I did when overcome with feelings of awe and grief during the journey to my in-laws' home in East Legon. In that poignant moment, Amy felt an intense yearning to connect with the people there, recognising a kinship that transcended time – a sentiment was expressed in her autobiographical writings:

> I hesitated for a moment – was it real, or only the outline of a land of chimera? As if to dispel any illusions I might have, there came clambering up the gangway, dark-skinned stevedores glistening with sweat, bustling with activity ... I longed to cry out greetings to my kinsmen. My heart went forth to meet those stalwart black labourers.[38]

As the ship prepared to dock in Dakar, Amy felt the conclusion of one chapter of her life and the beginning of another. Ahead of her 'lay a twofold destination – Africa the continent of tomorrow, and the Africa of my dreams'.[39] In Senegal, Amy was soon 'making friends with total strangers, no, not strangers but brothers whom I had not seen for two centuries' and immersed herself in the local politics, food, music, and art. An observant traveller, Ashwood Garvey was stuck by the French-ness of Dakar:

> I gazed at the well-arranged art shops, beautifully arranged and decorative shop windows, cafes, bars, restaurants, and licensed brothels. No this is not the Africa of my dreams, but an imitation of Paris. It seemed as if the French surrounded themselves with everything that reminded them of their country as a protection against the overwhelming forces of Africa.[40]

However, after engaging in lively discussions with Senegalese Pan-Africanists in Dakar, Amy felt the winds of change sweeping through the country. 'I was witnessing a peaceful revolution ... Africa was now finding its voice ... and I offered a prayer of gratitude for both God and Africa.'[41]

Freetown, Sierra Leone, was the ship's next port of call. Upon arrival, Amy marvelled at the natural beauty of the landscape, 'where the steep and wooded hills rise straight from the sea', reminiscent of the greenery of her childhood home in Port Antonio.[42] While in Freetown she connected with several women's groups, including the Business and Professional Women's Club.[43] Her journey continued to the rural villages in Moyamba, a district in the Southern Province of Sierra Leone, where she received an official welcome and a banquet from Chief Gualuma. Thousands turned out to greet her. 'Then,' she reported, 'the greatest spectacle of dancers and fairies that I had ever seen in my life appeared in a circle about a quarter mile in circumference and performed for some two hours.'[44]

When Amy heard about a woman chief 150 miles away, she embarked on a two-day journey to meet her. Her 'joy was complete,' she said, 'when the Queen of the Gallinas, Paramount Chief Madam Woki Massaquoi embraced me, and said, "Daughter of Africa, welcome home." To see a woman of my race, the great-granddaughter of Siaka, one of the first known kings of Sierra Leone, holding the reins of power in her hands made me very proud. Tell them to keep up their courage, Africa will live again as a free Nation.'[45]

Amy was captivated by the beauty of the art in the region. 'I can't describe how beautiful the artwork of the people in French West Africa is,' she expressed in a letter to Lionel M Yard. 'It is too beautiful for words.'[46] Already planning to collect pieces for an ambitious exhibition in New York and Chicago, her purchases included a 'circular African table' and a 'polished elephant stool'.[47] Ever business-minded, she saw opportunities to establish an art shop, intending to use proceeds to support underprivileged Black women worldwide.

The photographs Amy Ashwood Garvey took while traveling in West Africa offer a compelling glimpse into the diverse landscapes and cultural environments she encountered. One of her photographs captures traditional stilt houses with thatched roofs built over water, while another portrays a tranquil river scene with a solitary figure paddling a canoe. The calm expanse of the water and the distant horizon convey a sense of peace and openness. In another photograph, a straight, palm-lined pedestrian path offers a glimpse into the organised and verdant urban area. Amy's handwritten note on the back of this image, which reads, 'a road for pedestrians only. The straight and cemented road with the green foliage attracts me very much,' provides personal insight into her appreciation of the landscape.[48] Further images depict more rural scenes: one shows a blurry view of thatched huts, highlighting the simplicity and traditional living conditions. Another photograph of a fortified building, possibly a colonial structure, stands as a testament to the historical and architectural remnants of colonial influence in the region. These landscape photographs not only document Amy's travels but also reflect a Black diasporic visual practice that uses the camera to explore and connect with the cultural and historical landscapes. By capturing the natural beauty, traditional ways of life, and the enduring marks of colonialism, Amy's photography serves as a visual record of her journey, blending personal appreciation with a deeper awareness of the broader sociopolitical context. Her images offer a nuanced perspective on the regions she explored, embodying a diasporic desire to engage with and document the complexities of West African life and history, while also affirming a connection to the continent that resonates across time and space.

'THIS IS YOUR AFRICA, THIS IS YOUR LIBERIA'

Amy Ashwood Garvey departed Sierra Leone with excitement in May 1946, headed toward Liberia. Tony Martin notes that Amy's longstanding interest in Liberia was deeply rooted in the UNIA. Marcus Garvey envisioned Liberia as a homeland for the African diaspora, where repatriated Black people from the US and the Caribbean could escape racial and colonial oppression and build an independent nation on their ancestral soil.

On 8 June 1920, Elie Garcia, a UNIA commissioner, wrote to Liberia's President, C B D King, seeking support for the acceptance of UNIA members. The letter requested land to repatriate members and outlined the organisation's goals: establishing a universal fraternity of Black people, aiding the development of independent Black nations, protecting the African diaspora, providing educational opportunities, promoting international commerce, and improving living conditions for people of African descent. Garvey understood that these aspirations could only be realised in Africa, thus seeking Liberia's cooperation.[49] However, his ambitious plans, including the Black Star Line – a Black-owned steamship line to facilitate migration – were thwarted by financial setbacks, internal disputes and opposition from colonial powers. Despite these challenges, Liberia remained a symbol of Pan-Africanism and hope within the broader African diaspora for the UNIA.

Given this legacy, Amy's excitement upon arriving in Liberia is understandable. She was driven by the same diasporic aspirations that had motivated Marcus Garvey's vision: seeking freedom, self-determination, and contributing to the movement for African unity and liberation. However, Liberia's history as a settlement for Black Americans and Caribbeans is deeply intertwined with colonial projects. Established in the early nineteenth century by the American Colonization Society (ACS), Liberia aimed to repatriate freeborn people of colour and emancipated slaves to Africa. The ACS, founded in 1816 by Robert Finley, was born out of the belief that free people of colour could not integrate into US society, which was exacerbated by the growth of this population following the American Revolutionary War. As free Black communities began to establish themselves, slave owners feared that they might help those still enslaved to escape or rebel. Despite its long existence and headquarters in Washington, DC, until its dissolution in 1964, the ACS faced significant opposition from the abolitionist movement and figures like Frederick Douglass, who argued that Black Americans had lived in the United States for generations.[50]

After the American Civil War, financial support for the project waned, yet Black American and Caribbean populations continued to emigrate. By the time Marcus Garvey began looking to Liberia as a symbol of the African diaspora's quest for freedom and self-determination, the reality was far more complex. The Black settlers, or Americo-Liberians often perpetuated the same oppressive practices they sought to escape, displacing indigenous populations and treating them as second-class citizens. Americo-Liberians viewed the indigenous population with disdain, labelling them 'evil cannibals' and 'expendable country people.'[51] The cultural and linguistic divide further deepened the rift. Consequently, the settlement was established based on Western values and ideas, with little to no input from the indigenous population, highlighting the complexities and contradictions of Liberia's establishment as a safe haven for people of African descent.[52]

This context is crucial for understanding Ashwood Garvey's excitement and the criticisms of her views on Liberia. While she saw the potential for Liberia to be a beacon of Pan-Africanism, the underlying issues of oppression and exclusion present a more complicated picture. Despite these complexities, Ashwood Garvey was determined to see Liberia for herself and contribute to its development. As the early glow of the morning sun spread across the horizon, Amy made her way to the deck, eager to catch her first glimpse of the land that had captured her imagination for so long:

> What onlooker could have understood the intensity of my feelings as I sat so quietly and expectantly; yet even I was quite unprepared for that sudden emotional surge which arose in me when the Captain shouted down to me, 'Madame Garvey, this is your Africa, this is your Liberia.' The sun was rising as I gazed across the water towards the darkened outline of what to me was the unknown country of my dreams. The magic of peace and stillness was spread over this world. In a moment my heart was afire, for the spirit of the pioneers worked within me. I stood on the deck lost in reverie, but I was singing the song of Paul Lawrence Dunbar: 'O Mother Africa, to thee we bring this pledge of faith unwavering, this tribute to thy glory. We know the pangs which thou didst feel when chattel slavery crushed thee with its heel. With thy dear blood all gory.'[53]

Arriving in Monrovia was a moment of profound significance for Amy. As a Liberian official boarded the ship searching for her, he introduced himself as an emissary from the State Department,[54] Amy felt a wave of anticipation. His announcement of her diplomatic privileges was entirely unexpected but confirmed the significance of this new chapter. Stepping off the gangplank with her bags in hand, she was warmly greeted by a delegation of women, including Sarah Simpson George, who Ashwood Garvey later praised as 'Liberia's most astute and energetic political fighter.'[55] Amy was deeply moved by their warm welcome, finding a sense of comfort in the connections between women.

The President of Liberia, William V S Tubman, arranged for a special plane to bring Amy to his private estate.[56] Tubman, who hailed from an Americo-Liberian background, was a descendant of Black Americans who had settled in Liberia. Elected in 1944, he became Liberia's longest-serving leader, holding office until his death in 1971 after changing the constitution to extend his tenure. In the early postwar era, Tubman earned accolades as a significant statesman, advocating for African decolonisation and mentoring emerging African nationalists like Kwame Nkrumah. However, Tubman's twenty-seven-year rule has been subject to criticism.

Tubman's rule brought prosperity, with investments in health and education, and the adoption of a literacy program. He endeavoured to unite Liberia's population, making equal rights mandatory after years of Americo-Liberian dominance over indigenous groups. Additionally, he was celebrated for extending political rights to women. However, his close ties to the US and opposition to communism were seen by some as compromising Liberia's independence. Furthermore, he faced criticism for expanding opportunities for Western companies to exploit Liberia's natural resources and for repressing political opposition, with many labelling him an authoritarian who maintained his power and wealth through violence and intimidation.

President Tubman recognised and respected Amy's pivotal role in the formation of the UNIA and the propagation of Garveyism. Aware of the historical injustices she faced in the feud with Marcus and Amy Jacques, he was resolute in honouring Ashwood Garvey during her time in Liberia. Tubman's fascination with Amy extended beyond mere admiration; he went so far as to throw an extravagant party in her honour. There was speculation that they were dating.[57] Amy even told Lionel M Yard that Tubman proposed marriage to her. In a letter to Lionel she explained, 'marrying him would bring plenty of glory to us all, but my whole life would change, would no longer be free. The first lady has a tradition and would have to adhere to it – I can only say that I am very confused ... I shall make no decision until I talk to you but the whole nation is fascinated with me.'[58] Amy, unwavering in her feminist convictions, respectfully declined. Her independence was sacred to her, and she remained devoted to her mission of spiritual and social liberation. Amy refused to conform to the traditional role of a president's wife, just as she had refused to be Marcus's helpmate, preferring to focus on her advocacy work.

*

I was introduced to Amy and President Tubman's relationship through Lionel M Yard's biography, where I found a striking photograph of Tubman in the fourth chapter. In the photograph, President Tubman cuts a dignified figure. Dressed in a tailored suit and tie, he presents himself with professionalism. His facial features are framed by a pair of glasses, adding a scholarly touch to his appearance. The angled side profile captures his presence as he gazes off into the distance, seemingly lost in thought. I was left pondering the significance of this image – did Tubman present it to Amy as a symbol of their camaraderie or a keepsake of their shared endeavours? Such musings sparked my interest in the role of photographs as tangible reflections of social relationships.

In the 'Amy Ashwood Garvey Photographs, 1930s-1950s' collection at the John Hope Franklin Research Center, I encountered yet another portrayal of President Tubman that highlighted their long-standing personal connection. In this image, his features are more youthful and vibrant, devoid of the glasses that often adorned his face in later years. However, the quality of his presence remains unchanged, dignified in his direct gaze into the camera. The suit he wears in the photograph bears a striking resemblance to the one he wore in the previous image. What sets this image apart is the handwritten note in Amy's script, '[William Tubman, Liberian President],' adding a personal touch to the historical record.

A recent encounter with Tubman's images made me reflect on the multifaceted nature of photography itself – how it acts as a bridge between the past and the present, a medium that connects us to stories otherwise relegated to the shadows. In this sense, photography transcends mere documentation; it becomes a potent narrative tool that encodes emotions, memories, and relationships within the frame. Engaging with these images prompted me to delve more deeply into Liberia's history, to explore the legacy of Tubman, and to understand why he was so significant to Amy Ashwood Garvey, who remained close to him throughout her life.

This exploration led me to integrate Liberia's historical context more thoroughly into my research, recognising the profound impact that figures like Tubman had on Amy's worldview and activism. Tubman, a central figure in Liberian politics and an influential leader in Pan-Africanism, played a crucial role in shaping the political landscape of the region, a role that Amy deeply respected and valued. Their enduring friendship and mutual respect underscore the interconnectedness of the Black diasporic struggle for liberation, transcending geographic boundaries.

In this way, my engagement with Tubman's photographs became more than an academic exercise; it was a personal journey into the depths of diasporic memory and connection. The images invited me to ask questions, to speculate about the unspoken narratives they hold, and to experiment with the archive as a living, breathing entity that continues to inform and inspire.

This process is emblematic of the visual practice of diaspora, where photography serves as both a record and a catalyst. It prompts us to engage with history in a way that is dynamic and participatory, encouraging us to not only preserve the past but to actively interrogate and reimagine it. Through this practice, photography becomes a tool for uncovering hidden stories, for bridging temporal and spatial divides, and for fostering a deeper understanding of our shared histories. In this way, Amy's photographs, and those of her contemporaries like Tubman, are not just relics of the past; they are active agents in the ongoing work of diasporic memory, shaping how we see, interpret, and engage with the world around us.

*

Despite declining Tubman's proposal, Amy and the president remained close, with Tubman even offering to support her application for Liberian citizenship. Yet, Ashwood Garvey knew that this came with challenges. Since 1822, when Black settlers from the US first arrived in Liberia, tensions had arisen between them and the indigenous population. The settlers imposed their cultural and political dominance, leading to ongoing conflicts over land and power. This history influenced Liberia's sociopolitical landscape deeply. In a letter on 27 May 1946, Amy addressed these issues with Tubman directly. The previous year, Eslanda Robeson, Amy's Pan-Africanist ally and wife of Paul Robeson, criticised Liberia in autoethnographic monographic called *An African Journey,* labelling Americo-Liberians a 'disgrace' for their treatment of indigenous people.[59] Amy, familiar with Esanda's critiques, likely felt compelled to write to Tubman about these persisting conflicts:

> Over a period of years, I have read many books, Newspaper Articles, published on Liberia and noticed that the trend has invariably been to degrade, expose the country to ridicule and make capital out of any deficiencies from which all countries founded on similar grounds must struggle to fulfil their destiny.
>
> Because of the pride I now feel in becoming a Liberian Citizen and because I also know of the aims, aspirations and hope of millions of denationalized Blacks who look with jealous pride to the only Black Republic in Africa; I not only beseech or recommend, but demand that this Cultural Relations Department, be established to work as a separate Department in conjunction with the Department of Information and thereby bridging the seemingly, interminable and mysterious Gulf [sic] which exists between Liberia and other races.[60]

Amy initially hoped to manage the department, but her influence was truly felt in the lecture hall, where she connected with her audience through powerful speeches filled with profound insights and heartfelt words. Her presence was dynamic, and her authoritative voice left lasting impressions. Amy's lecture topics ranged from health, hygiene, and education to family and community relationships and the history of African peoples in the diaspora. Ashwood Garvey delivered many of these transformative lectures to women in Liberia, working closely with Sarah Simpson George, founder of the Liberian Women's Social and Political Movement. This collaboration allowed Amy to reach and empower a wider audience, reinforcing the importance of women's voices in the ongoing struggle for social and political equality in the country.

Sharing Amy's belief in women's political emancipation, Tubman supported her efforts. He also supported her desire to write a book on the history of Liberia from an 'African Woman's perspective'. He provided access to historical documents about Liberia's governmental politics and decision-making processes, a gesture of trust that Amy greatly appreciated. Amy sifted through these archives with meticulous care, crafting the manuscript *Liberia, Land of Promise*, which documented Liberia's development, celebrating the country as a homeland for the Black diaspora. Ashwood Garvey would complete various drafts after she returned to England.[61] While the manuscript was never published, Amy did publish an essay called 'The Liberian Woman' in a June 1946 issue of the *People's Voice,* in which Amy highlights the contributions of Americo-Liberian to building the nation. In it, celebrates the first Black American women who arrived in Liberia in 1820, such as Martha Ricks, Sarah Blyden, and Florence Barclay, while celebrating figures like Matilda Newport who reportedly fought in battles against indigenous tribes. She acknowledges the pivotal role of Susannah Lewis and other Liberian women in presenting the nation's first flag in 1847 and highlights the leadership of Sarah Simpson George, who established Liberia's first women's political party and advocated for mass education, economic opportunities, and suffrage for women.

Amy's endorsement of the settlers' efforts makes a nuanced analysis of her perspective on colonialism necessary. While advocating fervently for the upliftment of African women, her approval of the displacement of indigenous populations appears to contradict her broader intention to advocate for all women of African descent. Moreover, the very language she uses seems to reify the colonial ideologies and practices enacted by Black settlers. The essay includes three photographs, one of Sarah Simpson George, whose image is captioned accordingly, and two of indigenous women, whose names are unreported. Printed on the first page of the essay, to the right of the photographs of Simpson George, a photograph of a topless girl wearing a necklace and headwrap is captioned 'Native African belle of 16', creating the types and classifications common in colonial photography. The second image is of another young woman with a child strapped to her back. Its caption is more detailed, but it strikes a similar tone:

> Native Liberian women, shown here, are fast taking on the ways of Western civilization. These women live in the interior. On the streets of Monrovia, the capital, the women dress and act like any other Western woman. Above pix (sic) is a 16-year-old native belle in her native dress. At right a native woman goes to market. Like native women in other primitive areas, she carries her baby strapped to her back and her bundle on her bead. So-called civilized women can pattern the graceful walk that the native women have developed because of keeping their head bundles in proper balance. They swing along at beautiful, measured, graceful pace, when not burdened with a child on their backs.[62]

This quote from Amy's essay underscores her complex relationship to African women's experiences. On the one hand, Amy's attempt to document and bring visibility to the lives of women in Liberia aligns with her broader feminist goals. By highlighting these women's roles and daily lives, she provides a lens through which their contributions and struggles can be acknowledged and appreciated. However, a critical Black feminist analysis reveals several problematic elements. Amy's descriptions, such as 'native belle' and the notion of indigenous women 'taking on the ways of Western civilization,' echo colonial discourses that not only exoticise and objectify these women but also imply a hierarchy where Westernization is seen as a marker of progress and civilization.

Such perspectives inadvertently reinforce colonial ideologies that devalue indigenous cultures and practices. Moreover, by framing indigenous women's ways of life as something for 'civilized women' to emulate in terms of grace and balance, Amy others their traditional practices while simultaneously presenting them as something to be adopted by the West. This duality reflects a tension in her writing: while she seeks to celebrate these women, she also frames them within a Western gaze that fails to fully respect their cultural context and autonomy.

ASHANTI ANCESTRAL TIES

Following a brief return to Sierra Leone Amy Ashwood Garvey headed to the Gold Coast, now known as Ghana. She arrived in Accra in October 1946, where she reconnected with friends and acquaintances from London, before heading to Kumasi on 2 December 1946. Amy's arrival in Kumasi marked a significant chapter in her journey. Accompanied by her two adopted daughters, Eva Morris and Lizzie Wilson, Amy embarked on a quest to reconnect with her African heritage and reaffirm her ancestral ties. Amy first met Ghanian politician Joseph Boakye Danquah (known as J B Danquah) in London in 1924, when the latter was studying law, and they would go on to become longstanding friends. It was during this meeting that Amy shared the story of her grandmother Boahimaa, fondly referred to as 'Grannie Dabas,' and inquired about the locations mentioned in her narrative – Darman and Juaben. Danquah suggested that Grannie Dabas might have been referring to the State of Juaben in Ashanti. Nearly a decade later, in 1935, Amy crossed paths with another Ghanaian, Barrister Cobbina Kessie, who concurred with Danquah's interpretation. It was Kessie who accompanied Amy to the Asantehene's palace in 1946, initiating the series of events that would ultimately verify and conclude Grannie Dabas's narrative.

Shortly after arriving in Kumasi, Amy shared the story of her grandmother, Grannie Dabas, with a journalist from the *Ashanti Pioneer*. She recounted:

> My grandmother made me promise that someday when I became a woman, I would visit Ashanti our homeland. Ever since that time the desire to see Ashanti has been the moving impulse of my life. In fact, I have been living in Ashanti spiritually. I am here now in happy and dutiful fulfilment of that great promise.[63]

Eager to connect with local dignitaries who could help confirm her Ashanti roots, Amy sought a meeting with the King of Ashanti, Osei Tutu Agyeman Prempeh II, expecting a warm reception consistent with his reputation for hospitality. Her excitement to meet the king quickly turned to disappointment when she was met with a formal and reserved demeanour, quite different from the warmth she had anticipated. Unbeknownst to Ashwood Garvey, rumours sown by Amy Jacques Garvey had preceded her arrival, casting doubt over her character. A cautious King Prempeh, mindful of his reputation, chose to observe and evaluate Amy's intentions before extending his hospitality. Eventually, after uncovering the truth behind the accusations, Prempeh offered Amy a gracious restitution, welcoming her warmly into his circle. Amy was provided with a lodging at Manhyia Palace, receiving lavish care and provisions as a special visitor in the court of the Ashanti king. This gesture marked the beginning of a two-year period during which Amy forged a close bond with Prempeh, engaging in profound discussions on the history of the Ashanti, the struggle for independence, and the preservation of cultural customs. As they exchanged ideas, Amy shared her insights from her travels and activism, highlighting the injustices of racism and colonialism and advocating for Africa's emancipation.[64]

While living at Manhyia Palace, Amy Ashwood Garvey had the unique opportunity to witness a grand durbar – a major celebration that attracted people from all walks of life, including politicians and religious leaders. It was a colourful traditional ceremony honouring the Ashanti king. Amy's observations of the event reflect her keen eye for the intricate and vibrant culture of the Ashanti people. Her descriptions convey a deep appreciation for the ceremonial splendour and the complex social hierarchy on display. Her account of the durbar is deeply illustrative, painting a picture of the Ashanti community's unity and their devotion to preserving their heritage:

> A motley of colors. Innumerable were the broad lace-rimmed embroidered state umbrellas of quilt work containing every color of the rainbow. Each of these bespoke the presence of a ruler in the Ashanti Confederacy. And molding all sound into one was the flow of African music. Over two hundred Paramount, Divisional and Sub-Divisional Chiefs wearing golden crowns and golden sandals came bedecked in beautifully woven silk Kente cloth. With their multi-colored umbrellas swinging in the dewy-morning breeze they formed a spectacle of beauty passing fair ...
> Suddenly the murmur of the expectant crowd rose to a pitch and the drums in the background reverberated in a new tune announcing the appearance of the head of the Ashanti Nation; for the Asantehene, Otumfuo Nana Sir Osei Agyeman Prempeh II had arrived at the park. His beautiful purple, black and gold umbrella stood way above the crowd as the trumpets and pipes gave him a melodious welcome. To the center of the space occupied by the chiefs, four supported by eight men conveyed him in a palanquin of raffia work which had the inside lined with leopard skins and rich soft velvet. Thrown over his body was a costly blanket of Ashanti make. His head was encircled by a crown magnificent in designs of purest gold. On his feet he wore golden sandals. His robe twelve yards in length and two yards wide was laden with golden insignia worth the ransom of a king. Why, all over his body were drapplings of gold: gold on his arms, his leg, his neck, gold everywhere. No wonder the European adventurer christened that country the Gold Coast. His seat rested beneath the thing of beauty that was a canopy and glittered in the exquisite splendor of polished gold. There he sat, the true monarch of Ashanti, believed to be the most powerful king within the framework of imperialist sway in Africa ...
> For many the climax in that grand display of splendor came when the chiefs returned greetings to the Governor,

who had ascended the dais. It was a sight healing every curiosity of the eye. For who could behold the gorgeous beauty of those princes and princesses and yet desire anything more magnificent. All were clad in their full regalia of native artistry and immense worth. They paraded to the tune of martial music and the sound of sweet melody which made the crowd react in the peculiar and fascinating movements of African dances...

In the midst of the leisured procession came the Asantehene and the Golden Stool of Ashanti. In front walked the members of his court with the emblems of their office – key bearers and sandal bearers, porters of the silver bowls and goblets, executioners, clowns clad in red garments. The armor bearers carried the ancient battle dress of the warlike Ashanti Kings. Tradition traces the origin to the fifteenth century, whence it has come down, the precious heritage of each succeeding king, whose lot it was to lead the army in times of war ... With measured gait bespeaking dignity, Prempeh II advanced to shake hands with the Governor ...

Before him was borne the Golden Stool of Ashanti - the emblem of Ashanti Nationhood. It was delivered in the reign of Osei Tutu the founder of this renowned dynasty, through the ministration and power of the great fetish priest Okomfo Anotchi. It was a Stool which never had been sat upon... Following the Asantehene was the Asantehemaa, the Queen Mother of Ashanti. In Ashanti, woman occupies a very exalted political position in the state.[65]

This captivating portrayal likely describes the Akwasidae Festival, celebrated every six weeks on a Sunday by the Ashanti people and their chiefs, as well as the Ashanti diaspora. During this festival, the Asantehene meets his subjects and subordinate chiefs in the courtyard of the Manhyia Palace. The Golden Stool is prominently displayed in the palace grounds, symbolising the unity and continuity of the Ashanti nation. People from all over gather in large numbers, participating in traditional song and dance.

The festival serves as a critical cultural touchstone, and Amy's detailed account underscores the deep connection and pride the

Ashanti people have in their customs. Her narrative not only provides a window into the grandeur of the event but also emphasises the political and cultural significance of such gatherings. The procession, the adornments, the music, and the rituals – all these elements came together to create an unforgettable experience for Amy. Her observations highlight the prominent role of women in Ashanti society, particularly through the figure of the Asantehemaa, demonstrating the respected and influential positions women held in their political structure.

Amy Ashwood Garvey's time in King Prempeh's court culminated in a significant public reception in her honour in February 1947, attended by prominent local dignitaries, including the Chief of Juaben, Osekyerehene Yaw Sarpong II. She was formally recognised as a member 'of the family of Darmanhene, a native of Juaben and an Ashanti' during a lineage and naming ceremony. This induction was not only a powerful affirmation of her African identity but also a transformative experience that instilled a deep sense of belonging and fuelled her commitment to the rights and welfare of her people. In April 1946, she presented her case before officials in Juaben, where the community's historical records – traditionally passed down orally by a linguist – confirmed her ancestral ties. By January 1947, after deliberations involving the chief of Juaben and Prempeh II, her Ashanti ancestry was officially recognised, setting the stage for her formal introduction to the community.

In his telling of this experience, Lionel M Yard says that Amy arrived to the ceremony in a Cadillac flanked by locals in traditional kente. Inside a large hut, elders and the linguist recounted the authenticated history of Amy's family, solidifying her place within their lineage. With her African roots affirmed, Amy embraced her new Ashanti name, Yaa Boahimaa, which was also the name of her grandmother, Grannie Dabas. This choice reflected her deep connection to her heritage and her desire to honour her lineage. She adopted traditional Ashanti clothing, primarily kente, a practice she continued for the rest of her life. Among her most prized possessions were two kente cloths presented to her by the Asantehene, symbolising her accepted return and integration into her ancestral community.[66]

Unfortunately, a planned documentation of the ceremony was aborted due to a last-minute decision by Amy, a choice she later regretted deeply. Photography was not just a means of capturing moments for her; it served as a powerful medium to communicate and cement her personal and political identity within the African diasporic and Pan-African community. The absence of comprehensive visual documentation for this significant event was a missed opportunity to capture a pivotal moment in her journey. However, a single photograph survived, which has become a poignant testament to the ceremony's cultural and personal significance.[67]

This image, prominently featured in Lionel M Yard's biography of Amy, captures her dressed in Ashanti cultural attire, surrounded by a diverse group of attendees in a mix of traditional and Western clothing, highlighting the fusion of cultures at the event.[68] Amy's warm, animated expression and the attentive faces around her illustrate a shared moment of cultural reverence and personal triumph. The photograph not only encapsulates the atmosphere of Amy's ceremonial induction but also underscores her influential presence in Ghana and her deep connection to her ancestral roots.

Decades later, during Tony Martin's 1990 research trip to the region, Amy's visits to Kumasi and Darman were still vividly remembered. Asantehene Otumfuo Nana Opoku Ware II recalled her time at the Asantehene's palace from his childhood, highlighting the enduring legacy of her influence and the cultural bridge she helped fortify between the African diaspora and her ancestral homeland.[69]

*

In September 2021 I embarked on a research trip to Kumasi, aiming to retrace Amy's journey through the Ashanti region. My partner, Kobna, and his cousin Nana Yaw took turns driving my mother-in-law's truck from Accra. Our trip lasted about five hours, as we paused to take photographs and enjoy lunch along the way. Once we arrived, we checked into our rooms at Asantewaa Premier Guesthouse in Kumasi, a place named after the Queen Mother of Ashanti, Yaa Asantewaa, who famously led her people in resisting British colonial forces during the Ashanti-British War for the

Golden Stool in 1900. After settling in, I took a moment to reflect on the significance of our surroundings – not just in terms of Amy's legacy, but the enduring lineage of women who have been pivotal in the struggle against colonialism in Africa and the diaspora. This place, infused with the legacy of Yaa Asantewaa's resistance, serves as a powerful reminder of the historical and ongoing contributions of women like Amy who have fought tirelessly for freedom and justice across generations and continents.

From the outset of my research trip, it was evident that Amy's legacy is intricately woven into the cultural tapestry of Ghana, a country that gained independence under her friend Kwame Nkrumah, its first democratic president. Amy's influence in Ghana is ubiquitous, even though she might not always be recognised in official spaces like museums and archives. Unveiling details of Amy's time in Ghana led me beyond formal archival records and into enriching conversations with historians, archivists, and others. This exploration brought me to the iconic Manhyia Palace Museum, the seat of the current Asantehene in the Ashanti Kingdom. Situated in the heart of Kumasi, this palace is a shrine to Ashanti history and traditions, showcasing clothing and artefacts that highlight Ashanti heritage dating back to precolonial times. Originally a royal dwelling, the palace was officially established as a museum in 1995 and now attracts millions of visitors annually.

According to Amy's own accounts, she took up residence here around 1946, living within the women's quarters of the palace. In letters to President William Tubman, Amy described her close friendship with the king, who provided her with a plot of land to build her home and start a business. An unexpected conversation with a guide outside the museum, inspired by a photograph I showed of Amy, illuminated her lasting impact within the palace community, underscoring the significance of community memory in preserving her legacy.

Unfortunately, when I arrived the museum was closed for remodelling, rendering the entire collection inaccessible. I had hoped to explore the physical space; I longed to wander through the museum, imagining the places where Amy might have lived, entertained, and slept. Despite the museum being closed, showing the guide a photograph of Amy Ashwood Garvey with Prempeh II at Manhyia Palace sparked a rich dialogue about her time in the region. The guide animatedly described the events held at the palace and the way international dignitaries were hosted. He detailed the historical layout of the house, making it feel as though I was actually there. He pointed out where visiting women like Amy would have stayed – specific quarters at the back of the house beside the castle. This conversation allowed me to glean more about Amy's time there than I might have if the museum had been open.

Visiting Kumasi to conduct research on Amy Ashwood Garvey provided a profound moment for me to reflect on my own family history and lineage. My grandmother, Iris Sinclair, has often recounted stories passed down from her grandfather, Robert Plummer, who spoke of his own grandfather – one of two brothers torn from their homeland in West Africa and enslaved in Jamaica. According to him, they were from a village in the Ashanti region known as Koromantse. My grandmother recalls that these stories about our ancestors always concluded with the powerful affirmation, 'Coromantee blood run in all ah we.'

The Coromantees, or Coromantins, were a group of Africans from the Gold Coast region, their name derived from Fort Kormantine – also known as Fort Amsterdam – a former slave fort in Kormantse, Ghana's Central Region. Known for their fierce resistance to enslavement, particularly under the legendary leadership of Nanny of the Maroons, the Coromantees have become an enduring symbol of resistance to colonial oppression in Jamaica.

In May 2024, I visited my grandmother in Chicago, accompanied by my partner Kobna and our son Adali. During that visit, I had the opportunity to view photographs of these ancestors – her parents and grandparents – that she keeps in her home. Seeing those images made the stories she shared even more tangible and poignant. As she told me the story of our Coromantee ancestors once again, she emphasised how her grandfather's tales always ended with that powerful line about our bloodline.

Reflecting on Amy's quest to confirm her own family history and ancestral ties inspired me to pursue a similar journey. To replicate her experience, I decided to arrange a naming ceremony and kente weaving experience through Bilson Tours, a company established in 2019 to offer homecoming and heritage tours for descendants of enslaved Africans visiting Ghana. This initiative began during the Year of Return, which has since evolved into Beyond the Return, an annual programme commemorating the first recorded arrival of enslaved Africans in the English Colony of Virginia in 1619. My decision to engage in this ceremony was deeply rooted in a desire to honour my ancestors and solidify my connection to my African heritage, much like Amy did. My father-in-law provided a beautiful traditional wax print fabric, which I had previously made into a dress but had not yet worn. On the day of the tour, wearing that dress, I waited for an hour and a half for the delayed guide. Once we finally met, we drove through scenic Kumasi to Adanwomase, a town renowned for its cultural tourism.

The drive was picturesque, with fields of coconut and palm oil passing by, showcasing the region's agricultural bounty. Upon arrival, I was greeted warmly by a man named Kwame, who appeared to be around my father's age, and shown the kente shop, where the rhythmic clicks of wooden looms echoed the intricate artistry of kente weaving. After trying various fabrics I explored the village, observing young men and boys weaving kente in a large factory. I even had a chance to try my hand at weaving myself. As I immersed myself in the bustling atmosphere, I could not resist sharing pictures of Amy Ashwood Garvey in kente with the skilled artisans working around me.[70] Their eyes lit up with recognition, and soon animated discussions ensued about the symbolism and significance of the fabrics she wore. In that moment, I realised that Amy's connection to kente was not merely a personal choice but a profound statement of cultural identity and pride. These interactions became an unexpected facet of Amy's archive, illustrating how her embrace of traditional Ghanaian attire transcended the boundaries of time and space, forging a link between past and present, individual and community. In sharing her story with the artisans, I witnessed firsthand the enduring legacy of Amy's sartorial choices, woven into the fabric of kente.

The tour also included a visit to a small cocoa farm, where I paused frequently to take photographs of the regional flora, in an attempt to archive the land that both Amy and my ancestors were connected to. The richness of the earth beneath my feet felt like a bridge between past and present, linking me to the generations before me. Back at the shop, the preparations for my naming ceremony began. I was dressed in kente, covering my head and body, the vibrant colours and intricate patterns of the fabric wrapping around me, and leather slippers with decals painted in gold were placed on my feet. My head was brimming with anticipation as we made our way to the town's main square, where I was introduced to the chief of Adanwomase's traditional council, Nana Kwadwo Ntlamo Panin II, and other leaders, including the Queen Mother, Nana Korama Brimpomaa. The moment of naming was intimate and profound. They asked for my birthdate, and after some deliberation, they declared my new name: Ama Mansah, which means a woman born on a Saturday, who is courageous, sincere and hardworking. As the sash with the name 'Ama' was placed over my shoulders, I felt the weight of centuries of tradition and identity. The chiefs prayed over me, their words flowing like an ancient river, each syllable bringing me a step closer to understanding who I am and where I come from.

The ceremony concluded with a series of photographs. Standing there, newly named and deeply moved, I felt a connection to the African diaspora that I had never fully experienced before. More than a ceremony, it was a journey into the heart of my ancestry, offering me a profound and beautiful understanding of what Amy Ashwood Garvey might have felt during her own naming ceremony. It was a moment of reclamation, of honouring the past while stepping proudly into the future.

The next day, my journey to trace Amy's steps in Ghana took me to Juaben, a town rich with history and significance in the Ashanti region. Accompanied by Kobna and Nana Yaw, we set out early, packing our essentials and carefully mapping out our route. Our destination was the Palace of Juaben, a place where Amy Ashwood Garvey once sought to reconnect with her ancestry through a naming and lineage ceremony. Our short but bumpy drive from the hotel, guided by Google Maps, led us to the palace in the midst of a heavy downpour. As the rain subsided, we stepped out of the car into the damp air and made our way to the palace gates.

Nana Yaw, who had graciously taken on the role of translator, engaged the palace guard in conversation, explaining my purpose: to uncover more about a woman named Amy Ashwood Garvey, who visited the palace in the 1940s. I presented the guard with a photograph of Amy that I first saw printed in Lionel M Yard's biography in a section on Amy's homecoming, with a caption that reads 'Mrs Garvey, Paramount Chief, and Queen Mother'.[71] This sparked the guard's interest, and he soon directed us to meet with the palace's senior registrar, Kwaku Ankomah Asare.

As we were led further into the palace, I felt a sense of anticipation. This was more than just a research trip; it was a pilgrimage to understand Amy's journey, to walk where she had walked, and to uncover the layers of history that connected us both to this place.

Sitting across from the registrar, I articulated my intention to find archival records related to Amy Ashwood Garvey's stay and to gather information about the chief in her photograph. He guided me through the requisite paperwork for access. When I handed him the photograph of Amy posed with the chief Nana Yaw Sarpong II, the Queen Mother, Nana Juaben Serwaa II, and other dignitaries, a glint of recognition crossed his face. Ankomah Asare spoke of an elderly man, a former palace linguist, who had served for three decades. This linguist, an oral historian, carried the palace's history and the lore of its band and relationship with the Ashanti region in his memory, passed through generations. The linguist, it seemed, would be a vital source of information regarding Amy and the chief.

We awaited the former linguist's arrival. After half an hour, he greeted us warmly in Twi, and the registrar translated his words for me. We explained our research to him, which he acknowledged with a knowing nod as I shared Amy's photograph. As I presented him with a photograph of Amy seated alongside the chief of Juaben, his eyes lit up with recognition, and he uttered the words 'me papa,' identifying the man figured in the image as his own father. The linguist, whose name was Osekyerehene Sarpong III, recounted his father's stories of Amy's visit, describing her as a long-lost ancestor and recalling the grand celebrations commemorating her arrival. With vivid recollection, he spoke of Ashwood

Garvey's visit, describing how his father announced the return of a long-lost ancestor and hosted a grand feast in her honour. He painted a vibrant picture of the celebration and ceremony that welcomed Amy back. Through this simple yet powerful exchange, I gained a deeper appreciation for the significance of Amy's presence in Juaben and the profound impact she had on the lives of those she encountered.

This encounter underscored the importance of oral histories and the memories preserved within the community, highlighting how photography plays a pivotal role in unlocking these narratives. The photograph I presented acted as a bridge, connecting the past to the present, and enabling the retrieval of stories that might otherwise have remained untold. The image, passed through various hands and contexts, had its own 'social life' that allowed it to accumulate diasporic meanings and attachments to the photograph. This particular photograph of Amy Ashwood Garvey, once a static representation, became a dynamic tool for accessing historical knowledge, deepening my understanding of Amy's legacy.

It reminded me of Tony Martin's dedicated efforts when he journeyed to Ghana to find Ashwood Garvey's relatives and anyone who had connected with her. Martin's work seamlessly weaves these encounters into a wider historical fabric, demonstrating the use of oral history as a method for bridging gaps in Amy's biography. For me, this process embodied a form of Black feminist practice: engaging personally with the archive and comprehending her story by physically inhabiting the spaces she once did. Through this immersive experience and interaction with individuals having personal memories of Amy, I developed a profound appreciation for her life, work, and archival significance. This journey highlighted the crucial role of researchers being able to travel and engage with lived human repositories of knowledge, particularly when access to physical archives is limited or non-existent. The photograph was more than just an areifact; it was a conduit for reactivating memories, fostering connections, and continuing the biography of Amy Ashwood Garvey.

AUTOETHNOGRAPHY AS A BLACK FEMINIST ARCHIVAL PRACTICE

Travel to the continent further transformed how Amy Ashwood Garvey imagined herself in relation to people of African descent and created new opportunities for her to expand her feminist networks. She learned extensively about the conditions of women in regions and villages that she visited, taking detailed notes from her observations throughout the trip. One of Amy's primary aims for this journey was to write a book about the conditions of women of Africa and the diaspora. Inspired by the women she met on the tour, Ashwood Garvey began a multi-volume manuscript called *Mother Africa*, which examined the history of West Africa and the position of women in local cultures. In one of her surviving manuscripts, she wrote:

> In my travels of West Africa, I was interested mainly in the problems and affairs of my sex. As I went from place to place, I was forcibly struck by the condition of African women in the home. More often than not the hard cement or mud floor formed the bed and a single mat for the bedding. Some of the women were well clad, but there were regions where one or two loincloths sufficed and places where leaves and beads supplied their need. For the last however, custom and superstition were largely responsible, though poverty was a determining factor too. Poverty is one of Africa's main handicaps; poverty in the midst of plenty.[72]

In an outline for an essay called 'The Black Woman,' Ashwood Garvey expressed concern about the 'problems facing African women in their attempt to gain self-realization.' She identified 'rigid customs and taboos', 'limited education facilities' and 'government indifference' as significant barriers to their development. She also examined the African woman's role in the family, proposing that her 'function as a mother', 'role as wife' and 'sexual life … under a system of polygamy' hindered her 'rights of dignity and independence.' Amy attributed these issues to the lack of women leaders who could define and address these problems. However, she saw hope in 'recent advances' in education, women's 'greater involvement in business activity', a 'growing consciousness' of their rights, and an awareness of scientific advancements in promoting health. She argued that 'exposure to foreign influences' had changed the outlook of many women.[73]

Amy's efforts to improve conditions for women in Africa were often intertwined with colonial notions of modernity and progress. Despite her ties with radical movements and contemporaries, her solutions frequently revolved around private enterprise and small businesses, reflecting an overreliance on capitalist frameworks. Moreover, Amy's writing during this period suggests a lack of critical engagement with her own position as a middle-class Black woman of the African diaspora, who, despite financial troubles, led a life of relative privilege. Nevertheless, her work was always focused on empowering women, particularly the most marginalised. Amy's solution in this instance was to form women's organisations, and she aimed to raise funds in the US, the UK and the Caribbean to support this cause. She later reported that she helped to establish fifteen such groups during her three-year tour of West Africa.[74]

Photographs taken by Amy that are held at the John Hope Franklin Research Center beautifully capture the essence of the young women she engaged with during her time in West Africa.[75] In the first photograph, four young women stand in a row outside a building, dressed in simple yet elegant traditional West African garments made from Ankara – a vibrant cotton fabric with bold, intricate designs. Although Ankara originated in Indonesia, its deep association with African culture reflects the entanglements of colonial trade and the diasporic circulation of goods. The women exhibit a sense of calm and composure, standing tall and looking directly at the camera. The backdrop of the building with open windows frames them, suggesting a school or community centre setting.

The second photograph features a group of eight women also adorned in Ankara, including headwraps.[76] They stand and sit together, the lush natural surroundings hinting at a village or rural setting. This photograph emphasises the collective spirit and solidarity among the women, showcasing their cultural identity and the bonds of community. Both photographs reflect Amy's dedication to capturing the lives and experiences of the women she met, offering a visual narrative that celebrates their cultural heritage and contributions. These images are a testament to the impactful work Amy engaged in while traveling through West Africa, providing a window into the lives of the women who were part of her advocacy work.

Another black-and-white photograph captures a moment of camaraderie and purpose, featuring Amy Ashwood Garvey standing alongside a group of women on a wooden dock, with a boat in the background.[77] I believe this photograph was taken in Kumasi, Ghana. The backdrop and the boat suggest a setting near water, possibly framing the group before or after a journey on the river. This image became a pivotal reference point for my own trip to Lake Bosumtwi, an ancient impact crater lake situated in the Ashanti region, where I sought to trace Amy's footsteps and gain a deeper understanding of the places and experiences that shaped her work and advocacy. The photograph not only captures a historical moment but also serves as a visual testament to Amy's commitment to uplifting and empowering women. It underscores the importance of her contributions to the communities she engaged with and highlights her efforts to promote unity among women of African descent.

Another photograph from Amy's collection, dated 1949 and annotated 'Accra', captures a group of seven women seated in a row of chairs, likely at an outdoor event or gathering.[78] The women are dressed in a mix of light-coloured and patterned attire. Two of the women, seated prominently in the middle, wear white dresses and hats, their postures relaxed yet composed. One woman, also in white, is captured in a moment of contemplation, resting her chin on her hand, while the other looks forward with a thoughtful expression. The woman next to them, dressed in a darker dress and a headscarf, gazes straight ahead, seemingly engaged in the event unfolding before them. The rest of the women, including one in a checked dress and another in a patterned outfit, complete the scene, each embodying a unique presence and style.

The photograph's background suggests foliage and a fence or barrier, possibly at an organised outdoor function. The women's attire and the overall composition of the photograph reflect the social and cultural dynamics of the time. Amy's handwritten note on the back adds the personal touch of an archivist, connecting the viewer to the geographical context of the image. This photograph reflects the rich, multifaceted lives of the women Amy encountered during her travels, capturing the bonds of Pan-African sisterhood in a postwar African setting.

*

Amy Ashwood Garvey's use of photography alongside her research firmly establishes her role as a Black feminist auto/ethnographer. Through her lens, Amy not only documented her encounters but highlighted the beauty, strength and cultural heritage of the African people she met. Her images provide a powerful visual narrative that complements her written accounts, both revealing a layered, intricate understanding of the African societies she explored. Her manuscripts, many of which remain unpublished, also reflect her deep commitment to Black feminist autoethnography. Her writings focus on the conditions and experiences of African women, blending personal reflection with broader social and political analysis. This approach bears a close resemblance to Eslanda Robeson's methodology in *African Journey,* where personal experience intertwined with scholarly observation provided a more holistic view of African cultures.

Both Eslanda Robeson and Amy Ashwood Garvey's works were groundbreaking for their time. They offered rare and valuable insights into African societies from the perspective of women from the US and the Caribbean, emphasising the interconnectedness of the African diaspora. Their use of photography was a crucial element of their Black feminist autoethnographic practice, providing a means to document and validate the lived experiences of African people, particularly women. Robeson's *African Journey* and Garvey's photographic archive and manuscripts serve as important historical documents. They challenge colonial narratives and provide an empowering counter-narrative that celebrates African heritage and the contributions of African women. Through their work, both women underscored the power of personal and collective memory in shaping identity and resistance. By examining Amy

Ashwood Garvey's life and work, I theorise autoethnography as a Black feminist archival practice. Her efforts continue to inspire and inform my scholarship, highlighting the crucial role of both written and visual documentation in the creation and preservation of the visual archive of the African diaspora.

Standing on the land in Kumasi, tracing Amy's steps, felt like more than just research; it was a deeply personal pilgrimage that connected my academic inquiry with the spirit of my ancestors. The experience of being in the Ashanti region, where the legacy of the Coromantees began, was a profound reminder of the deep roots that link my personal history to the broader narratives of resistance and resilience in the African diaspora. This journey highlighted how Black feminist autoethnography not only shapes our understanding of others but also deepens our understanding of ourselves as women of the African diaspora. Through Amy's life and legacy, and my own journey, I continue to explore the powerful connections between past and present, and between the academic and the deeply personal, underscoring the enduring relevance of Black feminist archival practices in documenting and honouring our collective heritage.

NOTES

1. Brent Hayes Edwards, 'The Taste of the Archive', *Callaloo* 35, No 4, 2012, p945.
2. Tina Campt, *Image Matters: Archive, Photography, and the African Diaspora in Europe*, Duke University Press: Durham, NC, 2012, p6.
3. Ibid.
4. Lionel M Yard, *Biography of Amy Ashwood Garvey, 1897-1969: Co-Founder of the United Negro Improvement Association*, The Associated Publishers, Inc: New York, 1988, p88.
5. Campt, op cit, p170.
6. Ibid, p26.
7. Ibid, p7.
8. Campt, op cit.
9. Deborah Willis, *Reflections in Black – A History of Black Photographers, 1840 to the Present*, 1st edn, W W Norton & Company: New York, London, 2000, p42.
10. See David Boxer, 'The Duperly Family and Photography in Victorian

Jamaica', in Tim Barringer and Wayne Modest (eds), *Victorian Jamaica*, illustrated edn, Duke University Press: Durham, NC, 2018, pp322-356.
11. Leigh Raiford, 'Notes toward a Photographic Practice of Diaspora,' *English Language Notes* 44, No 2, 1 September 2006, pp209-216.
12. Amy Ashwood Garvey Photographs, David M Rubenstein Rare Book & Manuscript Library, Duke University.
13. Amy Ashwood Garvey Portrait Collection, Schomburg Center for Research in Black Culture, Photographs and Prints Division, New York Public Library.
14. 'Amy Ashwood Garvey', 1 October 1945, John Deakin/Stringer/Picture Post, Getty Images; 'Ethiopian Sympathizers at London Meeting', 2 September 1935, Bettman, Getty Images; 'Pan-African Congress', 1 October 1945, John Deakin/Stringer/Picture Post, Getty Images.
15. Leigh Raiford, 'Marcus Garvey in Stereograph', *Small Axe* 17, No 1, 2013, pp263-280; Emilie Boone, *A Nimble Arc: James Van Der Zee and Photography*, Duke University Press, 2023; Mark Sealy, *Photography: Race, Rights and Representation* Lawrence Wishart: London, 2022, pp77-80.
16. Raiford 2013, op cit.
17. Raiford 2006, op cit; Campt, op cit.
18. Leigh Raiford and Heike Raphael-Hernandez, (eds), *Migrating the Black Body: The African Diaspora and Visual Culture*, University of Washington Press, 2017.
19. Campt, op cit, pp163, 170, 192.
20. Amy Ashwood Garvey Portrait Collection, Schomburg Center for Research in Black Culture, Photographs and Prints Division, New York Public Library.
21. 'Ethiopian Sympathizers at London Meeting', 2 September 1935, Bettman, Getty Images.
22. Amy Ashwood Garvey Portrait Collection, Schomburg Center for Research in Black Culture, Photographs and Prints Division, New York Public Library.
23. 'Amy entertains guest at Afro-Women's Centre', Yard, op cit, p205.
24. 'Oration at the grave of Late H Macaulay', Amy Ashwood Garvey Photographs, David M Rubenstein Rare Book & Manuscript Library, Duke University.
25. 'Unidentified event attended by, left to right, Claudia Jones, Paul Robeson, Amy Ashwood Garvey, Eslanda (Essie) Robeson, and unidentified couple', Schomburg Center for Research in Black Culture, Photographs and Prints Division, The New York

Public Library, 1959, https://digitalcollections.nypl.org/items/a2dce264-6027-361b-e040-e00a18060eae.
26. 'Women's International Magazine Planned as One Avenue to Lead to World Unity', *New York Amsterdam News,* 1 April 1944, ProQuest Historical Newspapers Database, http://proquest.umi.com/pqdweb?did=1089245182&Fmt=10&clientId=4273&RQT=309&VName=HNP
27. Ibid.
28. Ibid.
29. Tony Martin, *Amy Ashwood Garvey: Pan-Africanist, Feminist and Mrs Marcus Garvey Number 1, or, A Tale of Two Armies,* Majority Press: Dover, Mass, 2008, p177.
30. Rhoda Reddock, 'The First Mrs Garvey: Pan-Africanism and Feminism in the Early 20th Century British Colonial Caribbean', *Feminist Africa,* 1 January 2014, p70.
31. Ibid.
32. *Barbados Observer,* 21 March 1953, cited in Reddock, op cit, p70.
33. Martin, op cit, p252.
34. Thelma Rogers to 'Dear Friends', 1 August 1989, Amy Ashwood Garvey Memorabilia Collection, University of the West Indies, St Augustine, Trinidad.
35. 'The Alma Jordan Library - About the Library,' accessed 31 July 2024, https://libraries.sta.uwi.edu/AJL/index.php/about-the-library/about-the-library.
36. Raiford 2006, op cit, p213.
37. Amy Ashwood Garvey Unpublished Manuscript, 'Liberia', quoted in Yard, op cit, p136.
38. Ibid, p137.
39. Ibid, p136.
40. Ibid, p138.
41. Ibid, p139.
42. Ibid.
43. Letterheads, Lionel M Yard Papers, quoted in Martin, op cit, p212.
44. Amy Ashwood Garvey, Unpublished Manuscript, *Britain's First Out-Post of Colonialism in West Africa,* Lionel Yard Collection, quoted in Martin, op cit, p212.
45. Ibid.
46. Amy Ashwood Garvey, 'My dear Comrade,' Freetown, Sierra Leone, 30 April 1946, Lionel M Yard Papers.
47. Receipts from Milner-Brown and Co, Kumasi, 8 March 1947, Lionel M Yard Papers, quoted in Martin, op cit, p222.

48. Amy Ashwood Garvey Photographs, David M Rubenstein Rare Book & Manuscript Library, Duke University.
49. Vashti Lewis, 'Marcus Garvey's Impossible Dream', *Negro History Bulletin* 40, No 6, 1977, pp770-3.
50. Paul Cuffee, Jehudi Ashmun, and American Colonization Society, 'Colonization - The African-American Mosaic Exhibition: Exhibitions (Library of Congress)', 23 July 2010, https://www.loc.gov/exhibits/african/afam002.html.
51. Anita K Dennis, *Slaves to Racism: An Unbroken Chain from America to Liberia*, Algora Publishing, 2008, p32.
52. Naomi Anderson Whittaker, 'On Racialized Citizenship: The History of Black Colonialism in Liberia', *CERS Working Paper*, Leeds University, April 2015.
53. Ashwood Garvey, 'Liberia', op cit, p139.
54. Yard, op cit, p141.
55. Amy Ashwood Garvey, 'The Liberian Woman', *The People's Voice*, 8 June 1946, Garvey Era Materials, Robert A Hill Collection, David M. Rubenstein Rare Book & Manuscript Library, Duke University.
56. Yard, op cit, p141.
57. Ibid, pp141-2.
58. Ashwood Garvey, 'My dear Comrade,' op cit.
59. Eslanda Goode Robeson, *African Journey*, V Gollancz Ltd: London, 1946.
60. Amy Ashwood Garvey, William V S Tubman Papers, microfilm, Liberian Collections, Indiana University Libraries: Bloomington, IN, 2008.
61. Amy Ashwood Garvey Memorabilia, Alma Jordan Library, University of the West Indies, St Augustine, Trinidad & Tobago.
62. Ashwood Garvey, 'The Liberian Woman', op cit.
63. *Ashanti Pioneer*, 4 December 1946, quoted in Martin, op cit, p216.
64. Yard, op cit, p165.
65. Martin, op cit, pp213-5.
66. Yard, op cit, p167.
67. Ibid.
68. Yard, op cit, 'Amy's Reception in Juaben', p164.
69. Martin, op cit, p220.
70. Ashwood Garvey, 'Britain's First Out-Post', op cit.
71. Yard, op cit, 'Mrs Garvey, Paramount Chief and Queen Mother', p172.
72. Amy Ashwood Garvey, Unpublished Manuscript, Lionel M Yard Papers.
73. Amy Ashwood Garvey, 'The Black Woman', quoted in Martin, op cit, pp377-8.

74. Hillal H Nadji, 'A Garvey Comes Home to Africa', *Chicago Defender*, 15 September 1945.
75. Amy Ashwood Garvey Photographs, David M Rubenstein Rare Book & Manuscript Library, Duke University.
76. Ibid.
77. Ibid.
78. Ibid, 'Accra'.

4

The Future of Black Feminist Archives

THREADS OF SOLIDARITY: HISTORY, ACTIVISM, SCHOLARSHIP

Just two weeks shy of my final semester at Sarah Lawrence College, I found myself strolling familiar streets in London. I arrived on a frigid, rainy Sunday morning in January, a weather pattern that persisted throughout the week. Despite the dreariness and my jet lag, I left my cousin Nadeen's flat bright and early on Monday morning, determined to uncover additional archives documenting Amy Ashwood Garvey's life in London.

My research had led me once again to the Local Studies Archive at the Kensington Central Library, where I sought references to the Afro People's Centre, the residential club and community centre Ashwood Garvey operated from her home in the local neighbourhood of Ladbroke Grove. Sitting in a quiet corner of the library's west wing, nestled among rows of leather-bound volumes, I carefully flipped through Electoral Registers for the Parliamentary Borough of Kensington, searching for Amy's name. In the records from 1955 to 1961, 'Amy A. Garvey' is listed as an occupant of 1 Basset Road, indicating her eligibility to vote and to serve as a juror. This small but significant discovery supported my argument that, despite her travels, this city was her home.

I also returned to the Black Cultural Archives (BCA), which houses a significant collection chronicling the rise of the Black Women's Movement in Britain. My intention was to situate Ashwood Garvey within a genealogy of early Black feminists who lived, worked and organised in postwar London. I sought out Kelly Foster, then operations manager at BCA, known for her expertise in Black women's history and its intersections with London's social history. Kelly provided a succinct yet comprehensive overview of Black feminism in the UK, highlighting how it was forged by women of African and Asian descent who championed 'Afro-Asian solidarity' and embraced a collective political identity as 'black' women. Her insights reminded me of Carole Boyce Davies's pivotal work *Black Women Writing and Identity: Migrations of the Subject*, which engages with the postcolonial and diasporic frameworks in writings by 'Black British feminism.'[1] This includes influential texts such as *Black British Feminism: A Reader, Charting the Journey: Writings by Black and Third World Women*, and *Many Voices, One Chant: Black Feminist Perspectives*.[2] Our conversation also brought to mind a seminal text by Southall Black Sisters that I had studied in my Revolutionary Women course at Sarah Lawrence – the class that first sparked my research on Amy.[3]

An hour later, I found myself holding a pamphlet of the speeches given at the First National Black Women's Conference, hosted by the Organisation of Women of African and Asian Descent (OWAAD) in Brixton, on 18 March 1979. I read through the introductory speech with intense curiosity:

> It is necessary to define exactly what we mean by black women. The term black can have a variety of definitions and does not necessarily refer only to skin colour. It can be used very liberally to refer to all those whose origins lie outside Northern Europe, or more narrowly to refer only to those who came originally from Black Africa. It can have both racial and cultural implications, and as a result of the development of the Black Power Movement in the 1960s, it can also have political implications where black people use it to reassert their identity and self-esteem, rejecting the negative labels and roles which we have been forced to accept in the past. For our purposes, we will use the term 'black' to refer to the two major ethnic groups of Black people in this country, namely: Those people who came originally from the Indian subcontinent, many via East Africa and the Caribbean. Those

people who have their origins in Africa, and who as a result of slavery, have their own immediate origin in a number of Caribbean countries.[4]

Something clicked in my mind, and I suddenly remembered that Amy had women of African and Asian descent living at the Afro Women's Centre, and that she often advocated multi-racial and transnational feminist networks. This marked a significant departure from the separatist racial politics of the UNIA and Garveyism. While Marcus Garvey had vehemently opposed interracial relationships and collaborations of any kind, Ashwood Garvey had evolved to embrace a broader, more inclusive vision of solidarity, one based on shared histories of colonialism, displacement, and struggle rather than just skin colour.

Amy's feminist politics were inherently intersectional, rooted in an understanding that the struggles of Black women could not be separated from those of other marginalised groups. Her approach anticipated the very ideas expressed in the OWAAD speech, where blackness was framed not only as a racial identity but as a political and cultural one. By fostering alliances with women of different ethnic backgrounds, Amy recognised the power of collective resistance against the interconnected oppressions of racism, sexism, and imperialism. This approach placed her at the forefront of a feminist politics that sought to unite women across lines of race, ethnicity, and nationality – a politics that OWAAD would later carry forward, building on Amy's legacy of transnational solidarity.

Realising the significance of this archive, I took photos of everything I could and paid the fee to get scanned copies of the rest. Later that evening as I sat on the couch beside my cousin Nadeen, clicking through the images while she asked me about my day I resolved that when the time came to pursue a PhD, my work on Amy and the insights sparked by my introduction to this speech would be my foundation. The connections between Amy Ashwood Garvey's life and the broader narratives of Black feminism and Pan-Africanism had begun to crystallize in my mind. As I explored the materials I had gathered, I realized that Amy's work was not just a vital part of history but also a critical lens through which to view contemporary struggles for racial and gender justice.

The seeds of my research were sown in those early moments of discovery, and I became determined to delve deeper into how her legacy could inform and inspire contemporary Black feminist thought. The journey I was about to embark on felt like a natural continuation of the work Amy herself had begun, weaving together threads of history, activism, and scholarship.

*

When I moved to London in August 2012 to enroll in the doctoral program at the Centre for Gender Studies at SOAS University of London, I would bump into Kelly Foster from time. Although she was no longer working at BCA, Kelly remained a prominent figure in spaces where discussions about Black history, memory and archives were taking place. As a public historian and London Blue Badge Guide with over fifteen years of experience in community and independent archives, Kelly has cultivated a distinctive Black feminist archival practice. Among the various strands of her practice, Kelly uses oral history and archival research to deliver walking tours that bring to life the city's hidden histories.[5] One of her most impactful tours, 'Black Women/Black Power in Brixton,' delves into the networks and organisations that fuelled the Black Women's Movement of the 1970s and 1980s.[6]

Nearly thirty-six years after the First National Black Women's Conference, in March 2015 I had the privilege of joining one of Kelly's walking tours. This event was part of a day of activities hosted by The Body Narratives at BCA and the Karibu Centre, formerly the Abeng Centre, where OWAAD had held their historic conference. Curated by British South Asian scholar and writer Hana Riaz, 'Black British Feminism: Past, Present and Futures' brought together archivists, artists, and activists for a day of discussion, exploring the history of OWAAD and the politics of Afro-Asian unity within the Black Women's Movement.

A key part of the programme, Kelly's tour offered a powerful exploration of the historical and contemporary contributions of women of African and Asian descent to social justice movements in Britain. As we walked through Brixton's vibrant streets, she highlighted significant landmarks and events, beginning with the arrival of the *SS Empire Windrush* and the pivotal role of women in Britain's postwar settlement. Standing before the commemorative plaque honouring the passengers aboard the ship, Kelly connected their arrival to the emergence of the Black Women's Movement, weaving together the narratives of figures like Olive Morris and the Brixton Black Women's Group.

When we stopped outside the Abeng Centre, Kelly delved into the history of OWAAD, emphasising the politics of Afro-Asian unity that shaped much of the activism of the time. Pausing at landmarks such as the former Brixton Black Women's Centre and Sabarr Bookshop, she vividly illustrated the rise of Black Power in 1960s Brixton and the enduring influence of these organising efforts on contemporary Britain. Her tour brought to life the layered histories embedded within Brixton's everyday spaces, showing how the legacies of these contributions to activism are woven into the very fabric of our cities, yet often remain underacknowledged. The experience deepened my understanding of the rich heritage of activism in Brixton, reinforcing the importance of Black feminist archival practices in preserving these narratives for future generations.

Kelly's practice exemplifies the collaborative and exploratory nature of contemporary Black feminist archiving. Beyond leading tours, Kelly has been deeply involved in several digital archiving initiatives. In an episode of the Black Digital Archiving Podcast, Kelly delves into the evolving landscape of Black archival work in the UK, offering critical insights into the roles of institutions, the enduring impact of British imperialism on archiving practices, and the changing dynamics of archival access and digital literacy. From the founding of BCA to the innovative use of digital platforms like Wikipedia, Kelly emphasises the necessity of empowering Black communities to actively participate in the archiving process.[7]

As a founding member of TRANSMISSION, a collective of archivists and historians of African descent – including the influential Ego Ahaiwe Sowinski – Kelly's work continues to inspire new approaches to Black feminist archival practices. Meeting Ego at a Black Feminists UK event, an organisation forged under the banner of Afro-Asian unity in the spirit of OWAAD, marked a significant moment in my activism and research. An archivist and mixed media artist, Ego has profoundly influenced my approach to archival work. Her impressive background includes a collaborative PhD at Chelsea College of Arts (UAL) and Tate Britain, alongside notable scholarly contributions like the chapter, 'Recasting Jamaican Sculptor Ronald Moody (1900-1984): An Archival Homecoming,' and her recent book *Ronald Moody: Sculpting Life*, which was released the same week as a major exhibition on Moody's work at The Hepworth Wakefield. Ego also holds an MA in Archives and Record Management from UCL and has co-edited *Mirror Reflecting Darkly: The Rita Keegan Archive*.[8]

Ego's archival practice, which encompasses research, writing, art-making, and curation, underscores the necessity of a reflective and inclusive approach to Black feminist archiving. Her influence on my practice has been invaluable, inspiring me to employ a Black feminist archival consciousness to expand traditional boundaries of archival work. When we met, Ego was the director of the Lambeth Women's Project (LWP), a feminist community space in London deeply inspired by the legacy of Amy Ashwood Garvey, who opened the first Black women's centre in London in 1954. Over 150 women passed through LWP each month, accessing a range of services such as counselling, mentoring, meditation, yoga, self-defense classes, art and music workshops. Run entirely by volunteers – Ego herself went unpaid for many years – LWP also served as a meeting space for numerous women's groups, particularly Black women's groups like the Remembering Olive Collective (Ego was a founding member), Muslim Sisters Jaamat, Eritrean Women's Action for Development, and Black Deaf Sisters. It was also the site where Black Feminists UK hosted its first public event.[9]

In July 2014, I spent eight intensive hours interviewing Ego for my doctoral research. Surrounded by archival materials and personal artefacts at her dining table, we discussed the history of LWP and the financial and structural issues that resulted in its forced closure in 2012, reflecting on how it carried forward the work of Brixton Black Women's Group, which was also forced to close for similar reasons in 1985. Our dialogue naturally flowed from the Black past, rooted in the politics of OWAAD, to our shared dreams for the future, as members of contemporary Black feminist groups, exploring how we see ourselves as Black feminist activists, archivists, and artists. We spoke about the transformative power of art in preserving and reimagining our histories. This exchange was more than just a discussion – it was a merging of our passions and aspirations. Recognising the importance of our conversation, we decided to record it, symbolising our commitment to a collaborative archival practice.

Our collaboration continued as we joined forces with Yula Burin to develop a workshop inspired by Emma Wolukau-Wanambwa's installation about Amy Ashwood Garvey at the Showroom Gallery. This workshop was part of the *Women on Aeroplanes* international artist research project, developed by Annett Busch, Marie-Hélène Gutberlet, and Magda Lipska. The London exhibition and accompanying public programme at the Showroom were curated by the Otolith Collective, a collaborative effort between Kodwo Eshun and Anjalika Sagar.[10]

Me, Ego and Yula were incredibly excited to work together on this project, and our plans were ambitious. We aimed to create a space where the archival practices of Black women could be explored, celebrated, and expanded. Drawing from my research on Amy, the papers of Stella Dadzie and Jan McKenley at BCA, Ego's archive from LWP, Yula's archive from Black Feminists UK, and our individual creative practices, we envisioned the workshop as a platform to showcase how collaborative art projects using archives could offer innovative ways of documenting and celebrating Black women's lives, particularly their friendships and solidarities across time and space.

Our workshop was also designed to explore digital storytelling as a method to document and celebrate Black women's lives. We planned to encourage the use of digital platforms like Twitter and Instagram throughout and after the workshop, using the hashtag #BlackHerstoryArchives to facilitate the sharing of stories and memories, creating a living archive that could evolve over time. These creative methods would not only preserve the past but also engage new generations in the ongoing project of documenting and honouring Black women's lives.[11]

However, our experience developing this workshop was not without its challenges. Despite the enthusiastic acknowledgment from Emma and The Otolith Collective that her installation was informed by my research, the lead curators of the program positioned Marika Sherwood as the primary expert on Amy Ashwood Garvey and her archive, and despite requests from me and Emma, our names were never added to the 'In Flight Magazine' that was intended to showcase all of the 'passengers' who worked on the project.[12] This subtle sidelining of our Black feminist expertise felt like a deliberate oversight, undermining the very premise of our workshop. Furthermore, when we advocated for the Black Herstory Archive workshop to be an exclusive space for women of colour our request was dismissed by the lead curators, who also asked that we not use Twitter or Instagram. This decision led to an atmosphere of surveillance during the workshop, with white women participants observing from the sidelines, which created an undercurrent of discomfort and tension.

Despite these setbacks, we were determined to make something meaningful out of the experience. We recognised the critical importance of creating spaces where Black women's contributions and struggles are not only acknowledged and celebrated but also meticulously documented. To ensure that the day's events were preserved, we turned on an audio recorder and captured every interaction – the passionate contributions from the women of colour who attended and the awkward silences and tensions whenever white women entered the room. This experience underscored the necessity of documenting and preserving Black women's herstories, fostering a Black feminist archival consciousness that ensures our legacies remain a crucial part of our collective future.

Reflecting on this experience, I saw clear parallels to Amy Ashwood Garvey's life and activism. The subtle undermining of Black women's contributions in academic and curatorial spaces was not just a personal frustration; it mirrored a pattern that Amy herself encountered throughout her life. Like many Black women in history, Ashwood Garvey was often sidelined in the very movements she helped to build, particularly within male-dominated Pan-African circles. Yet, her resilience and unwavering commitment to creating spaces where Black women could articulate their experiences and advocate for their rights resonate deeply with the challenges we faced during this project. Amy understood the importance of documenting and preserving the voices and experiences of Black women, ensuring that their contributions were not erased from history. Her relentless commitment to creating spaces for Black women, whether through her community work, writing, or organising, continues to inspire the way I theorise Black feminist archives and archival research.

I draw inspiration from Amy Ashwood Garvey's dedication to curating a personal archive, however fragmentary. She meticulously took and kept photographs that captured both intimate and public moments, including her interactions with prominent Pan-African leaders, community events, and everyday life in West Africa and the Caribbean. These photographs are not merely images but visual narratives that document the richness of her experiences and connections. Amy's letters from friends and colleagues offer a glimpse into her personal and professional relationships, filled with discussions on political strategies, cultural preservation, and personal reflections. These correspondences reveal the depth of her involvement in various movements and her commitment to the causes she championed: Pan-Africanism, women's liberation, and the rights of Black peoples in the diaspora.

Additionally, her collection of newspaper clippings depicted significant historical events, such as anti-colonial protests, cultural festivals, and notable achievements within the Black community. These clippings served as both a record of the times and a testament to her role in these pivotal moments. Her practice of preserving extra copies of her letterhead and magazine covers showcases her pride in her work and her awareness of its historical significance. Collectively, these artefacts reflect a life dedicated to activism, cultural preservation and the empowerment of Black communities. Amy's archival efforts have in turn inspired me to see the value in documenting and cherishing the multifaceted aspects of our lives and legacies. Furthermore, Ashwood Garvey's efforts towards cultural preservation resonate deeply with futurist ideals, consistently acknowledging the influence of ancestors and the continuum of past, present and future. Through this lens, Amy's archives are not static collections but living, breathing entities that speak to contemporary struggles.

Amy Ashwood Garvey's contributions did not merely end with her own life's work; they have set a powerful precedent for future generations. The engagement with her archives and the ways Black feminist researchers have built upon her foundation reflect the dynamic, evolving discourse around Black feminist archives today.

My collaboration with Ego Ahaiwe Sowinski and Yula Burin further deepened my understanding of Amy's tenacity and her foresight in recognising the power of documenting Black and African women's lives as a tool for resistance and empowerment. This experience reinforced my belief in the significance of Black feminist archival practices as a means of safeguarding our legacies and continuing the work that Amy began. It marked a turning point in my research, creative and curatorial practice. I began to perceive Amy Ashwood Garvey's legacy not solely through historical documents but through the living, evolving practices of contemporary Black feminist archivists, artists and curators. These creatives reinterpret the 'archive' in innovative ways, transforming it into a dynamic space for storytelling, resistance and community-building.

In this concluding chapter, I aim to bridge the archival life and activism of Amy Ashwood Garvey with the work of these contemporary artists. By investigating their creative practices, I will highlight the ongoing evolution of Black feminist archives. Furthermore, I will reflect on the development of my own creative practice, including the motivations behind my self-portraits and the objectives of my artist film centred on my research into Amy's life. Through this exploration, I seek to illuminate how the past informs the present and inspires future generations of Black feminist thought and activism.

BLACK DIASPORA FEMINISM AND THE ARCHIVE

An awareness of feminist thinking was central to Amy Ashwood Garvey's activism and her archive suggests that she even identified herself as a feminist. Her activism operated at the intersection of women's empowerment and global Black political struggles, making it fair to situate the Black diaspora as a central element of her feminist politics. I theorise Black diaspora feminism as a political practice and consciousness that consolidates Black feminist thinking and consciousness with the lived experience of diaspora as a social and cultural formation, and a site for transnational solidarity and resistance.[13] To prefix 'Black' to 'diaspora' encapsulates the internationally dispersed but interconnected Black identities and cultures that have emerged from the social and psychic effects of enslavement, colonialism, migration and settlement, and have evolved in dialogue with the dominant discourses of race, class, gender and nation. The term Black diaspora feminism therefore names how Ashwood Garvey's identity as a Black Jamaican woman, the descendent of enslaved Africans, born and raised in a British colony, who lived and travelled in many countries, shaped her approach to organising, writing and speaking on behalf of herself and women of colour around the world.

I first used the phrase 'Black diaspora feminism' in my PhD research on Black feminist organising in the UK, beginning with the historical context of OWAAD and the contemporary ethnographic context that led to the formation of its successor, Black Feminists UK.[14] But I can see how my earlier work on 'Pan-African Feminist Amy Ashwood Garvey' shaped how I viewed the work of OWAAD and Black Feminists UK. My thesis examined the creation and curation of a Black feminist narrative in the archive, while engaging ethnography as a Black feminist archival practice. Using narrative vignettes that move across time and space, I traced a genealogy of Black feminism in Britain. I analysed the way the archive documents the emergence of the Black women's movement and preserves this legacy for future generations. I also reflected on the ways in which present-day Black British feminists made use of the archive for activist and consciousness-raising purposes.

The archive of OWAAD, preserved across the papers of Stella Dadzie and Jan McKenley, as well as periodicals donated by The Runnymede Trust, offers a tangible connection to the genealogies of Black feminism in Britain. The printed documents, including organisational records, membership cards, flyers, posters and other ephemera, reflect the vibrant campaigns and initiatives of Black women's groups formed in the 1970s and 80s, such as OWAAD, the Brixton Black Women's Group (BBWG), and the East London Black Women's Organisation. This material, which includes newsletters like *FOWAAD!* and *Speak Out*, speeches from the first

National Black Women's Conference, and photographs of iconic figures like Olive Morris, provides a deep view of the historical and political landscape these women navigated. The oral history collection themed around *Heart of the Race: Black Women's Lives in Britain* further enriches this archive, grounding it in the lived experiences of Black women who shaped the feminist movement in the UK.[15]

Through my research trips to the BCA, I have come to see this archive not merely as a repository of historical records but as a 'living archive of diaspora,' to borrow from Stuart Hall's description.[16] This archive, situated in the diaspora space of London, reflects the ongoing, never-completed project of documenting the lives and struggles of Black women in Britain. It occupies a disjunctive space between the metropolis and the periphery, 'coloniser' and 'colonised,' embodying the historical entanglements between 'there' and 'here.' By engaging with this archive, I have been able to situate Amy Ashwood Garvey within a broader genealogy of Black diaspora feminism in Britain, linking her legacy to the work of OWAAD and other Black feminist groups, and the contributions of Black feminist researchers, artists, and curators, in the UK and the wider Black diaspora. This archive is not just a collection of past records; it is a living, breathing testament to the ongoing struggle for Black women's liberation and empowerment in the diaspora.

PRESENCING AND PRODUCTION: WOMEN'S LABOUR, EDUCATION AND THE ARTS

Amidst the burgeoning movements for independence across the Caribbean, Amy Ashwood Garvey returned to Jamaica in April 1939 as the tour manager for Sam Manning's vaudeville show *Harlem Nightbirds*. This return was not just a professional move but also a significant moment in her ongoing commitment to social and political activism. The island at that time was rife with political fervour, fuelled by widespread discontent with British colonial rule, economic hardships, and social inequalities. Local populations were organising strikes, protests and political campaigns, all aiming to carve out a path towards self-governance and improved living and working conditions. Amy's return came at a pivotal moment, with the population increasingly advocating for political and economic autonomy.

Amy's reputation preceded her; she was described in the *Jamaica Gleaner* as an 'Internationally Known lecturer and traveller' and an 'ardent worker in the cause of negro culture.'[17] Her involvement in organising a 'memorable mass meeting' in London's Trafalgar Square alongside fellow members of the International African Friends of Abyssinia further underscored her commitment to the cause.[18] This backdrop of political activism is crucial to understanding Amy's ventures in local politics and community development for Black Jamaican women from the working classes. Her efforts to advance women's rights and promote economic opportunities were integral to the broader Jamaican independence movement.

Amy's engagement with the arts, particularly theatre, was an essential aspect of her activism. She believed that the arts were a critical modality for critiquing and responding to issues of race, class, gender and colonialism, and for documenting Black histories and Black women's experiences. Before her return to Jamaica, Amy had branched out into the world of theatre in Harlem, staging musical shows such as *Brown Sugar*, *Hey! Hey!*, and *Black Magic*. These productions were not just entertainment but served as platforms to explore and challenge societal norms, with *Hey! Hey!* even critiquing the legacy of her former husband, Marcus Garvey. The plays tackled themes of race and class, offering commentary on the social dynamics of the time. Amy saw theatre as a powerful tool to engage the public in discussions about pressing social issues, making it a vital component of her broader activism.

In 1943 Amy threw herself into local politics, founding the JAG Smith Political Party, named after the renowned Jamaican politician. This independent political entity was committed to promoting Jamaican nationalism and advancing the island on the journey towards autonomy. In a political landscape dominated mostly by men, Ashwood Garvey emerged as a pioneering figure who championed the cause of women's rights and empowerment. At the core of her political campaign was the objective to uplift working-class Black Jamaican women. She recognised their potential and believed in their capability to contribute meaningfully to both local and international spheres. Amy envisioned a society where women stood shoulder to shoulder with men, playing active roles in the socioeconomic development of their communities

During the inaugural meeting of the JAG Smith Political Party, Amy underscored her commitment to advancing feminist causes, specifically focusing on women's labour and education through a 'domestic science training' programme.[19] Her establishment of The Garvey Memorial Institute of Domestic Science Training in 1944 was a testament to her dedication to offering career training for underprivileged girls.[20] Amy was deeply concerned about programmes in Jamaica that trained young girls to become domestic workers, calling it 'quasi-slavery under a thin camouflage of philanthropic solicitude.'[21] She worried that schoolgirls were being forced 'into the service of brown people or fair people of the middle class who envied the 'domestic entourage of the upper class' and 'desired a servant or two,' considering the system to be an 'outrageous outcrop of a rotten economy' that consistently ignored creating adequate employment opportunities for women.[22]

What set the Garvey Memorial Institute apart from other programs was Amy's keen awareness of the intersecting issues of class struggle and colourism. She was starting to believe that the primary issue in Jamaica was socioeconomic conditions, which was stratified by ethnicity due to colonialism. On the issue of class struggle, Ashwood Garvey said:

> I have for a great portion of my active life been a militant champion of the rights of my people; I have railed and perhaps ranted against established privilege, and the bar of color, [sic] but here [in Jamaica] I came face to face with the revealed fact that 'condition' and not 'color' [sic] was the vital problem.[23]

Confident that working-class Jamaican women could find better opportunities abroad, Amy Ashwood Garvey aimed to secure US work permits for 25,000 women. Her vision extended beyond mere employment; she was committed to ensuring fair working conditions, including a maximum nine-hour workday and a minimum wage of eight shillings per week.[24] To bring her plan to fruition, Amy sought the support of Eleanor Roosevelt, the First Lady of the US. Drawing on Roosevelt's first-hand observations of economic conditions in the Caribbean, Amy hoped to find an ally in the First Lady. In an article that appeared in the *Chicago Defender*, Ashwood Garvey explained that she had reached out because she knew Mrs Roosevelt would 'seriously consider the plight of unemployed women in the West Indies' and might sympathise because she recognised 'the problems facing women generally.'[25] Roosevelt's favourable response led to what became known as the 'Garvey-Roosevelt plan,' a collaborative effort to alleviate economic distress in Jamaica while addressing the wartime shortage of domestic workers in the US.

However, not everyone agreed with this approach. Jamaican-born journalist A M Wendell Malliet expressed concern that Jamaica's national policy should not include the exportation of its citizens in order to support the nation's economy, and he criticised the arrangement as just another form of imperialist exploitation.[26] Such immigration projects usually involved exporting workers from a developing country while maintaining a low standard of living in the country of origin. This served as a compelling force that drove people out of their home country, never to return. Malliet's concern was that often immigrant workers entered a workforce in which they were demeaned and humiliated, and in the worst case scenarios even killed after their work had come to an end.[27]

Ashwood Garvey's initiative aimed to empower women economically and promote their economic independence. In the short term, her plan was to train young girls, recruit prospective employers in the United States, and ensure they would provide reasonable working conditions. In the long term, she hoped that after the war these women would return to Jamaica equipped with savings and new skills to contribute to the nation's sociopolitical and economic development.

*

The vision that Amy Ashwood Garvey had for empowering working-class women through education and advocacy is mirrored in the mission of the Sistren Theatre Collective, whose important book, *Lionheart Gal: Life Stories of Jamaican Women* has informed my Black feminist politics and research. Established in Kingston in 1977, Sistren emerged to tackle of issues faced by women in Jamaica – particularly those linked to race and class through the legacies of transatlantic slavery and colonialism. Their introductory play, *Downpression Get a Blow*, which spotlighted the tough conditions within a women's garment factory and the fight for unionisation, set a definitive tone for Sistren's commitment to women's labour issues. [28]

Sistren – a Jamaican patois term of endearment derived from the word 'sisters' – was founded by women intimately connected to the working-class communities they aimed to elevate. Many founding members were Black Jamaican working-class single mothers who forged a space where their voices and experiences could find recognition and validation. Their work draws directly from their lived experiences, exploring themes such as unemployment, domestic violence, alcoholism and racism, often communicated through the Jamaican patois used by their audiences. Fusing Brechtian techniques, Caribbean folk culture and improvisation, their performances served as a potent vehicle for social change and community engagement. [29]

Reflecting on the work of the Sistren Theatre Collective reveals strong parallels with Amy Ashwood Garvey's efforts to empower working-class Black Jamaican women and her belief in solidarities grounded in shared histories and experiences that cut across lines of race and gender. Like Sistren, Amy was dedicated to creating environments where marginalised voices could express their experiences and struggles. Her activism revolved around empowering women through education, community organisation and cultural preservation, efforts that align closely with Sistren's mission.

At the Afro Women's Centre in London, Amy welcomed women from different backgrounds, including women of Asian descent, and later opened the centre to white working-class women and sex workers, recognising that their struggles with housing and labour were intertwined with those of Black women. This inclusive approach mirrored the founding principles of Sistren, which, despite being a collective primarily for working-class Black

Jamaican women, also included members from diverse backgrounds. Notably, Honor Ford-Smith, one of Sistren's founding members, was of mixed race and was considered a white Jamaican. Her involvement underscored the collective's commitment to solidarity that transcended racial and class divides.

Ashwood Garvey's belief in collective action, the politics of solidarity and multiracial, transnational feminist networks also had resonances in OWAAD. Many members of OWAAD were simultaneously involved in women's groups that collaborated with white women on shared issues such as employment, sexuality, gender and reproductive justice. Others engaged with Black empowerment groups that included men, focusing on tackling racism and broader systemic injustices. This approach mirrored Amy's own expansion of the Afro People's Centre to include men, recognising that the fight for social justice required the solidarity of all marginalised people. Sistren's evolution similarly reflects this inclusive vision, as the collective has also expanded to include men in its efforts, particularly in their work on violence prevention.[30]

Amy's legacy, much like the work of Sistren and OWAAD, continues to inspire today's movements striving to uplift and empower Black women's voices against systemic oppression. Their shared belief in the power of solidarity across race, class, and gender remains a guiding principle for contemporary activists committed to building a more just and equitable world, the Black feminist future that, to borrow from Tina Campt, has not yet happened but must.[31]

Sistren played a pivotal role in the Caribbean women's movement, steering various social initiatives and outreach programmes rooted in personal testimony and group analysis of women's issues. One of Sistren's most impactful projects, *Sweet Sugar Rage*, epitomizes collective and creative Black feminist archiving. The film immerses viewers in the lives of women labouring in the sugarcane plantations of Clarendon, Jamaica, uncovering the brutal realities they face. Under the scorching sun and often neglected by trade unions, these women wage a relentless battle to sustain their families. Their stories, gathered through interviews, form the backbone of a theatrical portrayal within the film. These narratives were captured and transformed into performances through 'drama-in-education workshops.'[32] These workshops functioned not only as tools for feminist consciousness-raising but also as platforms for addressing women's issues and channels for making radical ideas accessible through alternative modes of Black feminist archiving.

Following a screening of *Sweet Sugar Rage* at *Translation/Transmission: Women's Activism Across Space & Time,* a screening of feminist films held in Bristol in 2014, Gail Lewis, a foundational figure in OWAAD and the Brixton Black Women's Group, shared her memories of Sistren's visit to the UK. She provided a rich analysis of how their feminist efforts transcended borders, situating them within a Black feminist movement that championed anti-imperialism and internationalist politics. This dialogue became a lens for examining how the cultural memory of the Black Women's movement in the UK is preserved and its ongoing influence on contemporary feminist knowledge production. Gail posed a crucial question: 'What can be achieved through cultural production to unveil the structures of inequality?'[33]

These reflections further shaped my understanding of Amy's legacy and how her presence is felt in Black feminist spaces, even when she is not explicitly mentioned. This 'practice of presencing', to borrow from Gail Lewis,[34] not only honours Ashwood Garvey's contributions but also serves a vital connection between past struggles and envisioning Black feminist futures. Amy's groundbreaking work laid the groundwork for the cross-cultural and transnational dialogues that Sistren, OWAAD, and other Black feminist collectives attempted to nurture and archive, reminding us that the struggle for justice and Black liberation is both local and global, personal and political.

Recently, *Sweet Sugar Rage* was screened at the Institute for Contemporary Arts (ICA) in London as part of *The Work We Share,* a broader series showcasing newly digitised works from the feminist film and video distributor, Cinenova.[35] Curated by Black feminist multimedia artist Moira Salt and feminist curator Louise Shelley – whose work often foregrounds the creative practices of Black women in Britain – this program highlighted the legacy of feminist collaboration and the powerful impact of diverse groups of women coming together to explore their shared work.[36] This mission aligns closely with the objectives of OWAAD, the Sistren Theatre Collective and Amy Ashwood Garvey.

Louise Shelley, a steadfast supporter of my work since Emma's exhibition at the Showroom Gallery, extended an invitation for me to share my artist research for the first screenings of *The Work We Share* programme. This invitation held particular significance for me as Louise was the only non-Black curator working on the *Women on Aeroplanes* project who truly understood the importance of creating spaces exclusively for Black women, where our voices and experiences could be centred without compromise. For this programme, I was asked to respond to three deeply resonant films: *Back Inside Herself* (1984) by S Pearl Sharp, *Now Pretend* (1991) by L Frank Gilliam and *A Place of* Rage (1991) by Pratibha Parmar, a founding member of OWAAD.[37]

Watching these films together felt like encountering a Black feminist archive in motion, each film articulating a distinct but interconnected practice of Black feminist archiving. Sharp's *Back Inside Herself* captivated me with its visual poetry on identity, revealing the quiet interiority of Black womanhood. Gilliam's *Now Pretend* moved me with its experimental layering of personal memory and theory, a meditation on the emotional landscapes shaped by the lived experience of being a Black woman. Drawing inspiration from the powerful autobiographical stories of feminist icons like Angela Davis, June Jordan, Trinh T Minh-ha, and Alice Walker, Parmar's *A Place of Rage* echoed with the profound understanding that the personal is indeed political. This film delves into the pressing need for political action against racism and homophobia, emphasising their interconnectedness. Furthermore, it shines a light on the multiracial and transnational feminist solidarities that were vital to both OWAAD and Amy Ashwood Garvey's activism.

In response, I crafted my own visual poem on identity, weaving together family photographs and autoethnographic footage from my research trips in Accra and Kumasi, and from family trips to Lucea and Harvey River, a town and village in the parish of Hanover, Jamaica, where my family has lived for generations. I drew on personal memories, integrating them with excerpts from my writings, alongside the words of my cousin, Canadian-

Jamaican poet and painter Lorna Goodison, passages from Zora Neale Hurston's *Dust Tracks on the Road*, and reflections from Carole Boyce Davies's *Black Women, Writing, and Identity*.[38]

The work also included reflections drawn from OWAAD's archive, utilising documents I had acquired from the Black Cultural Archives (BCA) during my PhD research and those early days of my research on Amy. Each piece was carefully chosen to speak to the intersections of diaspora, identity and memory.

In this work, I also incorporated images from Amy Ashwood Garvey's archive, connecting her legacy to the ongoing conversation about Black women's identities across time and space. This project became a form of Black feminist archival practice – a way to embody the past, trace the threads that bind our past to our present, and envision a future where our stories are fully recognised and honoured. Through this process, I sought to create something that transcended mere documentation; it was an articulation of a Black diaspora feminism that is alive, dynamic, and deeply rooted in both the personal and collective experiences of Black women.

Following our earlier collaborations, Louise Shelley later invited me to participate in an exciting project with Black Blossoms as part of their collaboration with Art on the Underground, where she was now a curator. Founded by Bolanle Tajudeen, Black Blossoms is an innovative curatorial platform and online art school. It is dedicated to providing an in-depth exploration of contemporary art, with a particular focus on Black and underrepresented artists. The Black Blossoms School of Art and Culture, in partnership with Art on the Underground, launched a new series of short courses in 2022, free and open to all. These courses expanded on the ideas explored in the artworks and practices of artists like Joy Labinjo, Larry Achiampong, Rhea Storr, and Shanti Panchal.[39]

I was invited to develop a course in response to *Uncommon Observations: The Ground that Moves Us*, a multi-site artwork by London-based artist Rhea Storr. Launched in July 2022, this series of large-scale captioned photographs was exhibited across four London Underground stations: Stratford, Bethnal Green, Notting Hill Gate and Heathrow Terminal 4. Rhea's work engages deeply with the production and circulation of images of Black subjects, raising critical questions about how images can share knowledge, build community, and project joy and liberation.[40]

In response to Storr's work, I developed a course on the history of photography, focusing on its origins as a technology of control and racialisation during colonialism. Scheduled to begin in January 2023, the four-week course aimed to explore how photography, historically used as a tool of surveillance and documentation rooted in colonial notions of Blackness as otherness, has influenced cultural meanings of Blackness to the present day. We would examine how Black artists have used the camera to challenge photography's colonial legacies and to create their own conceptions of Blackness, diasporic identity, and culture. Despite the unfortunate cancellation of the course due to safety concerns, following critiques from writers in the *Daily Mail* and the *Telegraph*, this collaboration opened doors for future work with Bolanle.

Bolanle and I would have the opportunity to collaborate again in October 2023 during the *Harlem Renaissance in London* programme at Tate Britain. Curated by Ese Jade Onojeruo and Tram Nguyen in collaboration with the Tate Collective, this programme aimed to explore Black feminist practices within the historical context of anti-colonial cultural activism in the UK. This event, which included a panel discussion about the recent publication of *Speak Out!: The Brixton Black Women's Group* with founding members Suzanne Scafe and Sindamani Bridglal, also provided a platform for me to reflect on Amy Ashwood Garvey's legacy.

In our wide-ranging panel discussion, Bolanle, Ese and I shared our journeys as Black women creative practitioners from migrant and working-class backgrounds, navigating the arts, culture and heritage sectors in London. Bolanle spoke about her motivation for founding Black Blossoms, emphasising the urgent need for inclusive spaces where Black and marginalised communities can learn about and engage with art on their own terms. Reflecting on my previous work with The Politics of Pleasure, a curatorial project at the ICA co-curated with Rita Gayle and Ifeanyi Awachie, I delved into how Black feminist pleasure, joy and playfulness serve as acts of resistance against the pervasive racial and gendered oppressions we face.[41] Together, we discussed the intricate challenges and complexities of collaborating with other Black women, especially when our work is shaped by cultural institutions whose involvement may inadvertently steer the direction and outcome of our projects.

We also explored the significant struggles Amy Ashwood Garvey faced in maintaining the Afro Women's Centre, later the Afro People's Centre, in Ladbroke Grove. Much like many of us today, Amy relied on financial support from benefactors who, while essential to her work, often introduced complications that made her mission even more challenging. I drew parallels between Amy's experiences and those of later Black feminist organisations like the Brixton Black Women's Group, which, despite their determination to remain independent, struggled to sustain their operations without external funding.

Within this framework, I responded to a deeply evocative image of Amy Ashwood Garvey during a protest against the Italian invasion of Ethiopia in Trafalgar Square. This powerful image, reinstalled by curator David Bailey for Windrush Day 2023, sparked a rich discussion about Amy's enduring influence. Sharing this image in such a space felt profoundly resonant, as if we were collectively reawakening Amy's legacy for a new generation. I also presented a rare photograph of Amy standing with two friends on the steps of the Afro Women's Centre, which I uncovered at the Schomburg Center, and pointed out its location in Ladbroke Grove. Bolanle, who grew up in the area and had passed that street countless times since her teenage years, confessed that she had never noticed the Blue Plaque on 1 Bassett Road or realised the historical significance of the location.

These images and narratives underscored how Amy Ashwood Garvey's life and activism embodied the creation of physical spaces as a Black feminist tool – spaces that became vital epicentres for community building, resistance and cultural preservation that would later result in the foundation of projects like Black Blossoms. Our discussion highlighted the immense challenges of sustaining such spaces, the often-undervalued labour that goes into maintaining them, and how these efforts continue to inspire today's Black feminist cultural practices. By positioning Amy within this ongoing narrative, I sought to bridge the gap between past activism and contemporary Black feminist creative work in the UK, offering insights into how we might continue to create and sustain these essential spaces in the future.

WEAVING A LEGACY: THE KENTENESS OF KENTE

When Amy Ashwood Garvey returned to England in July 1949, she carried with her a wealth of memories and a deepened connection to her heritage as a woman of the African diaspora. Her travels through West Africa marked a pivotal chapter in her life, enriching her understanding of the region's diverse cultures and complex political landscapes. During this journey, Amy forged connections with Pan-African leaders, anti-colonial activists, scholars, writers, and artists, and played a crucial role in establishing several women's organisations.

Departing the Gold Coast in April 1947, Amy made Nigeria her home base for the next two years, where her dedication to women's issues continued to be a central focus, this time with a particular emphasis on education. In Port Harcourt, she was instrumental in establishing a Women's Political Action Committee and visited a Catholic school for girls, reflecting her commitment to the empowerment of young women through education. Amy also engaged with members of the Zikist movement, a radical nationalist group advocating for Nigerian independence, and visited the University College of Ibadan, further immersing herself in the intellectual and political currents of the time. Additionally, she visited the Ricketts Industrial Mission at Agbowa Ijebu, an educational institution founded in the late nineteenth century by Jamaican missionaries Reverend J E and Letitia Ricketts. These encounters not only deepened her African diasporic identity but also reinforced her commitment to Pan-Africanism, solidifying her role as a bridge between Africa and its global diaspora. For Amy, Africa represented a continent in transition, grappling with the complexities of colonisation, urbanisation, industrialisation and political change. Her nuanced perspective on these social and political challenges increasingly complicated the straightforward ideals of Blackness and African unity that had been central to UNIA and Garveyism. Yet, she remained unwavering in her belief that Africa was the future – a homeland for all Black people in the diaspora, where they could reconnect with their roots and build a free and united continent.[42]

Back in England in the autumn of 1949, Amy Ashwood Garvey maintained correspondence with her friends in West Africa, though she believed that due to financial constraints and her poor health she might never return to the continent she had grown so deeply connected to. Among her letters is a particularly poignant exchange, an unsigned and undated letter attributed to J B Danquah, a key figure in the Gold Coast's struggle for independence and a prominent intellectual in the fight against colonial rule. This letter, found in the Lionel M Yard collection, insists that Amy must return to Africa to visit him:

> The genuine African woman cannot die and you are her – the personification of one of the finest ideals that ever walked God's earth. If so, then you must change your plans – do not go to Africa at all, I mean any other part of Africa. Come to me. Here you will not die, you will not be allowed to die. You must live to be the grandest thing in Africa – for your life has a story to tell.[43]

The letter requests Amy's return to Ghana to participate in celebrations following an upcoming election: 'I am bound to win in the end because what I want is not me, but her – Ghana.'

Tony Martin references this letter as being from Danquah, but the letter in Yard's collection is unsigned and was saved alongside a photograph of Kwame Nkrumah, raising questions about its true authorship.[44] Adding to the speculation, a 1951 letter from Danquah to an individual in England has recently surfaced online, in which Danquah rejects a call from Kwame Nkrumah regarding Ghana's independence.[45] This revelation complicates the narrative, making me wonder whether the letter urging Amy to return for the independence celebrations was truly from Danquah or if it was written by another close friend, possibly Nkrumah, in an attempt to draw her back to this momentous occasion.

Nonetheless, the significance of the letter – whether from Danquah or another key figure – lies in the recognition of Ashwood Garvey's contributions to Pan-Africanism and the belief that her presence would not only be symbolic but also a testament to the unity and collective effort that had driven the Pan-African movement. As a founding member of the United Gold Coast Convention (UGCC), a pro-independence nationalist movement, J B Danquah's request, if authentic, would have carried considerable weight. He, along with Kwame Nkrumah, another towering figure in the push for independence, understood Amy's vital role in the broader Pan-African struggle. Nkrumah, who would become the first Prime Minister and later the first President of Ghana, had long been inspired by the ideals of Pan-Africanism. He attended the Fifth Pan-African Congress, signing his name to the list of signatures on the blue paper now held in the Len Johnson Collection at the Working Class Movement Library.[46] Nkrumah's commitment to creating a united Africa resonated deeply with Amy's aspirations for the continent, making her involvement in the independence celebrations profoundly meaningful to both him and, presumably, Danquah.

In the spring of 1957, Amy returned to the Gold Coast to witness and take part in Ghana's independence celebrations. The event was emotionally charged and historically significant, marking the realisation of dreams set forth at the fifth Pan-African Congress in Manchester, England, where the independence of African nations had been a central goal. When Kwame Nkrumah proudly announced the creation of a new African state, governed by its own people and standing proudly on the global stage, it was a defining moment in the history of the continent.

Being part of these celebrations was a moment of immense pride and emotion for Amy. Ghana's independence was more than just a political milestone; it was a declaration of self-governance that resonated across the African continent and beyond. For Ashwood Garvey, this achievement represented the first concrete step toward broader African liberation – a vision she had tirelessly championed throughout her life. Her participation in the independence celebrations underscored her deep commitment to the cause and reaffirmed the importance of her lifelong dedication to Pan-Africanism.

In 1961, Amy returned to Ghana with Sam Manning, who, despite being married, seemed to have rekindled their partnership.

They had been working on several projects in London, and now they endeavoured to establish a diamond business. During this period, Sam's health began to falter due to consumption. Despite his physical decline, Sam maintained his cheerful spirit, often playing his guitar to lift the atmosphere around him. A dedicated doctor would make the fifty-mile trip every two weeks to prescribe medicine for him, though the efforts proved futile. Amy tenderly cared for Sam until, on 11 December 1961, he passed away in her embrace, a moment that etched profound sorrow into Amy's heart. His death left not just a bereaved spouse and two children, but also an emotional void for Amy that seemed insurmountable. Sam was laid to rest in Accra, Ghana, beneath a simple wooden cross.[47]

A striking photograph from this era, now part of the John Hope Franklin Research Center collection, captures the solemnity of Sam Manning's funeral. This black-and-white image reveals Amy standing beside his freshly dug grave adorned with flowers. Positioned slightly to the left, framed by two stark bare trees, the photograph provides both a sense of structure and a visual metaphor for Amy's solitude. Dressed in traditional mourning attire and adorned with a floral wreath or garland, Ashwood Garvey's posture is reflective and contemplative. The outdoor burial site, characterised by its uneven ground, loose soil, and barren trees, naturally draws the viewer's gaze to Amy and the grave. This poignant photograph not only symbolises Amy's deep connection to Sam but also encapsulates a moment of profound personal grief and introspection.[48]

Decades later, as I made my own return to Accra after a research trip in Kumasi and Juaben, the legacy of Amy Ashwood Garvey was ever-present in my mind. My journey through these historically rich regions of Ghana had already steeped me in a deep sense of connection to the past, particularly the cultural and political heritage that figures like Amy helped to shape. The landscapes, the people, and the cultural traditions I encountered seemed to echo the very principles that Amy had stood for – principles of Pan-Africanism: cultural pride and preservation, and the deep connections that bind Africa and the diaspora.

Upon my arrival in Accra, I found myself drawn into the currents of Pan-African thought and activism that have long defined the city. In the weeks that followed, I revisited key historical sites: the W E B Du Bois Memorial Centre for Pan-African Culture, the Kwame Nkrumah Mausoleum and Memorial Park, and Black Star Square, where Ghana's Independence Day Parade has been celebrated every 6 March since Amy Ashwood Garvey witnessed the inaugural event in 1957. I even attempted to find Sam Manning's burial place but proved unsuccessful. Standing in these historic spaces, I could feel why Amy was so profoundly connected to Ghana. As someone of African descent with roots tracing back to the region, I too felt a deep resonance – each step through these landmarks revealed an archive of African ancestry, where every monument and memory echoed the ongoing struggle for liberation and unity. This sense of connection deepened as I prepared to attend the 3rd annual Kwame Nkrumah Pan-African Intellectual and Cultural Festival at the University of Ghana, Legon. The festival's theme, 'Pan Africanism, Feminism, and the Next Generation: Liberating the Cultural Economy,' struck a chord, reflecting the principles Amy championed throughout her life: self-reliance, freedom from imperialism, and the vital role of African cultural production in the pursuit of a united and liberated Africa.

Although the ongoing COVID-19 pandemic meant that most of the festival was online, the spirit of Pan-Africanism was palpable. The festival was a platform for intellectual debate, cultural showcases, and discussions on how to transform Africa's resources into sustainable livelihoods. The week-long event was a convergence of minds dedicated to the liberation and flourishing of Africa, celebrating the beauty, ingenuity and creativity of African cultural production.

During the festival, I attended a panel on Pan-African Feminism that was both enlightening and deeply moving. The panel featured Carole Boyce Davies and Rhoda Reddock, two leading scholars whose work has profoundly shaped the discourse on Black feminism and Pan-Africanism. Carole Boyce Davies, a scholar and activist renowned for her work on Claudia Jones, discussed the complexities of Jones's life and contributions to Black internationalism. She highlighted how Jones navigated the intersections of race, gender and class, and how her activism laid the groundwork for a global Black feminist consciousness. Boyce Davies emphasised that Jones's life was a testament to the power of diasporic connections and how these connections were instrumental in shaping a transnational feminist movement. Rhoda Reddock, an influential Caribbean feminist scholar based at the University of West Indies in Trinidad, turned her focus to Amy Ashwood Garvey, shedding light on aspects of Amy's life that are often overshadowed by her association with Marcus Garvey. Reddock's discussion delved into Amy's role as a pioneering feminist who operated at the intersections of Pan-Africanism and feminism. She explored how Amy's activism extended beyond her support for her husband's work, emphasising her independent contributions to the liberation of Black people, particularly Black women in Trinidad. Reddock illustrated how Amy's efforts in organising women and advocating for their rights were pivotal in laying the foundation for the development of Black feminist thought in the Caribbean and beyond.

The discussion between Carole Boyce Davies and Rhoda Reddock revealed the profound connections between two remarkable women – Claudia Jones and Amy Ashwood Garvey – highlighting how their legacies continue to shape contemporary feminist and Pan-Africanist thought. Their insights brought to life the shared struggles and triumphs of Black women who fought for liberation across different continents and historical moments. This session illuminated the intertwined legacies of these trailblazers, underscoring the continuity of their influence on modern Pan-African feminist discourse. The discussions further enriched my understanding of the historical and present-day dimensions of Pan-African and Black diaspora feminism, reinforcing the enduring relevance of Amy's work.

While I participated in most of the convening online, I made it a point to visit the campus in person on the final day to experience the exhibition firsthand. Stepping into the Kwame Nkrumah Building at the Institute of African Studies, University of Ghana, I was surrounded by lively conversations in various languages, blending seamlessly, as scholars and enthusiasts engaged with the displays. This Black feminist curatorial project was an exemplary archival effort, celebrating the radical contributions of Black and African women, forging connections between the continent and its diaspora.

The exhibition showcased photographs of notable Pan-African women whose work bridged Africa and its diaspora. Among the figures featured were Una Marson, the Jamaican feminist, poet, and playwright who boldly challenged colonialism and advocated for gender equality; Adelaide Casely Hayford, the Sierra Leonean educator and nationalist who passionately supported African women's education; Amina Mama, the Nigerian-British feminist and scholar known for her extensive writings on African women's rights and activism; Ama Ata Aidoo, the acclaimed Ghanaian author and playwright who powerfully explored African women's lives and struggles; Angela Davis, the African American political activist and scholar whose work on racial justice, feminism, and prison abolition has inspired global movements; and Sylvia Tamale, the Ugandan feminist legal scholar challenging patriarchal structures and advocating for sexual rights in Africa.

As I explored the exhibition, a familiar portrait of Amy Ashwood Garvey caught my eye. Before leaving Kumasi I had visited Bonwire, a renowned kente weaving village in Juaben, where I purchased a piece of kente that closely resembled the one Amy wore in the portrait. This visit was not merely about acquiring a piece of fabric; it was about connecting with a cultural legacy passed down through generations. Showing the photograph of Amy to the shop manager, he confirmed the significance of the patterns and the name *Emmaada*, which means 'first of its kind,' signifying something unique, unprecedented, or rarely seen before. The intricate designs woven into the *Emmaada* fabric held deep symbolic meanings, making it a fitting choice for a woman who established herself as a trailblazer in both the Pan-African and feminist movements.

Amy Ashwood Garvey's presence seemed to permeate both the virtual and physical spaces of the exhibition and the kente village. The experience of being in Bonwire, surrounded by the rhythmic sound of the looms and the vibrant colours of the cloth, was deeply moving. It felt as though I was retracing Amy's footsteps, reconnecting with the cultural heritage that had been so important to her. At the exhibition, a portrait of Amy strategically placed at the entrance of building named after Kwame Nkrumah served as a grounding force, reminding all who entered of her pivotal role in Pan-Africanism's feminist past and the promise of its future. It underscored the profound impact of Amy's contributions to the Pan-African movement, deeply rooting our contemporary conversations in the legacies of the Black and African feminists who paved the way.

The following week I arranged to meet with Adjoa Armah, a Ghanaian British artist living between London and Accra. Adjoa's work is deeply rooted in a Black feminist archival practice that draws on West African approaches to social and historical mediation. As the founder and curator of Saman Archive, she focuses on collecting photographic negatives across Ghana, exploring innovative ways to build institutions that are grounded in Akan concepts of time and cultural memory.[49] Her practice spans installation, sculpture, sound, public education and photography, all with an emphasis on Black Atlantic histories and the environmental impacts of racial capitalism. Guided by the Akan word 'saman,' meaning both photographic negative and ghost, her work challenges conventional archival methods and seeks to expand our understanding of history and memory.[50]

I first became familiar with Adjoa's work through Curatorial Tactics, a UK network of Black curators, practitioners, and artists interested in curation. This network was brought together online by Languid Hands, a London-based artistic and curatorial collaboration between Rabz Lansiquot, a filmmaker, curator, and DJ, and Imani Mason Jordan, a writer, live art practitioner and prison abolitionist. Their fellowship at Cubitt Gallery in London, titled *No Real Closure*, and the platform they create with Curatorial Tactics, became a vital space for artistic and curatorial exchange during the pandemic and lockdowns in 2020.[51]

Connecting with Adjoa felt essential as I sought to deepen my work on Amy Ashwood Garvey and her life in Ghana. Adjoa's approach to Black feminist archiving, with its emphasis on rethinking history through West African perspectives, offered a rich framework for understanding Amy's legacy. Our meeting would provide me with new insights into how to honour and preserve the complex layers of Amy's contributions to Pan-Africanism and Black feminism. We met at a cosy café in Accra, where she arrived with her camera, as if ready to document our conversation and life of the city around us.

Over glasses of water and iced sobolo – a spiced hibiscus drink beloved in Ghana, known as sorrel in Jamaica – I recounted tales from my latest research journey, focusing on deciphering the meaning behind the various kente cloths Amy donned in photographs. Adjoa then shared insights from her previous work on an artist research project that explored the cultural significance of kente. She emphasised how these fabrics are symbols of identity, resistance and continuity across the African diaspora. As we savoured our drinks, we discussed the deep meanings and cultural symbolism embedded within kente – what she called the 'kenteness of kente'. Adjoa explained that kente is not merely a fabric; it is a language, a medium for conveying values, history and identity. She told me how kente has been integral in numerous ceremonies and rites of passage, representing themes ranging from unity and strength to wisdom and spirituality.

Our conversation deepened my understanding of kente and its significance not only in Ghana but across the global African community. Adjoa's insights into the symbolism of the patterns and the cultural practices surrounding kente resonated with me, linking Amy's legacy to a broader narrative of African identity and heritage.

After our meeting, I felt inspired to honour Amy's legacy in a tangible way. I decided to recreate the iconic images of Amy dressed in kente using the fabric I had purchased in Bonwire. Back at my Airbnb in Cantonments, Accra – a place called Afro Gbede Mansions after Komla Agbeli Gbedemah, a Ghanaian politician and Minister for Finance in Nkrumah's government who was also a member of the UGCC – I began to prepare. The space itself, rich with the history of Ghanaian politics and Pan-African activism, provided a fitting backdrop for my undertaking.

Having recently returned from Kumasi, where I had attempted to visit the places Amy lived such as Manhiya Palace, and met with people who remembered her, like the linguist in Juaben, I felt a deeper sense of purpose and connection to the history I was engaging with. My research trip had culminated in my own naming ceremony, an experience that was more than just a ritual; it was an act of reclaiming my place within the ongoing narrative of African diasporic heritage. With this renewed focus, I wanted to use my body as an archive, a vessel to transmit some of the experiences Amy Ashwood Garvey carried and felt during her time in Ghana.

I draped myself in the kente, its patterns connecting me to Amy and the generations of women who had come before her, and those who would come after. Through a series of self-portraits, I sought to embody her spirit, channelling her strength, wisdom, and commitment to documenting and amplifying the experiences of women in Africa and the diaspora. Each click of the camera preserved the dialogue between past and present, between Amy's legacy and my contemporary interpretations of it. These images are more than just photographs – they are a visual homage to Amy Ashwood Garvey's influence on my identity as a Black diaspora feminist researcher and artist, intertwining it with the rich cultural heritage she so proudly represented.

In these moments, I realised that Amy's legacy continues to live on in the creativity, curation, and archival practices of Black diaspora feminism even when she is not overtly named. Her impact is woven into the fabric of our collective history, much like the kente cloth she often wore. Through my portraits, I hope to keep her memory alive, ensuring that her contributions to Pan-Africanism and Black feminism remain visible and celebrated for generations to come.

SANKOFA: BLACK FEMINIST GENEALOGIES OF FRIENDSHIP

Amy Ashwood Garvey's move to England was also influenced by the need to escape the bureaucratic entanglements and relentless scrutiny of US immigration authorities. Her archive within the Robert A Hill collection reveals the extent of the FBI's surveillance, which had shadowed her for years.[52] This scrutiny ranged from her public divorce from Marcus Garvey and her contentious battle with Amy Jacques Garvey to her involvement in Pan-African movements and her relationships with well-known communists, including Claudia Jones, who had been deported from the US for communist activities. Even as she attempted to re-establish her right to residency in the US, the FBI kept a close watch, further driving her to seek refuge and continue her work in England.[53]

Opportunities to publish her writing and an international women's magazine had drawn Amy back to Harlem from Jamaica in 1944, where she immersed herself in a fervent array of political and social activism. Ashwood Garvey played an instrumental role in Adam Clayton Powell Jr's landmark campaign to become New York's first African American Congressman. On the primary election day, 1 August 1944, a pro-Powell handbill swept through Harlem's streets, capturing the essence of the moment. Titled 'Adam Clayton Powell, Jr.: The Women of Harlem Say', this flyer showcased photographs and endorsements from several notable women, including Ashwood Garvey herself. Her assertion was powerful: 'Adam Clayton Powell, Jr., is equipped by experience and knowledge to fight the battle in Congress to preserve Americanism against home-grown fascists and bigots. No one has a greater stake in this fight than the Negro women.'[54]

Upon unearthing this handbill in Lionel M Yard's collection, my heart surged with excitement. This discovery was not only historically potent but also personally resonant since I lived on a street named after Clayton Powell, creating an intimate connection, a bridge between me and Amy.

In Harlem, Ashwood Garvey also forged alliances with C L R. James, George Padmore, and Paul Robeson – individuals deeply intertwined with Marxist movements and consequently monitored by the FBI. Her involvement with progressive organisations like the Council on African Affairs, co-founded by Robeson and Max Yergan, and her connections with Caribbean-American radicals in the West Indies National Council (WINC), intensified the FBI's scrutiny. Her every move and interaction with prominent figures was closely watched and recorded. The FBI's deep-seated paranoia about her supposed communist leanings cast a constant shadow over her activities, with the threat of deportation ever-present.[55]

Taking advantage of her status as a British colonial subject, Amy found herself grounded in a thriving Black community, amidst the postwar waves of Caribbean migrants reshaping British urban landscapes. Determined to continue her social and political pursuits, Amy immersed herself in this community. Her meticulous habit of archiving is evident in the extensive collection of newspaper clippings she amassed, particularly from 1948-9. These scrapbooks were filled with articles on race relations in Britain.[56]

Amy's activities in England soon garnered her a new public reputation, not just as an activist and lecturer, but also as a writer and scholar. Her published works from her time in West Africa resonated in England, which lead to speaking invitations including an address to the Ballets Nègres Society at King's Theatre in Hammersmith in November 1949, and an invitation from African students at Trinity College, Dublin in 1950. Her insights even caught the attention of an African PhD student at Edinburgh University, who sought her perspectives for his social anthropology dissertation.[57]

By February 1950, Amy was residing in Birmingham, Britain's second-largest city, in the neighbourhood of Handsworth, a community marked by the struggles of its new Black residents against exclusion and discrimination. Her activism now focused on the local Black schoolchildren, advocating directly with school authorities when she heard of incidents of racial exclusion. She prophetically warned, 'as more workers come here to compete in the labour market, Britain will have its own colour question – just like America.'[58]

In December 1952, Amy Ashwood Garvey earned a diploma in short story writing and literature, a significant step in her ongoing efforts to refine her craft and amplify her voice through writing.[59] With this degree, Amy hoped to bring to fruition several writing projects she had long envisioned. Among these was her ambitious *Mother Africa Series*, which she planned to publish in a style similar to Eslanda Robeson's *African Journey*, incorporating both autoethnographic writing and photographs.[60] This approach would allow Amy to blend personal narrative with broader cultural and historical insights, creating a rich tapestry that documented and celebrated the diversity of African heritage.

Although her book *Liberia, Land of Promise* remained unpublished, it garnered attention and praise from notable figures like English feminist E Sylvia Pankhurst, who previewed the manuscript and hailed it as a pivotal contribution to Liberian studies.[61] Another significant work Ashwood Garvey endeavoured to complete was *Black Millions*, a biography of Marcus Garvey, which she envisioned as a comprehensive portrayal of his life and legacy. Amy also attempted to publish *Africa and the New Era*, which was to be a history of West Africa with an emphasis on the Gold Coast. Through these works, Amy was engaging in a Black feminist archival practice that sought to document, preserve and share the stories of African and African diasporic experiences. Her commitment to this mission embodied the principles of care, community and cultural preservation that are central to Black feminist thought, even as she encountered significant challenges in getting these works published.

While Amy's influence grew, she faced considerable difficulties in sustaining the Afro People's Centre, in Ladbroke Grove. The Afro People's Centre, purchased with the assistance of Sir Hamilton Kerr, was envisioned as a hub of cultural activity dedicated to service and community. Initially established as the Afro Women's Centre, it reflected Amy's commitment to creating a safe and nurturing space for people of African descent, particularly women, who were navigating the challenges of life in postwar Britain. The centre quickly became a sanctuary for individuals from Africa and the Caribbean during their sojourns in England, offering much-needed lodgings for students fulfilling their college matriculation requirements.

However, Amy's inclusive vision gradually expanded beyond its original focus. Recognising that the struggles with housing, labour, and social integration were shared across different marginalised groups, she began welcoming people from various backgrounds. Despite this broadening of its mission, Amy chose to retain the name 'Afro People's Centre,' likely to emphasise the space's origins and primary dedication to the African diaspora. The name served as a reminder of the centre's foundational purpose, even as it grew to embrace a wider community in need.

The centre, though modest, was significant. It provided not just shelter but also a sense of belonging, hosting various group meetings and serving as a home for political organisation. However, Amy's renowned generosity, while deeply impactful, presented significant challenges to the centre's financial sustainability. The space became a refuge from the harsh realities of English life, attracting tenants who often lacked the means to afford accommodation elsewhere. This constant demand for lodging led to substantial wear and tear on the property, with continuous repairs that strained Amy's limited resources. The centre's tenants, though grateful, were often unable to pay rent consistently, resulting in difficult-to-collect arrears. The mailbox frequently overflowed with creditors' slips and threats of legal action, reflecting the centre's precarious financial situation.

Complicating matters further was Amy's association with Claudia Jones, a communist who had been deported from the US. The two women shared a close friendship, as evidenced by letters between them, and Amy supported Claudia during her time in England, helping her to set up the *West Indian Gazette and Afro Asian News*.[62] Ashwood Garvey even published some of her writings from her time in Africa and her tour of the Caribbean in the newspaper, copies of which I acquired during my research at the Lambeth Archives, which holds a small collection on the newspaper and Jones. And Claudia looked after Amy's affairs in London during her travels.[63] However, this relationship reportedly caused significant issues with Sir Hamilton Kerr. When Kerr learned that Ashwood Garvey was not merely a social acquaintance but also a project partner with Jones, he threatened to withdraw his financial support due to Jones's alleged communist ties. Amy's response was blunt and defiant: 'Go to hell. Claudia is my friend. You can stick your 500 pounds where the monkey put the ripe banana.'[64]

Despite Amy's resolve, the financial strain and numerous obstacles eventually took their toll. By the 1960s, the situation at 1 Bassett Road had deteriorated significantly. On 23 and 25 June 1964, Amy reached out in desperation to Claudia in London through two heartfelt letters outlining the critical financial burdens she faced. She revealed that her property at Bassett Road was dangerously close to being 'embargoed,' leaving her with only a few days to salvage her possessions. 'Right now, I have no cash,' she implored on 25 June. 'I am still in the hospital and can't assist myself.' Ever resourceful, Amy suggested to Claudia that she might send some her items to be sold to alleviate her expenses, but her words unveiled the depth of her distress. 'Claudia, I am so sad,' Amy lamented, 'though my spirit remains unbroken. I have lost everything I had and I am nearly alone ... Please help me so my belongings don't end up on the street, for that is their aim. For the love of God, do not desert me at this moment.' On 2 July, Amy wrote another letter to Claudia, stating 'I can't sleep at nights. I am distressed beyond expression.'[65] The property at Bassett Road was eventually abandoned until 1970, when it was taken over by real estate agents for refurnishing. Although the Afro People's Centre could not last in its original form due to these challenges, its impact and the ideals it represented continue to inspire contemporary efforts to document and preserve the history of Black women's activism.

*

In June 2024 Barby Asante, a dear friend and collaborator, mentioned that she had seen a clip of Amy in *Beyond the Bassline: 500 Years of Black British Music*, an exhibition at the British Library in London. 'You have to go see it,' Barby told me over the phone, 'it's only a few minutes long, but I think she's standing in front of the community centre you were telling me about.' Two weeks later, Barby and I met in front of Brixton Underground Station to catch the tube to King's Cross St Pancras.

Mykaell Riley and Aleema Grey, promised an in-depth exploration of Black Britain's musical legacy. I first encountered Aleema when she was a master's student at the Centre for Migration and Diaspora Studies at SOAS, where I was a Teaching Assistant for her course. Since then, Aleema has earned the prestigious Yesu Persaud Scholarship for her doctoral research, 'Bun Babylon: A community-engaged History of Rastafari in Britain', and she was the Lead Curator for this exhibition at the British Library and as the founder of House of Dread, an anti-disciplinary heritage studio.

Aleema's curatorial approach is deeply rooted in Black feminist archival practices. Drawing on the lived experiences of the Black diaspora, her work places strong emphasis on memory, belonging, and engaging with the rich – albeit contested – heritage of Black communities in Britain. This made her the ideal curator for *Beyond the Bassline*, where she skillfully intertwines both personal and collective histories into compelling narratives.

As Barby and I emerged from the station into a sunny London afternoon, our first stop was Ititakizen, a charming vegan and gluten-free-friendly Japanese restaurant I frequented during my SOAS days. Over a delicious meal, we caught up on our lives and research. I shared details of my recent research trip to the Schomburg Center, where I photographed Amy's former home in Harlem and the former locations of the UNIA offices and Liberty Hall, retracing the streets Amy once roamed.

An artist, educator and DJ whose work intricately engages with the concept of archives, Barby has significantly influenced my thinking about Black feminist archival practices. Her creative practice highlights the fluidity of cultural memory and the ongoing impact of colonial histories. Barby's work invites audiences to reconsider whose stories are told and preserved in history, fostering a deeper understanding of shared cultural heritage.

Barby's practice has profoundly shaped my approach to artistic research within the realm of Black feminist archival practice. Her methodology is deeply rooted in speculation, experimentation and collaboration. Barby's artistry is fundamentally collaborative, performative and dialogic, often involving groups as contributors, collaborators or co-researchers. Through storytelling, collective actions and ritual, she not only explores the archival but also makes speculative propositions and maps out the stories and contributions of people of colour. Barby critically examines established narratives, challenging dominant histories with a keen focus on migration, the creation of safe spaces in hostile environments, and the significant roles individuals play within societal, cultural and political discourses.

Her ongoing project, *As Always a Painful Declaration of Independence: For Ama. For Aba. For Charlotte and Adjoa*, explores the social, cultural and political agency of women of colour as they navigate the legacies of colonialism, independence and migration, as well as the complexities of the contemporary global sociopolitical climate. Through performative actions that engage with historical spaces, archives and collections, Barby creates a platform for women of colour to assert their voices and reclaim their histories. These works emphasise the importance of creating inclusive, participatory archives that authentically capture the diverse experiences and histories within our communities. Furthermore, Barby's work encourages us to not only reflect on our past but also to envision and shape our collective futures, contributing to the ongoing evolution and futurity of Black feminist archives. This project exemplifies her commitment to cultivating spaces where Black feminist thought and practice can thrive, sparking new ways of engaging with archives and imagining what they can become.

I had the great fortune to participate in two episodes of Barby's recent project, which profoundly shaped my understanding of Black feminist archival practices. In February 2019 I took part in *Declaration of Independence* at BALTIC, Gateshead, a live-streamed performative forum designed to mirror the conference halls used to negotiate and formulate treaties of independence, coalitions, trade deals and manifestos. As a 'contributor-performer,' alongside a group of womxn of colour, I shared a personal story about my Aunt Gloria, who had recently passed away, connecting it to the legacy of slavery and colonialism, and responding to Ama Ata Aidoo's 1992 poem 'As Always a Painful Declaration of Independence'. This powerful experience underscored the importance of incorporating personal narratives into Black feminist archives, particularly those drawn from the lived experiences of Black women of the African diaspora.

Another evocative component of Barby's project, titled *To Make Love is to Create Ourselves Over and Over Again: A Love Poem for Audre,* was featured in July 2021 as part of the exhibition *UNTITLED: Art on the Conditions of Our Time* at Kettle's Yard. This segment, also live-streamed, involved a group of participants who were invited to record themselves engaging in rituals of self-care and reading excerpts from Audre Lorde's *Poetry Is Not a Luxury*. Additionally, Barby brought together me, Foluke Taylor and other collaborators to develop a live performance that included singing, reading and music, all inspired by Lorde's poem. The focus on collective memory and the creative process as acts of love and resistance in this work further exemplifies Barby's commitment to cultivating spaces where Black feminist thought and practice can thrive

These experiences both highlight the crucial role of art-making practices that draw on the lived experiences of Black women in developing Black feminist archives that are inclusive, dynamic, and reflective of the voices within our communities. Barby's work demonstrates how integrating personal stories, cultural memory and creative expression can transform archival practices, ensuring that the rich, multifaceted experiences of Black women are preserved, celebrated, and woven into the broader tapestry of history and cultural heritage.[66]

After collaborating with Barby on these projects, I became quite close with her and other women of colour that participated, something that I have noticed is a crucial and powerful outcome of her work. My bond with Barby deepened further during our time together in Accra, where Barby and I lived and worked together at Afro Gbede Mansions for four weeks. Just a year before, I had taken a series of self-portraits at Afro Gbede, using my body as an archive to explore Amy Ashwood Garvey's time in Ghana, an effort to channel her spirit and legacy through my own experiences.

In the sunny living room that became our sanctuary of creativity and reflection, Barby wrote for her doctoral thesis, *That Bird is Singing Us an Invitation to Meet Our Future: Listening to the Call of Sankofa to Develop Memory Practice Methodologies for Performative Practice.* Her research centres on the Akan Adinkra principle of Sankofa, which means 'go back and fetch it' – a concept deeply embedded in cultural and memorial practices of the African diaspora. Barby presents Sankofa as a memory practice methodology through a Black feminist and decolonial lens, exploring how this symbol of a bird with its head turned backward while gently holding an egg on its back, can guide the development of performative artistic practices that involve collective learning, remembering and storytelling. By examining the bird's act of nurturing the egg as a symbol of care and resilience, Barby's work ultimately fosters communities of support, recover and transformation, inviting us to meet the culture and wisdom of our past.

While Barby immersed herself in this work, I turned my focus to my manuscript on Amy Ashwood Garvey. I embraced Barby's conceptualisation of Sankofa, using it as an interpretive frame through which to revisit the autoethnographic narratives from my previous research trips in Kumasi and Accra. I returned to the self-portraits I had taken, placing them in juxtaposition with Amy's own photographs to better understand the embodied choices I made in those moments. The work of autoethnography, and the act of using the camera, are fundamentally performative – they serve as mediums for archiving the present, which later become invaluable in retrieving past Black feminist narratives and laying the groundwork for new archives for future generations.

This shared journey in Ghana, deeply rooted in the philosophy of Sankofa, continues to influence how I think about archives and the importance of remembering and reclaiming our histories. As we walked through the *Beyond the Bassline* exhibition, the spirit of Sankofa was palpable in our movements and interactions. Our exploration of the exhibition was not just about viewing artefacts and images; it was an active engagement with our past, pulling forward the memories and legacies that have shaped us. As we uncovered historical archives from nightclubs frequented by Black Britons, like the Florence Mills Social Parlour – co-run by Amy Ashwood Garvey and Sam Manning – we found ourselves engaging with, challenging and reframing the usual narratives about Black British cultural history.

The pinnacle of our visit was undoubtedly the video clip of Amy Ashwood Garvey. Standing together before this footage, we were not just viewers but participants in an ongoing dialogue with the past, honouring Ashwood Garvey's legacy, reconnecting with her journey and integrating it into our understanding of Black diasporic communities in Britain today. In this way, the exhibition became more than just a space of learning; it was a space of remembering and reclaiming.

In the archival footage from 1956, Amy stands in front of the Afro People's Centre, graceful and confident. Her hair is tied up, and she wears a black velvet top or dress complemented by a pearl necklace and matching pearl earrings. The clip captures Ashwood Garvey addressing whether immigrants face dislike in the UK. She responds thoughtfully, 'Well, I think they find a lot of ignorance displayed towards them. I do not think it is really dislike. Basically, I do not believe the British people hate anyone … Well, they ask silly questions – where did you learn to speak English? Are you naturalised? Have you always worn clothing? Things of this type.'[67]

Filmed as part of a segment about immigration from the

Caribbean and the racism faced by these communities, the clip highlights Amy's clarity of thought and her dedication to advocating for the rights and dignity of immigrants. Her attire and demeanour reflect her status and the seriousness with which she approached these pressing social issues. The footage, accessible online through Getty Images, offered a vivid glimpse into her contributions to Black British history. It was a profoundly moving experience that connected Amy's legacy to the broader story of Black British cultural heritage.

Guided by the principle of Sankofa – going back to fetch what has been left behind – I revisited the Getty Images archive after watching the clip at *Beyond the Bassline*, in hopes of uncovering more about Amy's life and work. My search led me to extended clips that provide rare footage of Amy, which I subsequently purchased for use in my artist film, *Amy and Me in the Archive*. This film explores the multiple ways I have attempted to curate an archive about Amy Ashwood Garvey, drawing on Barby's theorisation of Sankofa to retrieve and preserve these fragments of her legacy.

In one clip, Amy explains that people have come to England because 'they are Black Britons. They come because they have been under the domination of colonialism for over four centuries; and they look to England as their mother country.'[68] This moment situates Amy Ashwood Garvey within the broader genealogies of postwar Black Britishness, where the concept of the 'mother country' carried profound implications; it speaks to the nuanced expectations and disappointments experienced by Black Britons who, despite their hopes for a warm welcome, often faced the harsh realities of racism and exclusion.[69]

Another clip captures a more intimate scene: the camera pans from a window above the sign reading 'Afro People's Centre,' revealing three Black women smiling down at the world below.[70] Though I don't know their names, their presence inspires reflection on the intimate bonds forged at the centre, the relationships between Black women in such spaces, and the genealogies of Black feminism in Britain – particularly those that shaped the formation of OWAAD, and my collaborations with Barby, Emma, Ego and Yula.

Reflecting further on the principle of Sankofa, the friendships among these Black women can be seen as acts of retrieving what has been left behind, preserving the stories, support systems, and wisdoms that sustain and empower us. Historically, these relationships have been a cornerstone of community building, resistance and survival, providing networks of support, mentorship and collaboration in the face of intersecting oppressions. Within the context of the archive, these friendships offer insights into the lived experiences and collective strategies of Black women, revealing how they supported each other and contributed to broader social movements and cultural productions.

To further explore the significance of networks of solidarity among Black women, and specifically Ashwood Garvey and Claudia Jones's friendship, I am incorporating the clip of Amy in front of the Afro People's Centre into my film project, *Amy and Me in the Archive*. This work delves into the connections between their lives and the spaces they inhabited, capturing the essence of their solidarity and the powerful role that friendship played in their activism. Through this film, I aim to continue the archival work of documenting and celebrating these relationships, which have been vital to the genealogies and futurity of Black diaspora feminism in Britain.

TWO WOMEN NAMED AMY: BEYOND GARVEY'S GHOST

Amy Ashwood Garvey was devastated when she learned of Marcus Garvey's death on 10 June 1940. Despite not having communicated for nearly twenty years, the news marked a deeply emotional moment for her, as it did for the global Pan-African movement. Marcus Garvey, a towering figure in the fight for Black empowerment, passed away in relative obscurity in London at the age of fifty-two. His death not only represented the loss of a significant leader but also brought into sharp relief the challenges he had faced in his final years – challenges that had worn him down physically, financially and emotionally.

Garvey's later years were marred by relentless persecution by the US government, a campaign that began long before his eventual deportation to Jamaica. FBI records from the Robert A Hill Collection, along with the pioneering scholarship of Hill and Tony Martin, reveal the extent to which Garvey was targeted because of his powerful influence as a Black political activist. The US government, alarmed by Garvey's ability to galvanise millions of people around the world through the UNIA, sought to undermine his efforts to promote Black self-reliance and Pan-African unity. His imprisonment in the United States on charges of mail fraud, widely believed to be politically motivated, was part of a broader strategy to discredit and neutralise him.[71]

This persecution of Garvey was not an isolated case but a precursor to the later treatment of prominent Black American activists such as Martin Luther King Jr, Malcolm X and members of the Black Panther Party. Just as Garvey was hounded by the state for his political activities, so too were these later figures, whose efforts to challenge systemic racism and advocate for Black empowerment were met with surveillance, harassment, and in some cases, assassination. The government's actions against Garvey set a troubling precedent for its subsequent efforts to suppress Black political activism in the US.

In the midst of these difficulties, Garvey's health declined rapidly, and by the time he arrived in London in the late 1930s he was a shadow of his former self. The strokes that ultimately claimed his life were the culmination of years of stress, persecution and hardship. Yet, despite the modest circumstances of his final days, Garvey's influence continued to resonate across the African diaspora, inspiring generations of activists who would carry forward the ideals of Pan-Africanism and Black self-determination.

After his death in London, Amy Ashwood quickly obtained a court injunction that prevented the British Home Secretary from releasing Garvey's body to Amy Jacques, who was widely recognised as his legal widow. This legal battle over the custody of Garvey's remains underscored the deep, unresolved tensions between the two women, each of whom sought to claim Garvey's legacy. The struggle over Garvey's body symbolised the broader conflict between Amy Ashwood and Amy Jacques, reflecting their competing visions for how Garvey should be remembered and which of them held the truest connection to his life and work. The tensions between them were expressed through letters and public statements that further entrenched the divide between them.

Despite their bitter rivalry, both Amy Ashwood and Amy Jacques remained fiercely devoted to preserving Garvey's memory, albeit in different ways. Amy Ashwood distanced herself from the UNIA but remained dedicated to Pan-Africanism, supporting various initiatives aimed at African self-rule and collaborating with figures like W E B Du Bois. Meanwhile, Amy Jacques took on the role of custodian of Garvey's legacy, meticulously documenting his speeches and writings and surrounding herself with Garvey memorabilia in her Kingston, Jamaica home.

This commitment to Garvey's legacy was vividly captured in a 1960 issue of *Ebony* magazine in an article where Lerone Bennett interviewed both women about their perspectives on Garvey's influence. The article, accompanied by images of the two Amys in their respective homes – Amy Jacques in Kingston, Amy Ashwood in London – revealed the complexity of their relationships with Garvey and with each other. Despite their differences, both women articulated a shared belief in Garvey's prophetic vision for the Black diaspora.[72]

Seated in the front room of her well-appointed home, surrounded by old books, busts and pictures of Garvey, Amy Jacques passionately defended her late husband's ideas. 'He was no damn fool,' she told Bennett, her voice firm as she recounted Garvey's warnings about the limitations of integration. 'Integration is not enough,' she insisted, pointing to the shelves and walls lined with Garvey memorabilia. 'All around you,' she said, gesturing with her hands, 'you can see the things he saw then coming true.' Jacques, who could quote Garvey's speeches for hours, was in the process of writing a book about him, determined to ensure that his message was not forgotten. 'When I talk, I talk for Garvey,' she proclaimed. 'I feel I can interpret how he would feel if he were alive.'[73]

Meanwhile, across the Atlantic in London, Amy Ashwood was interviewed draped in a kente cloth, recalling her early days with Garvey and her role in the founding of the UNIA. 'His spirit is still a dynamic force in the world,' she told Bennett. 'The seeds he scattered in the 1920s are beginning to bear fruit.'[74] Despite the bitterness that had once marked their divorce, Ashwood expressed a deep respect for Garvey's contributions to Black consciousness. Reading from a manuscript she had written about him, she described Garvey as 'an enigma ... a prophet, student of mass psychology, and something of a healer.' She paused, removed her glasses, and smiled as she reflected on his legacy. 'More than any other man of his time, Garvey made a contribution towards awakening the masses of the world toward racial insecurity.'[75]

However, the publication of this article did not bring the two women closer together. Instead, it reignited old grievances. Amy Jacques was displeased that the article had featured Amy Ashwood alongside her. 'You did not tell me that you intended to write a symposium,' she wrote to Bennett, expressing her frustration that Amy Ashwood was given space to assert her connection to Marcus. Her son, Julius, shared her sentiments, arguing that it was 'not fair to give Amy Ashwood's statement [a] place' in the narrative, considering her 'campaign to down Garvey since they were divorced.'[76]

The rivalry between the two Amys, which had once been rooted in personal and marital conflicts, had evolved into a battle over the ownership of Garvey's legacy. Yet, despite their differences, both women remained committed to preserving and promoting Garvey's ideas, each in her own way. This shared commitment, even in the face of personal animosity, speaks to the profound impact Garvey had on their lives and on the broader Pan-African movement.

As I reflect on the lives of Amy Ashwood Garvey and Amy Jacques Garvey, it becomes clear that their stories are inextricably linked, not only by their shared connection to Marcus Garvey but also by their contributions to Black nationalist thought and activism. Their rivalry, though deeply personal, also reflects broader questions about the role of women in movements historically dominated by men. By examining their lives together, we gain a more nuanced understanding of the complexities of the Garvey movement and its lasting impact on the world.

In my artist film *Amy and Me in the Archive*, I weave together the stories of both Amy Ashwood and Amy Jacques Garvey, using the principle of Sankofa as a conceptual framework. By looking back to recover and retrieve the histories and memories that shaped the lives and politics of both Amys, I aim to highlight the ways in which their contributions to Pan-Africanism and Black feminist thought continue to resonate today.

One of the most intriguing aspects of their intertwined legacies is the frequent misattribution of their identities, both in their lifetimes and in historical records. For instance, the *Daily Gleaner* incorrectly attributed Amy Jacques as the founder of the JAG Smith Political Party, a mistake that Amy Ashwood forcefully corrected, demanding a retraction.[77] Similarly, the *Baltimore Afro-American* newspaper captioned a photograph by James Van Der Zee of Marcus and Amy Jacques Garvey with Amy Ashwood Garvey's name instead.[78] This error led Marcus Garvey to advise Amy Jacques via telegram to employ a white lawyer to sue the publication. These misattributions are more than mere clerical errors; they reflect the broader challenges both women faced in being recognised for their distinct contributions and identities.

Through the lens of Sankofa, my film seeks to reclaim and recontextualise these stories, providing a space where the nuances of both Amys' lives can be fully explored and appreciated. In doing so, I hope to contribute to the ongoing project of building Black feminist archives that are not only inclusive but also dynamic and forward-looking. This approach allows us to not only honour the past but also to imagine new futures where the voices and experiences of Black women are central to the narratives we construct.

The Schomburg Center for Research in Black Culture holds a treasure trove of materials that further illuminates the complex relationships between these two women and Garvey's legacy. On one of my visits to the Moving Image and Recorded Sound Division (MIRS) at the Schomburg, I discovered a VHS cassette containing interviews with both Amy Ashwood and Amy Jacques, each discussing Marcus Garvey, his work, and his influence. Although the dates and locations of these interviews are not identified, and the interviewers are not named, the recording offers a rare opportunity to hear both women speak about Garvey and their own roles in his life and legacy.

As I sat in the medium-sized room at MIRS, filled with anticipation, I navigated through the digital archive, finding an audio recording titled 'Amy Ashwood Garvey – Up You Mighty

Race: Recollections of Marcus Garvey.' Released in 1968, this recording features Ashwood's own voice recounting her memories of Garvey, interspersed with performances by Thelma Massy and Lord Obstinate, accompanied by The Tony Thomas Orchestra. The crackling of the recording filled the room as Ashwood's voice emerged, strong and resolute yet warm, painting vivid images of struggle and triumph.

Another significant discovery in the archive was an episode of *Like It Is,* a groundbreaking television programme focused on issues relevant to the Black American community.[79] Hosted by Gil Noble, this particular episode featured an interview with Amy Ashwood Garvey, where she delved into her reflections on Marcus Garvey's life and legacy. The conversation took place against the tumultuous backdrop of the Civil Rights and Black Power movements. Ashwood discussed pivotal political issues, including the importance of embracing the term 'Black' over 'negro' and shared her admiration for Malcolm X, having read his biography and met his family.[80] She expressed belief in the revolution Malcolm was advancing, aligning it with her own lifelong advocacy for Black empowerment.

Gil Noble also prompted Amy to reveal insights into Garvey's private life and emotional state, which added a deeply personal layer to the discussion. Amy offered perspectives on historical events that influenced Garvey's politics, including his connection with Booker T Washington. Reflecting on her views of America, she remarked, 'In my prayers, I pray for everyone. I pray for America,' and optimistically added, 'I think a wonderful future lies ahead for this country,' referring to the US.[81]

When Noble inquired about her thoughts on the premature deaths of Marcus Garvey, Malcolm X, and Martin Luther King Jr, Amy offered a profound perspective rooted in her African heritage: 'Well, being an African, to me there is no death. But just a transitionary period from one to another world.'[82] This insight highlighted her belief in the continuity of existence, a belief that not only comforted her but also connected the legacies of these revolutionary leaders across time and space.

This interview, along with the others I found, reveals the deep sense of purpose and conviction that both Amys carried with them, even as they navigated their complex relationship with each other and with Garvey's legacy.

In the end, the legacy of Marcus Garvey is not just about his own achievements but also about the women who supported, challenged, and ultimately outlived him. The lives of Amy Ashwood Garvey and Amy Jacques Garvey offer a poignant reminder of how Black women have navigated and shaped the political and cultural landscapes of their time. By paying attention to their voices and the ways in which they have been represented in both popular and scholarly discourse, we can gain a deeper understanding of the multifaceted nature of Black feminist thought and activism.

Reflecting on these materials through Barby Asante's theorization of Sankofa, I began to see these interviews not just as isolated pieces of history but as tools for recovering and understanding the ideological parallels between these women as early Black Pan-African feminists. In this context, these interviews become more than just recordings – they are acts of reclamation. This approach allows me to see beyond the haunting presence of Marcus Garvey, as noted in the title of Lerone Bennett Jr's article, and instead focus on how both Amys contributed to the legacy of Black feminist thought and Pan-Africanism.

Amy Ashwood and Amy Jacques, despite their personal conflicts, were united in their commitment to documenting and uplifting Black women's lives. Amy Jacques Garvey's work on the Women's Page of *The Negro World* provided a crucial platform for Black women's voices, highlighting their struggles, achievements, and contributions to the global Black community. Her writings advocated for the education and empowerment of Black women, emphasising their role in the fight for racial equality.

Similarly, Amy Ashwood Garvey's travels in West Africa led her to conduct in-depth research, photography, and writing about the women she encountered. She documented their lives, work, and cultural practices, offering a rare and valuable perspective on the experiences of African women during the colonial period. Through her lens, Ashwood Garvey sought to bridge the gap between the African diaspora and the continent, reinforcing the Pan-African ideals that she and Marcus Garvey championed.

By engaging with these interviews and archival materials in my film, I aim to use Sankofa as a methodology for recovering and honouring the ideological parallels between these two women. Their shared dedication to documenting Black women's lives and their efforts to uplift and empower their communities resonate deeply within the broader narrative of Black feminist and Pan-African thought. In bringing their voices together through these archival recordings, I hope to contribute to a richer understanding of their legacies and to inspire future generations to continue the work of documenting and celebrating Black women's contributions to global struggles for care, community and Black feminist solidarity.

AMY AND ME IN THE ARCHIVE: BLACK FEMINIST ARCHIVAL BRICOLAGE

Back in Jamaica in November 1968, Amy Ashwood Garvey found herself in a country grappling with economic challenges and the weight of its colonial past. After consenting to the return of Marcus Garvey's body in 1964, Amy initially received VIP treatment from the Jamaican government. However, her later years were marked by financial difficulties and strained relations with Garveyites who remained bitter over her conflicts with Amy Jacques regarding Marcus's legacy. Despite her hopes for recognition, Ashwood Garvey faced the harsh reality of living in a financially struggling nation that was ambivalent about her role in Garvey's legacy. In desperation, she reached out to her friends seeking financial support.

In one of her letters from December 1968, she wrote to Yard, 'dear, time is not on my side, I am beginning to feel old. I can no longer stand up to the fray!'[83] This poignant admission reveals not only the physical toll that age was taking on Amy but also the deep emotional and psychological strain she was experiencing. Returning to Jamaica as an older woman, after a lifetime of activism and struggle, Ashwood Garvey faced the harsh realities of a society that had changed significantly since her earlier years. The once vibrant and determined leader now found herself grappling with feelings of isolation, vulnerability, and perhaps even a sense of abandonment. She urgently cabled President Tubman for help, but his replies came in cipher and were not immediately decoded. On 22 April, she penned, 'this may be my last letter to you, for I am sinking very fast and also my last wish.' Her final wish was for his help in paying off her debts and for her book, *Liberia Land of Promise,* to be published by her adopted daughter, Eva Morris, in Liberia. She signed off, 'there is only one thing I can give you, and that is my love, which you have always had. If I am unable to make this trip to America it's goodbye. Of course, you know that my funeral expenses will be up to you, and you will be informed of those concerned.'[84]

Amy's experience highlights the broader difficulties faced by older, single women, particularly Black women who have dedicated their lives to public service, as they navigate the complex intersections of gender, age, and societal expectations in their later years. Amid these struggles, Amy was deeply affected by the loss of her close friend and confidante, Claudia Jones, who passed away alone at her apartment in London on Christmas Eve in 1964, her body found two days later. This profound loss added to her sense of isolation and under-appreciation in her homeland. Even in the face of such grief, Amy remained resolute, striving to establish an organisation in Marcus Garvey's honour and continuing to push for the publication of her book.

*

On 27 April 1969, Amy Ashwood Garvey's health took a turn for the worse, leading to her admission to the University of the West Indies Hospital. Despite her deteriorating condition, she discharged herself on 30 April, against medical advice, and later explained to Yard, 'I can hardly dictate this letter, for I've been filled with so much sorrow since you heard from me last. I was taken ill again last week, very ill, and was admitted to the U.C. Hospital, and after I found out they could do very little for me, I had to get out.'[85] President Tubman, her steadfast friend, wired funds in response to her desperate pleas, but due to delays in decoding his telegrams, the money never reached her in time.

By the time of her passing on 3 May 1969 she was living in financial distress, far from the recognition she had so deeply desired. Amy had expressed a wish to be buried in Liberia, but her friends in Jamaica were unable to fulfill this request due to financial constraints. Instead, she was interred on 11 May at Kingston's Calvary Cemetery following a funeral service at Holy Cross Church, Half-Way Tree. Among the twelve attendees were veteran Garveyites like St William Grant, Frank Gordon, L Pinnock, and Z Munroe Scarlett, as well as her secretary, Ione Thomas, and Marcus Garvey's niece, Ruth Prescott. The auxiliary Roman Catholic bishop of Kingston delivered the eulogy, noting that both Marcus and Amy had converted to Catholicism shortly before their deaths.[86]

In November 1969, Lionel Yard organised a symposium in Harlem to honour Amy's life under the auspices of the Association for the Advancement of Caribbean Education. Yard spoke on 'The Personality of Amy Ashwood Garvey', while George Weston discussed 'Amy Ashwood Garvey as a Crusader.' Despite extensive publicity, the event drew only twenty-six attendees.[87]

The unveiling of her headstone at Calvary Cemetery in 1976, arranged by the Amy Ashwood Garvey Friends Association, was a poignant acknowledgment of her contributions. Funds for the headstone, donated by the New York Branch of AAG Friends, underscored the diasporic connections that continued to support her legacy. The ceremony, with its speeches and prayers, marked a bittersweet moment in recognising the complexities of Amy's life – a life deeply intertwined with her efforts to honour Black women's histories and contributions.[88]

*

In late December 2021, I received a series of WhatsApp messages from Adisa Vera Beatty inviting me to participate in a UNIA program 'in honor of Amy Ashwood Garvey's 125th birthday'. I was sitting on the couch at my mother's home in Winter Park, Florida, surrounded by photographs of family members, which had made me think about Amy and her life in Jamaica earlier that day. I was intrigued by the synchronicity and pleased to receive Adisa's invitation.

A poet and historian whose research examines the lives of Afro-Jamaican Garveyites in Liberia, Adisa was at that time a Fulbright scholar in the history department at the University of the West Indies, Jamaica. Adisa and I had never met in person but became acquainted when she emailed about the archives referenced in my master's dissertation, and we subsequently met over WhatsApp call to discuss her research on Amy's time in Liberia for her doctoral research. This led to a conversation about the condition of Amy's archive and the papers and photographs that were held by Yard's family.

Adisa had accessed Yard's collection in 2019 and 2020 at his daughter Patricia Malliard's home in Brooklyn, New York. Comparing quotes included in my master's dissertation, typed from digital copies of Amy's papers that I scanned at Patricia's home in 2009 and 2010, with what she saw during her research, Adisa concluded that several photographs, letters and pages of Amy's writing were missing. We spoke at length during our call about how to ensure the preservation of what remained of Amy's archive, along with Yard's personal papers, but we never continued the conversation. When Adisa invited me to take part in this UNIA event, it therefore felt important to present a biography of Amy's life through a curated selection of images and documents from her archive.

Following my WhatsApp exchange with Adisa, I spoke to Anya Thompson, director of Liberty Hall, the national museum in Jamaica dedicated to Marcus Garvey and the UNIA. Anya shared her vision for the program, 'Remembering Amy Ashwood Garvey', and its intended audience: 'UNIA Chapter Members, Garveyites… students of Garveyism'. I spent several hours over a few short days writing my presentation. With her insights, I spent several hours piecing together details of Amy's early life. My sources ranged from autobiographical essays referenced in Lionel M Yard's and Tony Martin's biographies, civil registrations, and passenger lists on genealogy websites, to immigration documents and FBI records in the Robert A Hill Collection.

As I compiled this documentation, I felt that Amy Ashwood Garvey would have appreciated knowing that her birthday would one day be celebrated by a UNIA chapter in Jamaica, with a programme curated by a Black woman who was the director of a museum dedicated to Garvey and Garveyism.

*

I had hoped to travel to Kingston to visit the National Library of Jamaica, which holds items from Amy's estate that were donated after her death. I also wanted to see the place where she last lived, the address from where she wrote to Lionel M Yard in her final letters, and to visit the Marcus Garvey Museum at Liberty Hall and the place where she was buried. I even planned to visit Port Antonio to see if I could find any confirmation of her origins there. Unfortunately, my plans were repeatedly thwarted – first by pregnancy, then by the birth of my child, and finally by Hurricane Beryl. At times, I wondered if I could ever finish this book, but I decided to go ahead and publish this work, while acknowledging these unavoidable limitations on my formal archival research.

This reaffirmed how my research on Amy has always extended beyond traditional archival work into what Tiera Tanksley calls 'Black feminist archival bricolage.'[89] Through this approach, I weave together the herstories of countless other Black women, starting with my own family. This extends to my use of self-portraiture in the film *Amy and Me in the Archive*, which is informed by Oumou Longley's essay 'Olive and Me in the Archive,' exploring the complexities of Black diasporic experiences and epistemologies. Longley's work draws from personal and cultural archives to explore the everyday, messy and fugitive ways that Black lives document and define themselves.

Inspired by Longley's autoethnographic approach to Olive Morris's life, which challenges hegemonic expectations of Black women, my film similarly aims to reclaim Amy Ashwood Garvey's place within historical narratives that have often overlooked the contributions of Black women. By engaging in the archival process, I celebrate the resilience and courage of women like Amy, recognising the power of shared herstories to reinforce my roots and inspire future generations. This archival practice is not merely academic; it's a deeply personal journey of self-discovery and empowerment.

Through *Amy and Me in the Archive*, I offer an artistic interpretation of the experience of being a Black woman conducting archival research. Featuring iconic photographs of Ashwood Garvey, juxtaposed with original photographs, film and text, the artwork seeks to position Ashwood Garvey within multiple histories and archives. It reflects on the research process, which involves applying autoethnographic methods to address the challenges of working with a dispersed and fragmented archive. The film explores how my identity as a Black feminist researcher of Jamaican parentage, born and raised in the US, now living in Britain, has evolved through this ongoing transnational archival research.

The journey to crafting *Amy and Me in the Archive* has provided me with a unique perspective on Amy's life and activism. Through a careful blend of still and moving images, I delve into her social relationships and political endeavours, painting a portrait of her vibrant life. This intimate connection humanises her legacy, making it more accessible and impactful to a broader audience.

As I contemplate the future of Black feminist archives, the importance of creative and speculative methods in engaging with historical records becomes undeniable. The story of Amy Ashwood Garvey, viewed through both archival documentation and imaginative reconstruction, serves as a powerful reminder of the untapped potential within our historical narratives. The continued work of Black feminist researchers and activists in preserving and interpreting these archives opens new avenues for understanding and celebrating Black women's contributions across different spheres.

By adopting innovative approaches that blend historical rigour with creative speculation, we can ensure that the legacies of figures like Amy Ashwood Garvey are not only remembered but also reimagined for future generations. These creative expressions allow us to envision a future where Black feminist archives are not static repositories but dynamic, evolving spaces that inspire and empower. In this journey, the work of Black feminist researchers, artist and activists remains crucial. Their dedication to uncovering, preserving and celebrating the stories of Black women ensures that the archives of the future are inclusive, diverse and reflective of the rich tapestry of Black feminist thought and activism.

As a curator and artist working with Amy Ashwood Garvey's archive, I often feel that I bear some responsibility for ensuring its preservation and accessibility for future generations. Beyond mere documentation, the images in her archive serve as a testament to Amy's spirit and her legacy as a champion of justice and equality. From photographs that freeze moments in history to moving images that breathe life into the past, each artefact serves as a testament to Amy's remarkable journey. As I explore and experiment with her visual legacy, I want to ensure that her image and voice echo through the corridors of history. By engaging with her visual legacy, I not only honour her memory but also reaffirm our commitment to the ideals she so passionately fought for.

Amy's archive thus becomes a bridge to the future, a testament to the power of Black women's resilience and creativity, offering a wellspring of knowledge and inspiration. The dynamic methods used by Black feminist researchers today – be it through futurist narratives or speculative histories – serve as a beacon, guiding the way towards an inclusive and emancipatory historiography. The futurity of Black feminist archives is not just about preserving the past but actively shaping the future. It is about envisioning a world where the contributions and struggles of Black women are not only recognised but celebrated and used as a foundation for constructing more equitable societies. Amy Ashwood Garvey's life and the diligent work of contemporary Black feminist scholars ensure that this vibrant legacy remains a crucial part of our collective journey ahead.

NOTES

1 Carole Boyce Davies, *Black Women, Writing, and Identity: Migrations of the Subject*, Routledge: London; New York, 1994.
2 S Grewal et al (eds), *Charting the Journey: Writings by Black and Third World Women*, Sheba Feminist Press: London, 1988; Valerie Amos et al, 'Many Voices, One Chant: Black Feminist Perspectives,' *Feminist*

Review, No 17, 1984; Heidi Safia Mirza, *Black British Feminism: A Reader*, Routledge: London; New York, 1997.

3   Rahila Gupta (ed), *From Homebreakers to Jailbreakers: Southall Black Sisters*, Zed Books Ltd, 2003.

4   Introductory talk: 'Black women in Britain' (nd), The Papers of Jan McKenley, Black Cultural Archives, London, ref. McKenley/1/4.

5   In August 2021 Kelly Foster hosted three walking tours in Brixton as part of the Brixton x Harlem Festival: *The Island of Brixton – Brixton & the Empire Windrush* on Friday 5 August; *Black Sound – 100 years of Black music in Brixton* on Saturday 6 August; and *Black Women/Black Power in Brixton* on Sunday 7 August. This description of the tours was drawn from an advertisement: https://www.brixtonxharlem.com/walking-tours-with-kelly-foster.

6   Ibid.

7   Formed by a team of experienced archivists, storytellers, artists, and educators, including Rudy Loewe, Tania Nwachukwu and Ghislaine Yimga, The Black Digital Archiving Project was conceived during the Covid-19 pandemic when the closure of local archives highlighted the scarcity of accessible digital archival material. As Black history became a focal point amidst the growing Black Lives Matter movement and the loss of older community members, the project emerged as an exploration into existing Black history collections in the UK. It aims to identify regional gaps, whether geographical, thematic, or related to the digitisation of materials. With a focus on curating and contextualising the history and culture of Black people, the project is guided by principles of community technology, showcasing the potential of digital archives for documentary storytelling and preservation, and fostering collaboration for future developments in Black archival practices. To learn more about the Black Digital Archiving Project and Kelly Foster's episode of the Oral Tradition podcast, see https://blackdigitalarchiving.netlify.app/podcast/kelly-foster.

8   Rita Keegan, Matthew Harle and Ego Ahaiwe Sowinski, *Mirror Reflecting Darkly: The Rita Keegan Archive*, MIT Press, 2021.

9   To learn more about Lambeth Women's Projects and the issues that resulted in their closure, see 'Lambeth Women's Project: Savelambethwomensproject,' accessed 27 July 2014, http://savelambethwomensproject.wordpress.com/tag/lambeth-womens-project; 'Petition Save Lambeth Women's Project,' accessed 14 August 2024, https://www.ipetitions.com/petition/lambethwomen.

10 To learn more about the *Women On Aeroplanes* project, visit https://woa.kein.org and explore the Otolith Group's involvement here:

https://otolithgroup.org/public-programme/women-on-aeroplanes. For full details of the exhibition and program at The Showroom, see https://theshowroom.org/exhibitions/women-on-aeroplanes.

11   To learn more about the Black Herstory Archives workshop, see https://theshowroom.org/events/black-herstory-archives-workshop-led-by-ego-ahaiwe-sowinski-yula-burin-and-nydia-a-swaby.

12   For more information about Women on Aeroplanes, see https://woa.kein.org/About.

13   Tina Campt and Deborah A Thomas, 'Gendering Diaspora: Transnational Feminism, Diaspora and Its Hegemonies', *Feminist Review*, No 90, 1 January 2008, pp1-8.

14   One strand of my PhD research focused on exploring the notion of political blackness as a diasporic consciousness. This involved examining the diasporic dimensions of political blackness and how it served as a mobilising concept for women of African and Asian descent to engage in collective activism. For a detailed analysis of this concept, see Nydia A Swaby, 'Disparate in Voice, Sympathetic in Direction': Gendered Political Blackness and the Politics of Solidarity,' *Feminist Review*, No 108, 2014, pp11-25, http://www.jstor.org/stable/24571917.

15   To learn more about the collection on the Black women's movement at the Black Cultural Archives (BCA), including its focus on work, health, education, and migration as detailed in *Heart of the Race: Black Women's Lives in Britain* by Beverley Bryan, Stella Dadzie, and Suzanne Scafe, please refer to the subject guide available on the BCA's website: https://blackculturalarchives.org/subject-guides. Additionally, you can access the papers of Stella Dadzie and Jan McKenley, as well as listen to the oral history interviews in The Heart of the Race collection. For more information about the oral history interviews, visit: https://collections.blackculturalarchives.org/repositories/2/archival_objects/1716.

16   Stuart Hall, 'Constituting an Archive', *Third Text* 15, No 54, 2001, pp89-92.

17   *Jamaica Gleaner*, 6 April 1939, p21.

18   Ibid. For more on the meeting and Amy's speech in Trafalgar Square, see *Jamaica Gleaner*, 11 September 1935, p18 and 13 September 1935, p18.

19   *Jamaica Gleaner*, 11 October 1943, quoted in Tony Martin, *Amy Ashwood Garvey: Pan-Africanist, Feminist and Mrs Marcus Garvey Number 1, or, A Tale of Two Armies*, Majority Press: Dover, Mass.; London, 2008, p165.

20   'Mrs. Garvey Still Active With Crusade: First Wife of Marcus

Garvey', *New York Amsterdam News*, 4 March 1944, ProQuest Historical Newspapers.
21. Amy Ashwood Garvey, Unpublished Manuscript, Lionel M Yard Papers.
22. Ibid.
23. Ibid.
24. Martin, op cit, p168.
25. 'Garvey Widow to Talk with First Lady about Jobs,' *Chicago Defender*, 1 April 1944, ProQuest Historical Newspapers.
26. A M Wendell Malliet, 'World Fronts,' *New York Amsterdam News*, 18 March 1944, ProQuest Historical Newspapers.
27. Ibid.
28. Honor Ford Smith and Sistren, *Lionheart Gal: Life Stories of Jamaican Women*, Sister Vision Press, 1987.
29. Ibid; Sophia Satchell-Baeza, 'The Work We Share: Sistren Theatre Collective's Sweet Sugar Rage,' ALT/KINO, 12 April 2022, https://www.altkino.com/writing/sweet-sugar-rage.
30. Smith and Sistren, op cit, p247.
31. Tina Campt, *Listening to Images*, Duke University Press Books: Durham, NC, 2017.
32. Smith and Sistren, op cit, pp246-251; Satchell-Baeza, op cit.
33. *Gail Lewis Responds to Sweet Sugar Rage at Translation Transmission 25 03 2014*, 2014, https://soundcloud.com/translation-transmission/gail-lewis-responds-to-sweet.
34. Gail Lewis, 'Questions of Presence', *Feminist Review* 117, No 1, 2017, pp1-19, https://doi.org/10.1057/s41305-017-0088-1.
35. 'ICA: Cinenova: The Work We Share: Programme 3,' accessed 10 August 2024, https://www.ica.art.
36. Cinenova is a volunteer-run organisation dedicated to preserving and distributing feminist film and video works, emerging from the merger of Circles and Cinema of Women in 1991. The organisation manages over 300 titles that explore themes such as gender, race, sexuality, and decolonial struggles. *The Work We Share* is an international public programme featuring newly digitised films from Cinenova's collection, addressing key social issues and supported by contemporary artist responses. For more information, see https://cinenova.org/about.
37. 'ICA: Cinenova,' op cit.
38. Boyce Davies, op cit; Zora Neale Hurston, *Dust Tracks on a Road: An Autobiography*, Harper Collins, 2010.
39. For more information, visit https://www.black-blossoms.online/art-on-the-underground-x-black-blossoms.
40. Rhea Storr's work delves into the production and circulation of images

of Black subjects, exploring how images can convey knowledge, foster community, and challenge audiences. Her latest project for London Underground features six sequences of photographic artworks created with aerochrome, an outdated military surveillance film. The images, captured during a photoshoot with artist Jade Blackstock in London's common lands, examine visibility, control, and the fluidity of Black bodies in public spaces. Storr's work is further enriched by research conversations with London Underground staff, leading to captions that read like stills from a film, making viewers experience the images as if they are in motion. Exhibited in public space, these images invite us to reconsider our experiences as passengers and individuals in constant movement under observation. For more information, see https://art.tfl.gov.uk/projects/uncommon-observations-the-ground-that-moves-us.

41 To learn more about *The Politics of Pleasure*, a series of Black feminist programmes exploring pleasure as a politics of refusal, you can visit the ICA's website archive. The project centred Black gender non-conforming, nonbinary, trans and femme audiences, engaging with the research and practices of a pioneering group of pleasure artists, authors, activists, speculative writers, dance innovators, visual artists, a vegan soul food chef and other participants. This series was curated by *The Politics of Pleasure Collective*: Nydia A Swaby and Rita Gayle, with ICA Assistant Curator Ifeanyi Awachie. The program built on ideas foregrounded at *Fugitive Feminism* at the ICA in July 2018. For more details, you can explore the archived programmes *The Politics of Pleasure* workshop: https://archive.ica.art/whats-on/politics-pleasure-workshop/index.html; *The Politics of Pleasure* installation: https://archive.ica.art/whats-on/politics-pleasure-installation/index.html. Additionally, you can find the full details in the ICA's PDF archive: https://www.ica.art/media/02195.pdf.

42 Martin, op cit, pp223-5.

43 This excerpt was taken from an undated and unsigned letter, likely missing its second page, written from Amy Ashwood Garvey's address at the Afro-Women's Service Bureau, 65 Edgerton Gardens, London, SW3. This organisation later relocated to 1 Basset Road, becoming the Afro Women's Centre and Residential Club. The letter is part of the Lionel Yard Papers.

44 Martin, op cit, p242.

45 'Read JB Danquah's 1951 Letter Actively against Nkrumah's Push for Independence,' GhanaWeb, 4 August 2024, https://www.ghanaweb.com/GhanaHomePage/NewsArchive/Read-J B-Danquah-s-1951-letter-actively-against-Nkrumah-s-push-for-independence-1943893.

46 Working Class Movement Library, Len Johnson: Pan African Congress 1945, 13-21 Oct 1945, PP/JOHNSONL/3/3.

47 Lionel M Yard, *Biography of Amy Ashwood Garvey, 1897-1969: Co-Founder of the United Negro Improvement Association*, The Associated Publishers, Inc: New York, 1988, p158; Martin, op cit, p280.

48 Amy Ashwood Garvey Photographs, David M Rubenstein Rare Book & Manuscript Library, Duke University.

49 In Akan cosmology, time is often perceived as a cyclical process rather than a linear progression, emphasising the continuity between past, present and future. This understanding of time is deeply connected to cultural memory, where the ancestors (*samanfo*) play a vital role in guiding the living. The concept of *saman*, often translated as 'spirit' or 'ancestor', embodies the belief that the deceased remain an integral part of the community, influencing the lives of their descendants. Cultural memory in Akan thought is preserved through oral traditions, rituals and symbols, ensuring that the knowledge and experiences of the past are continuously woven into the present. This cyclical perception of time and the reverence for ancestral memory underpin the approach to archiving and institution-building in contexts grounded in Akan philosophy, where the past is not merely recorded but actively engaged in shaping the present and future.

50 As the founder of the Saman Archive, Adjoa Armah gathers photographic negatives from across Ghana, exploring new models of institution building grounded in Akan temporalities and West African technologies of social and historical mediation. Her work, which spans installation, sculpture, sound, public education, and photography, has been exhibited internationally at venues including Auto Italia in London, fluent in Santander, Hauser & Wirth in Menorca, and Salone De Mobile in Milan. Armah is also a practice-led DPhil researcher in Fine Art at the Ruskin School of Art, University of Oxford, focusing on Black Atlantic historiography and the ecological implications of racial capitalism. Her publications appear in platforms such as *Afterall*, *e-flux*, *Frieze*, and *Vogue*. For more information, visit her website: https://adjoaarmah.net and the Saman Archvie website: https://www.samanarchive.com/about.

51 Curated by Languid Hands during their curatorial fellowship at Cubitt Gallery, *No Real Closure* (2020-2022) was a dynamic platform dedicated to the exploration and advancement of Black artistic practice across various mediums, including exhibitions, moving image, text, performance and public programming. Rejecting superficial approaches and mere representational focus, the initiative emphasised

collaboration, dialogue and the creation of relationships that collectively yield something greater than the sum of individual efforts. In the context of global pandemics and ongoing struggles against anti-Blackness, *No Real Closure* addressed the persistent wounds of racial injustice, asserting that there is no final resolution to the work of dismantling oppressive structures, nor to the collective resilience and grief within Black communities. Alongside the development of *Curatorial Tactics*, the exhibition program featured groundbreaking works by UK-based Black artists, including solo exhibitions by R.I.P. Germain, Ajamu X, Camara Taylor, and Shenece Oretha, each of which explored themes of death, mourning, Black queer legacies, and the complexities of belonging and migration.

52 Robert A Hill Collection, David M Rubenstein Rare Book & Manuscript Library, Duke University.
53 Martin, op cit, pp170-2.
54 Flyer in Yard Collection cited in Martin, op cit, p173.
55 SAC, New York to Director, FBI, 16 August 1944, FBI files, 100 - 309034-3, copy in Yard Collection; John Edgar Hoover, Director, FBI to Hon. Adolf A Berle, Jr, Assistant Secretary of State, State Department, 31 August 1944, R G 59, 811.20244D/8-3144, National Archives quoted in Martin, op cit, p173.
56 Martin, op cit, p237.
57 Ibid.
58 Ibid.
59 Ibid, p240.
60 For more information on Amy Ashwood Garvey's book *Mother Africa*, see 'Mother Africa – A Book by Amy Ashwood Garvey,' *The Daily Gleaner*, Monday, 19 December 1949.
61 'Liberia Land of Promise', Amy Ashwood Garvey Memorabilia, Alma Jordan Library, University of the West Indies, St Augustine, Trinidad & Tobago.
62 To dive deeper into the friendship between Amy Ashwood Garvey and Claudia Jones, explore Ashley Everson's article, *Tracing the Pan-African Foundations of Transnational Black Feminism*, available at https://www.aaihs.org/tracing-the-pan-african-foundations-of-transnational-black-feminism, and Carole Boyce Davies's book, *Left of Karl Marx: The Political Life of Black Communist Claudia Jones*, Duke University Press: Durham, NC, 2007. These works provide rich insights into their connection and its impact on transnational Black feminism.
63 Martin, op cit, pp271-3.
64 Quoted in Martin, op cit, p272.

65 Amy Ashwood Garvey to Claudia Jones, 23 and 25 June, and 2 July 1964. Claudia Jones Memorial Collection, Schomburg Center for Research in Black Culture, Harlem, New York, Box 1, File 1/17 quoted in Martin, op cit, p287.
66 For more about Barby Asante's artistic practice, which focuses on the social, cultural, and political significance of memory and place, see her website: https://www.barbyasante.com. You can also explore her in-depth research by reading her PhD thesis, which delves into her work on collaborative practices and performative interventions: https://westminsterresearch.westminster.ac.uk. To experience her powerful performance *Declaration of Independence*, you can watch a recording of the livestream on Facebook: https://www.facebook.com/balticgateshead/videos/barby-asante-declaration-of-independence-live-balticmill/411461299627832. Additionally, find out more about her performance at Kettle's Yard, *Untitled (Exhibition)*, which continues her exploration of the politics of memory and identity: https://oldsite.kettlesyard.co.uk/events/untitled-exhibition-online-launch-and-performance-barby-asante.
67 Amy Ashwood Garvey on ignorance towards immigrants, UK, *BBC Motion Gallery Editorial/BBC Archive*, 24 September 1956. Getty Images, Editorial #1497920191. Uploaded on 14 June 2023.
68 Amy Ashwood Garvey on reasons for migration to England, UK. *BBC Motion Gallery Editorial/BBC Archive*, 24 September 1956. Getty Images, Editorial #1497921994. Uploaded on 13 June 2023.
69 Ibid.
70 Amy Ashwood Garvey stands outside Afro Peoples' Centre, UK. *BBC Motion Gallery Editorial/BBC Archive*, 24 September 1956. Getty Images, Editorial #1497917450. Uploaded on 13 June 2023.
71 Tony Martin, *Literary Garveyism: Garvey, Black Arts, and the Harlem Renaissance*, New Marcus Garvey Library, Majority Press: Dover, Mass, 1983; Tony Martin, *The Pan-African Connection: From Slavery to Garvey and Beyond*, Majority Press 1st edn, New Marcus Garvey Library, Majority Press: Dover, Mass, 1984; Colin Grant, *Negro with a Hat: The Rise and Fall of Marcus Garvey*, Oxford University Press, 2010; Robert A Hill Collection, David M Rubenstein Rare Book & Manuscript Library, Duke University.
72 Lerone Bennett Jr, 'The Ghost of Marcus Garvey: Interviews with the Crusader's Two Wives', *Ebony*, March 1960, pp53-61.
73 Ibid, p53.
74 Ibid.
75 Ibid, pp60-1.
76 Amy Jacques Garvey to Mr Bennett, 6 May 1960, box 5, file 2, Amy

Jacques Garvey Papers, quoted in Ula Taylor, *The Veiled Garvey*, The University of North Carolina Press, 2002, pp225-6.
77 'Correction', *Jamaica Gleaner*, 29 April 1944.
78 Emilie Boone, *A Nimble Arc: James Van Der Zee and Photography*, Duke University Press, 2023, p105.
79 Interview with Amy Ashwood Garvey; interview with Amy Jacques Garvey; Marcus Garvey, toward black nationhood, Call Number: Sc Visual VRA-1117 [hereafter 'toward black nationhood']; oral history interviews with the wives of Marcus Garvey, Call Number: Sc Visual DVD-185, Schomburg Center for Research in Black Culture [hereafter 'oral history interviews'].
80 'toward black nationhood', op cit; 'oral history interviews', op cit.
81 Ibid.
82 Ibid.
83 Amy Ashwood Garvey to President William S V Tubman, 22 April 1969 quoted in Martin, op cit, p313.
84 Ibid.
85 Ibid, p314.
86 Ibid; 'Burial of Amy Ashwood Garvey', *The Daily Gleaner*, 12 May 1969, p8.
87 Ibid, p315; Programme for 'Symposium on Amy Ashwood Garvey', The Lionel M Yard Papers.
88 Ibid; Headstone for Garvey's Wife Unveiled', *The Daily Gleaner*, 17 January 1976, p24..
89 Tiera Tanksley, 'Towards a Method of Black Feminist Archival Bricolage: Memory-Keeping within, beneath and beyond the Archive', *A/b: Auto/Biography Studies* 38, No 2, 4 May 2023, pp559-581, https://doi.org/10.1080/08989575.2023.2221951.

POSTSCRIPT

Yula, Emma and Amy

The loss of Yula Burin on 2 March 2021, after her battle with cancer, marked a profound moment of reflection and action for the feminist community in London. Yula, a Black feminist poet, writer, and activist, had been deeply involved in numerous political and arts projects throughout her life, including the Women's Radio Group, X Marks the Spot, the Feminist Library, Lambeth Women's Project and Black Feminists UK. I first met Yula at a gathering at Lola Okolosie's house, and we quickly became friends. Our connection deepened when I interviewed her for my doctoral research and we collaborated on the Black Herstory Workshop at the Showroom Gallery, forging a bond that would continue to shape my work.

Still grieving her loss a year later, I collaborated with Terese Jonsson – who had met Yula at the Lambeth Women's Project – to edit a blog series for *Feminist Review* commemorating Yula's life and legacy. The series, featuring essays by Lauren Craig, Rashne Limki, Debbie Golt, Kavita Maya, Ursula Troche, Sabrina Qureshi, Chitra Nagarajan, and Lola Okolosie, now forms a permanent online archive on the *Feminist Review* blog. This project transcended a mere tribute; it embodied the resilience, creativity and collective spirit that are the cornerstones of Black feminist archiving practices. By preserving Yula's contributions, we underscored the vital importance of making space for Black women's stories and ensuring they remain accessible for future generations.[1]

Similarly, Emma Wolukau-Wanambwa and I had envisioned another collaborative project to honour the life and activism of Amy Ashwood Garvey. Alongside Black feminist artist and cultural producer Lauren Craig, we dreamed of creating a tribute to Amy's visionary work by curating a temporary social parlour and restaurant inspired by the Florence Mills. Although Emma's passing from a degenerative illness on 3 January 2023 meant our plans never materialised, the seeds she planted in our discussions continued to grow. Her persistent question – 'when are you going to write Amy's Black feminist biography?' – has echoed in my mind since our first meeting. It wasn't just a question; it was a catalyst that shaped my academic and artistic path, intertwining my narrative with that of Amy Ashwood Garvey.

Outside of our work together, Emma was a brilliant artist, researcher and convenor of the Africa Cluster of the Another Roadmap School. She was known for her 'radical and generative engagements with colonial archives, memorial practices, art education, and collaborative formats, as well as her unwavering commitment to anti- and decolonial thinking and practices'.[2] Working with Emma on her installation at the Showroom Gallery marked the beginning of my journey as a Black feminist artist and curator. Her unwavering belief in the importance of Amy's story – and her trust in me to tell it – laid the foundation for my approach to Black feminist archival practice. Writing Amy's biography has deepened my understanding of the intricate connections between a biographer and their subject, transforming me into both an archivist and curator of stories that might otherwise be forgotten.

The loss of Yula and Emma has only strengthened my resolve to continue this work. Their legacies of cultural activism, artwork and scholarship continue to inspire me as I navigate the complexities of Black feminist archiving, ensuring that the stories of Black women like Yula, Emma and Amy are preserved and passed down. Through their legacies, I am reminded that our work is never solitary; it is a collective venture that spans generations. It is through this collective that we keep each other's stories alive, and it is within this shared endeavour that the seeds of our futures are sown.

NOTES

1. 'Celebrating Yula Burin', 22 March 2022, https://femrev.wordpress.com/2022/03/02/celebrating-yula-burin.
2. 'In Memoriam: Emma Wolukau-Wanambwa, 1976–2023', accessed 18 August 2024, https://www.e-flux.com/notes/581880/in-memoriam-emma-wolukau-wanambwa-1976-2023.

Index

Accra 132, 143, 148, 157, 182, 189, 193-4, 203
Adanwomase 151-2
Adi, Hakim 18, 37
Afro People's Centre 14, 30, 91, 93, 96-7,107, 118, 122-3, 164, 180, 185, 198-200, 204-5
Afro-Women's Centre 76, 89-91, 96, 118, 122, 129, 166, 169, 179, 185, 198
Ahaiwe Sowinski, Ego 24, 26-7, 77, 168-170, 173, 205
Aidoo, Ama Ata 192, 202
Akwasidae Festival 146-7
Alma Jordan Library 17, 50, 91, 118, 128-9
Archive/s: activism 39-40, 66; Black diaspora archives 203; Black archives 13, 20-9, 31, 40, 77, 172-3, 202; Black feminist archival consciousness 24, 28, 169, 171; Black feminist archival practice 23-5, 27; cities as living archives 78; visual archive/s 28-30, 116, 117-120, 124, 129, 159. See also: Pauline Gumbs, Alexis; Farmer Ashley D; Ahaiwe Sowinski, Ego; Foster, Kelly; Hall, Stuart; Campt, Tina and Burin, Yula.
Armah Adjoa, 193-4
Ashwood, Claudius (brother) 45
Ashwood, Maudriana (mother) 41, 45, 47-8, 54-6
Ashwood, Michael (brother) 45
Ashwood, Michael Delbert (father) 40-1, 44-8, 55-7, 65
Ashwood Garvey, Amy: archives on 12-3, 15-8, 172; public speaking 14, 79; financial problems 15; creative pursuits 19, 57, 59-61, 81-4, 176, 177-8; Pan-Africanism 19, 44-5, 50-1,61-2, 77-8, 83, 87-8, 96, 104-5, 107,120-3,124, 133, 136, 148, 158, 166, 171-2, 174, 186, 188-9; autobiographical writing by 40-1, 50-2, 53, 54, 59-61, 132; birth, 40-1; early life 43-9; co-founding UNIA

52-5; feminism 91, 103-4, 124-130, 138, 142-3, 155-8, 166, 173-5, 180-2, 185; marriage to Marcus Garvey 58, 62-6; social spaces 87, 91-2; anti-racist activism 91-5; travel 115, in Africa 130-148, 155-156, in the Caribbean 84, 126-8; death 214-5.
Asante, Barby 200-5, 212
Asantewaa, Yaa 148-9
Ashanti Region 13, 47, 130, 143-8, 152-3, 157, 159
Association for the Advancement of Coloured People 93. See also Claudia Jones.
Autobiography 39, 42-3. See also Ashwood Garvey, Amy and Boyce Davies, Carole

Bailey, David 20, 121, 185
Beatty, Adisa Vera 117, 215-6
Bennett, Lerone 208, 212
Beyond the Bassline 20, 200, 204-5
Birmingham, England 197
Black British Feminism: Past, Present and Futures 167-8
Black Blossoms 183. See also Tajudeen, Bolanle.
Black Cultural Archives 18, 22-3, 164-5, 167-8, 170, 174-5, 183
Black feminism: autoethnography 25-7, 155-9; biography 37-40, 229; bricolage 213-4; curation 19, 27-8; in the UK 21-5, 80, 165-6, 167-9, 174-5, 180-2. See also diaspora; Ransby, Barbara; archives; Boyce Davies, Carole; Robeson, Eslanda; Lewis, Gail; Tanksley, Tiera; Taylor, Ula and Hurston, Zora Neale.
Black Feminists UK 168-170, 228
Black internationalism 13, 21
Black photography 115, 119; African diaspora photography 116, 120, 123, 139; social life of the photograph 113-116. See also Willis, Deborah; Raiford, Leigh and Campt, Tina.
Black Power: in the UK 22-3, 80, 165-6; Black Women's involvement 167-8, 180
Black Star Line 58, 79, 106, 116, 135
Black Women Radicals 19
Boyce Davies, Carole 38-9, 42, 165, 183, 190, 191
Bowyer, Jane 19
Boahimaa (great-grandmother) 44, 47-8, 52, 130 143-4, 147
Brixton 18, 22-3, 80, 165, 167-8, 200
Brixton Black Women's Group 168, 174, 184-5
Brooklyn 11, 15, 72, 117
Burin, Yula 24, 26, 27, 77, 170, 173, 205, 228-9

Campt, Tina 26, 114, 120, 180

Carnaby Street 30, 86, 88-9
Casely Hayford, Adelaide 193
Clayton Powell Jr, Adam 70, 73-4, 78, 106, 196
Colon 45-6. See also Panama
Combahee River Collective 165
Cooper, Anna Julia 50
Council on African Affairs 14, 106, 196
Critical fabulation 27-8
Curatorial fabulation 27-31, 59-60
Curatorial Tactics 193

Dadzie, Stella 22, 80, 170, 174
Danquah, Joseph Boakye/JB 143, 187-8
Davis, Angela 182, 192
diaspora 12-3, 16, 21, 23, 26, 30, 36, 38, 40, 58, 73, 81, 86-7, 99, 102, 129-130, 149, 152, 186-194, 207, 208, 212; feminism 173-5, 183, 191, 195, 206; African diaspora in Britain 89, 93, 95; solidarity 107, 125, 135, 148, 158,172; identity 124, 155-6, 183, 202; homeland 141. See also archives; Black photography.
Dillard, Mary 36-7
Douglas-Folkes, Sula 28
Douglass, Frederick 50, 136
DuBois, W E B 99-101. See also Fifth Pan-African Congress.

Edwards, Brent Hayes 113-4
Everson, Ashley 19

Famer, Ashley D 39
Florence Mills Social Parlour 30; 86-9, 107, 124-5, 204, 229
Foster, Kelly 78, 165, 167-8
Fraser, Rhone 20, 38

Garvey, Marcus 17, 38; Black Star Line 116; biographies by Amy Ashwood Garvey 40, 49-66, 129, 176, 198; co-founding the UNIA 52-4, 78-9, in Harlem 72-3; Liberty Hall Museum 216-7; *Negro World* 99; Liberia 134-7; relationship with Amy Ashwood Garvey 11, 14, 62-6, 81-4, 113, 115, 191, 195; photography 119; Garveyism 166; death 206
Garvey Memorial Institute for Domestic Science 177-8
Garveyism 66, 137, 166, 186, 216-7. See also Garvey, Marcus
Gilliam, L Frank 182
Grey, Aleema 18, 200
Gumbs, Alexis Pauline 26

Haiti 44
Hall, Stuart 175
Handsworth, England 197
Hanover 9, 182
Harlem 13, 17, 29, 50, 57-8, 61-2, 65, 72-4, 76, 78-80, 82-4, 93, 104-8, 118-9, 120, 125-6, 129, 176, 196, 201, 215

Harlem Renaissance 73-5, 78-9, 81-4, 94, 105, 119, 184
Hartman, Saidiya 27
Heart of the Race Oral History Project 22, 175
Hill, Robert A 17, 40-1, 50-1, 59, 195, 207, 216
Hurston, Zora Neale 25-6, 74, 82

International African Friends of Abyssinia 87-8, 121, 124, 176
International African Service Bureau 88

Jacques Garvey, Amy 11, 38, 48-9, 60, 84; relationship with Ashwood Garvey, 65-6; 144, 195, 207-213; relationship with Marcus Garvey 63-4; 137
JAG Smith Political Party 176-7, 210
Jamaica United Party 76, 121
James, C L R 14, 20, 88,196, 86-7
Jeffers, Audrey 127
John Hope Franklin Research Center 17, 50, 117, 138, 156, 189
Johnson, James Weldon 106
Johnson, Len 97-8, 198
Jones, Claudia 18, 38, 93-5, 98-9; photographs of 76-7, 123; friendship with Ashwood Garvey 14, 19, 190-1, 199; death 214
Jordan, June 182

Juaben 130, 143, 147, 152-4, 189, 192, 194

Kensington Central Library, Local Studies Archive 18, 37, 80
Kente: worn by Ashwood Garvey 19, 30, 96, 121, 122, 129; Ashwood Garvey's writings about 145, 147, autoethnography of 150-2; 186-195. See also Armah, Adjoa.
Kenyetta, Jomo 14, 86, 101. See also Fifth Pan-African Congress.
Kerr, Sir Hamilton 90, 198-9
Kingston 11-4, 17, 51, 54, 57, 118, 179, 208, 215, 217
Kumasi 143, 148-152, 157, 159, 182, 189, 192, 194, 203
Kwame Nkrumah Pan-African Intellectual and Cultural Festival, 190-3

La Badie, Ama 101, 103
Ladbroke Grove 14-5, 18, 90, 93, 96, 164, 185, 198
Lafayette Theater 82-4
Lambeth Archives 18, 23-4, 37, 199
Lambeth Women's Project 24-5, 169-170, 220, 228
Languid Hands 193, 224
Lansiquot, Rabz 193
Lewis, Gail 27, 181
Liberia 126, 129, 134-6, 139-143

Liberty Hall 58, 62, 73, 79, 82, 106, 201; The Legacy of Marcus Garvey Museum in Kingston, 216-7
Longley, Oumou 24, 217

Mama, Amina 192
Manchester, England 97-8, 100-2
Manhyia Palace 144, 146, 149-150
Manning, Sam 14, 83-4, 86, 175; death 188
Maroons, Nanny of 50
Marson, Una 86, 192
Martin, Tony 13, 15, 20, 29, 32, 37-8, 40-1, 87, 127, 134, 187, 207
Mason Jordan, Imani 193
McKenley, Jan 22, 80, 170, 174
Mills, Florence 14, 30, 82. See also Florence Mills Social Parlour
Minh-ha, Trinh T 182
Moore, Queen Mother 39
Morris, Eva 214
Morris, Olive 23, 168, 175
Murolo, Priscilla 35, 75

National Association for the Advancement of Colored People 73
Negro World 14, 58, 64, 78, 79, 82, 99, 212
New York City, see Brooklyn; Harlem
Nigerian Progress Union 85
Nkrumah, Kwame 100, 137, 149, 187-8, 190-2. See also Fifth Pan-African Congress and Kwame Nkrumah Pan-African Intellectual and Cultural Festival.
Noble, Gil 118, 211
Nomvele, Thandeka 19
Notting Hill Carnival 93, 95
Nubian Jack Community Trust 18, 95

Onojeruo, Ese Jade 183
Oral history 22-3, 74, 154, 167, 175. See also Heart of the Race
Organisation of Women of African and Asian Descent 80, 165-9, 174-5, 180-2
Otolith Collective 20, 170

Padmore, George 86, 88, 92, 100, 124, 196. See also Fifth Pan-African Congress.
Pan-African Congress 99-100; Fifth Pan-African Congress 14, 18, 97-8, 100-7, 118, 188
Pan-African Federation 100
Pan-Africanism 103-104, 141-2, 158, 166, 171,190-3. See also Ashwood Garvey, Amy; Pan-African Congress.
Panama 13, 15, 29, 45-6, 55-6; Canal, 45-6; City 56-7. See also Colon
Pankhurst, E Sylvia 129, 197
Parmar, Pratibha 182,
Port Antonio 40-4, 133, 217
Port Harcourt 186

Prempeh II, Osei Tutu Agyeman 144-7, 150

Raiford, Leigh 120, 130
Ransby, Barbara 38-9,
Reddock, Rhoda 190-1
Remembering Olive Collective 23-4, 169
Riaz, Hana 167
Riley, Mykaell 20
Robeson, Eslanda 25-6, 38, 123, 140, 158-9
Robeson, Paul,14, 19, 82 86, 123, 140, 196
Rogers, Laurie 129
Rogers, Thelma 91, 128-130
Roosevelt, Eleanor 178

Salt, Moira 181
Saman Archive 193
Sankofa 195-6, 203-6, 209-210, 212-3. See also Asante, Barby.
Sarah Lawrence College 18, 35-6, 72, 113, 164
Schomburg, Arturo Alfonso 75. See also Schomburg Center for Research in Black Culture.
Schomburg Center for Research in Black Culture 17, 19, 50, 74-8, 96-7,107, 118, 119-121, 129, 185, 201, 210
Senegal 131-3
Sharp, S Pearl 182
Sharpe, Samuel 50
Shelley, Louise 181-3
Sherwood, Marika 18, 171

Sierra Leone 133-4,
Sistren Theatre Collective 179-182
Solanke, Ladipo 85
Southall Black Sisters 35, 165
Storr, Rhea 183
Street strolling 78-81, 102, 108. See also Taylor, Ula and Foster, Kelly

Tamale, Sylvia 192
Tanksley, Tiera 217
Tajudeen, Bolanle 183-5
Taylor, Foluke 21, 202
Taylor, Ula Y 38-9, 65, 78
The Garvey Memorial Institute of Domestic Science Training 177-8
Thompson, Anya 216
Tierney, Gabrielle 19
Trafalgar Square 121, 176, 185
Trinidad 41, 84, 91, 127, 191
Tubman, William 137-141, 149

UNIA, see Universal Negro Improvement Association
United Gold Coast Convention 188, 194
Universal Negro Improvement Association 13, 14, 29; founding of 52-5, 72-3, 78-9, 82, 86, 106-7, 113, 116, 119, 127, 129; and Liberia 134-5, 137, 166, 186, 201, 207-8, 215-6

Walker, Alice 182
Walker, Madame C J 78

Washington, Booker T 50
Wells, Ida B 78
Westwood High School 46-7
West African Students Union 86
West Indies National Council 196
Willis, Deborah 115
Williams, Eric 86
Wilson, Lizzie 143
Wolukau-Wanambwa, Emma 20, 49, 117, 170-1, 205, 228-9
Women in Print 19-20
Women on Aeroplanes 20, 49, 170, 182
Working Class Movement Library 18, 97, 188

Yard, Lionel M 11-2